# A Kind of Journal

P.J. KAVANAGH was born in England in 1931, and has worked as a lecturer, actor and broadcaster, as well as a writer. His *Collected Poems* were published in 1992, the year in which he was given the Cholmondely Award for poetry. His memoir *The Perfect Stranger* won the Richard Hillary Prize in 1966, and his first novel, *A Song and Dance*, was awarded the Guardian Fiction Prize in 1968. From 1983 to 1996 P.J. Kavanagh was a columnist on *The Spectator*, and from 1996 to 2002 on *The Times Literary Supplement*. In addition to his four novels for adults and two children's novels, P.J. Kavanagh has written a 'travel autobiography' (*Finding Connections*), a literary companion (*Voices in Ireland*) and has edited *The Oxford Book of Short Poems* and *The Essential G.K.Chesterton*, and, for Carcanet, a new edition of his *Collected Poems of Ivor Gurney*. P.J. Kavanagh lives in Gloucestershire.

**P.J. KAVANAGH**

*A Kind of Journal*

*1987–2002*

CARCANET

First published in 2003 by
Carcanet Press Limited
Alliance House
Cross Street
Manchester M2 7AQ

A CIP catalogue record for this book
is available from the British Library
ISBN 1 85754 632 6

The publisher acknowledges financial
assistance from the Arts Council of England

Set in Monotype Garamond by XL Publishing Services, Tiverton
Printed and bound in England by SRP Ltd, Exeter

*With thanks to Alexander Chancellor,*
*Charles Moore and Ferdinand Mount*

# Contents

*Life and Letters* first appeared in the *Spectator* between 1987 and 1996; *Bywords* in the *Times Literary Supplement* between 1996 and 2002.

*Life and Letters*

# The True Undertaking

We hardly go in for 'experimental' writing in England, we leave that to the Irish, just as on the whole we left 'modernism' to a couple of expatriate Americans. This seems a pity, when you think how next-to-impossible it is to describe anything, and literary form, like language, becomes tired, and we think something has been described when really we have only been passed a used token. Much experimental writing is merely pretentious, but good writers in other languages are not afraid to have a try. Vittorio Sereni, the Italian poet, had a shot at impressionistically describing what it was like to go back, with his wife and young child, to where he was made a prisoner of war.

He refuses to flinch at the hopeless entanglement of past and present and involuntary falsifications and allows his language (almost) to become entangled, like memory itself when he looks at his companions: 'bewildered to see you making your début on this ground, to see you being, the two of you, the never supposed future of my being there then'. He mistrusts 'that distorted emanation of ourselves which writing is', but pushes on: 'I am standing at the limit where I have always stopped myself whenever I put pen to paper. The point at which the true adventure, the true undertaking begins.'

Almost everything is beyond that limit, even the atmosphere of an eventless walk I took on Christmas afternoon. Its qualities were light (a gathering dusk) and almost total silence, not a car, not a person, moving. Also, apart from the difficulty of putting across that silence, that diminishing light (which increased, rather than lessened the way the lichened tree-trunks glowed), there is the difficulty presented by facts.

After initial doubt about some yellowish birds (greenfinches? They went black in the sky-framed bush), I came to the roadside dairy. Once the centre of clanking, lowing life on Christmas Day and every other day, it is now a part of the silence. It has just been sold up, its prosperous owner rumoured to be bankrupt. Everything is still there, the tubes hang that were attached to udders, the vast milk tank shines; there is even a graph of recent milk-production, going upwards. Below it a rat has thrown up a mound through a new gap in the concrete. The floor is white with the droppings of 21 refugee racing-pigeons. Well, they are certainly not woodpigeons. What are they doing there? As useless to ask as to ask why the farm was so suddenly sold. No one knows, or no one will say. Something to do with the EEC milk-quotas, I think, as I stand counting the pigeons, trying to establish at least one fact, their number. But if facts are hard to come by, how much more difficult it is to convey a sense of abandonment there, that feels so long established I might be standing in something left by the Anglo-Saxons. Yet I saw that dairy built. It will never be used again.

So, on, for a few more miles, not a soul, not a sound, the tree-boles glowing more greenly, the grass also. No place here or anywhere else for the thoughts that accompanied each step, forgotten at once; without these, too, the picture is false. Then at last a man, in a field, with an enormous limp. A black silhouette against a reddening sky, scattering hay for cows. He see-sawed across the field splitting the tight-packed bales with his hands, breaking off biscuit-like slices and skimming them over the ground. This was followed by the dignity of black and white heifers slowly, very slowly, from a far corner of the field, coming to eat their hay.

Words, attempts at description, make tyrants uneasy. (They can manage facts.) A story from Elaine Feinstein's life of the Russian poet Marina Tsvetayeva: in 1940 the Moscow Writers' Union found it easy to starve her out – they doubled the price of her meals. Desperate, she goes to see her fellow-poet, Akhmatova. They walk. (They are only poets, describers.) Someone steps out of the shadows and follows. Akhmatova wonders, 'Her or me?'

*January 1987*

# Remembering the Ram

When I was about nine years old, in a field in North Wales, my father noticed that I seemed unduly nervous of a ram. He told me that I should never be unnecessarily afraid of anything, so I went up to the ram and patted it between the horns, whereupon it knocked me down. (My mother discouraged my father's occasional interventions in my upbringing, but I was on his side. Whenever I had the stomach for it

I have tried to follow his advice.)

Nevertheless, I remain uneasily nervous about many things. I recently saw a programme about 'dub' poetry, which I believe originates in Jamaica. It is in the language of the street and the market, very fast and rhythmical, with rhyme-vowels added, 'o' and 'a' and 'er'. At first I thought it was called 'dud' poetry, the name attracted me because of its punk honesty, but I had misheard. Anyway, so far so reasonable, until a white-haired Jamaican poet called it 'nation-language', which sounded worrying, and a young Jamaican in England suggested that standard English was a form of cultural imperialism and then, with his imitation of a bossy Englishman, made his group of English youngsters giggle. This caused me to be nervous for the survival of the English language.

However, I thought, bravely (patting the ram between the horns), much the same must have happened to post-imperial Latin. But I find that this is not so. Written Latin became hopelessly separated from the languages spoken around it, but these grew from different language-roots, which had been there before Latin had been imposed on them; which is why, for example, Spanish is different from Romanian. But so far as I know, Jamaican 'nation-language' is imposed on nothing except English played-about with and disguised, which, although fun, might become undernourished.

Another reason for nervousness has been the great battle about structuralism and deconstruction that has raged in the academies of English. Sometimes it seemed to tend towards the collapse of English itself. You have to have had a very secure childhood (or an unbearably insecure one) to relish any sort of important collapse. Besides, the whole thing seemed too much like a political game played out between tenured academics, to the confusion of their pupils, and extraordinarily joyless. As Kathryn Sutherland says in the *Critical Quarterly*, Winter 1986 – and despite the way she says it (give me dub poetry, any day) – she is on the side of the common reader: 'It is surely a pertinent fact that structuralism and its aftermath have fashioned from the levelling of universal textualities a platform on which to raise higher the coterie status and esoteric privileges of the initiated reading few.'

A sensible response has been to keep the head down and trust that it will pass. But bad news filters through, and it is certainly easy to notice how people flinch away from new poems. Does anyone, for example, apart from scornful and aspirant poets, read the poems printed in this magazine? Why should they; but if the resistance is instinctive, surely there must be something unusually off-putting in the way verse is presented in schools?

In order to cheer me up a retired schoolteacher of Islay, Mr Alistair Shanks, has sent me a cassette of poems that interested his pupils. He reads them with emphasis on rhyme and rhythm, and moves from the simple and amusing to things like 'My Last Duchess'. When one of his pupils suddenly died Mr Shanks found that the boy's school-mates sat dumb and stunned in his class. So, inspired, he read them 'Adonais' – 'they probably did not understand much of it' – but it set them free and helped them to talk about their schoolfellow. He sounds like a good teacher, there are surely many, and to say that Islay is not Isleworth is to say not much.

But to moan about matters is easy when you don't have to do anything about them. Last night, as though the house is bugged by thought-police, an astonishing call came that invited me to join a committee on how English *should* be taught. As nervous as when confronted by the ram, I remembered my father and so had to accept. I also remember how the ram reacted.

*January 1987*

# Here Comes the Bard

Bards are itinerant (they give 'readings') and afterwards, when they gather together, they compare scars. These are usually inflicted in 'Arts Centres'. Whereas, when they are invited by local literary soci-eties it is because some member has read them, wants to hear them, and they are treated accordingly, 'Arts Centres' are for all the arts, run by bureaucrats whose first interest is unlikely to be poetry, but they throw a bit in from a sense of duty and, having done so, consider their duty done. They seldom attend (too busy) and if they do so are too bossy. I remember Norman MacCaig's Edinburgh chilliness, when, after a hard day, we were told there was no time for a drink before our reading: 'I – think – ye'll – find – there – *is*,' he said, with a deadly slowness, ordering a dram and relishing it, in his own time.

I shall never forget the Bridgwater Seven. South West Arts sent Jon Stallworthy and me on a readings tour of the west. Stallworthy was in the public eye at that time, having won a prize for his biography of Wilfred Owen. All went well until, of course, we reached the Bridgwater Arts Centre, where the audience numbered seven. (Adrian Mitchell says that any organiser can drum up an audience of 60; if he doesn't it's because he hasn't tried.) The place held about 200, and the Seven shyly secreted themselves among the dark back rows, as people do in church. We exhorted them to approach, but it was difficult to make ourselves heard because there was a vinous party in the next room, a Private View. The organisers had invited two poor devils of poets to read, and had thrown a party for themselves and the arts-concerned of Bridgwater, in the same building, at the same time, on the same night. We found it funny. We had to. But we had come a long way.

Why, then, do we do it? I don't, much, but it is a way of getting our books known, even sold (or so we dream): and there are a faithful few who come and seem to enjoy it. Also, we forget how bad it was the last time.

My own most recent experience was the other day, the one on which the clocks went forward. It was a Sunday and I reluctantly drove the 75 miles to the 'Arts Centre' in Berkshire; it had not seemed too far when invited six months before, but now it did. No one met me, the place was locked. When at last I got in no one knew anything of the poetry-reading, there were no posters, few signs of life, no sign of my fellow-reader, Anne Stevenson. I had originally accepted because I like her, wanted to read with her, as I was led to believe she did with me. We both have new books out, perhaps we might sell some …

I lurked, spirits low. Come 12 o'clock, the time of the reading, there was still no sign of the organiser, (the host), nor of her. I went to the bar, which was slowly filling with Sunday-morning drinkers, and found to my great dismay that this bar was where we were meant to give the reading: it was almost wholly windows, the sun beat in; no chance at all in that noon-day bar-room of making that queer, exciting connection with an audience. Quarter-past twelve, half-past … Should I jump in my car and drive back home? What about the patient people who had turned up? Or had they? 'Are you here for a poetry-reading or a drink?' I at last found courage to croak. 'Both,' they replied, so there was nothing for it but to introduce myself, back to the wall or rather the bar, and pull out a book and begin to read my poems. That is not quite the same as reading from Max Miller's Gag Book.

Eventually Anne turned up, all of a dither (she had forgotten, until too late, the clock-change). Then the organiser, not nearly enough in a dither to my taste. All came to an end, as all things do, and of course at the end there was none of our books to sell; 'they had not arrived'. Of course, no lunch was offered. Even so, I should like to have talked to Anne, to one or two people there, but my only desire was to get away. I threw my book-bag in the back of the car and uttered a huge expletive, aimed at the whole set-up. Unseen, a small boy was sitting on my bumper and he rose about a foot in the air. Hazlitt has an essay, 'My first acquaintance with poets.' That was his.

*April 1987*

# Prester John

Recently there was published *The Faber Book of Diaries*, which extracted entries for a day of the year, from diaries written over the centuries, and put them all together under that date. The result is entertaining but thin. It proves that the real interest of a diary, or journal, lies in its *dailyness*. To get the full flavour of another's life we need to see the whole game, not edited highlights.

Now there is published, by Greymitre Books, as highly flavoured a day-by-day account as can be imagined, by a benignly obsessive and magical man: the diary, for one important year, 1930, of John Cowper Powys. (He is magical, if for no other reason, in that he grew healthier as he grew older.)

To those who know about him the diary is important for two reasons. First, it begins with an account of his last few weeks as the inspired improvising lecturer, to women's clubs and anyone else who would have him; half mage, half pantaloon, he had crisscrossed the United States doing this for 25 years. Then it describes his suddenly settling, at last, in a cottage on a bank in upper New York State, in his 58th year, to write *A Glastonbury Romance*.

He had written novels before, was well-known as a writer and lecturer, but that vast book turned out to be nothing less than a cosmography that exfoliated easily from ordinary people and daily doings in the distant Somerset town.

The insight into the scale of these lecture tours is alone worth the price of admission. In five weeks he went backwards and forwards through eight States, took eighteen vast train journeys, crossed the Mississippi six times and gave more than thirty extempore lectures.

All this with half a stomach and the constant nipping of fresh ulcers. He did it to support himself and his estranged wife and son in England, and seems either to have been cheated or very ill-paid. What is useful in his self-descriptions are the mental and spiritual devices he uses to cope with his endless travels and his physical pain. He taps some deep vein of the life-force and is nervous of the power it grants him. When he curses the vulgarity of an American woman who giggles at an exiled Russian singing sad songs – 'O damn the bitch!' – he adds quickly, fearfully, 'This is no curse upon her, may all be well with her.' Not long afterwards he is looking at some polar bears in a zoo: 'One was tenderly scratching its hurt paw. It was lame. It scratched absent-mindedly like one puzzled, pondering on past and future, faintly recalling some arctic moss that was the cure.' That is like a thumb-nail sketch for the cosmic sympathies and far, apt connections that are in *A Glastonbury Romance.*

At last he moves to the cottage, with Phyllis Playter, his companion for the previous nine years and, as the reader knows but Powys does not, for the rest of his long life. She hates the place; its pokiness, its smoking stove, the housework. He loves her, depends on her, agonises about his decision to bring her here, and it is as though he is required to summon all his devices and tricks and spells to be tested by the negative side of the female principle. Meanwhile, page by page, the great book grows and he reads it to her, the only critic he cares about. And she loves it.

Perhaps the source of Powys's mage-like power is his unshakeable faith in the value of the childlike, his lack of embarrassment. His supreme pleasure that summer is the rescuing of trout and flies from drying pools and watching them revive in deeper ponds. His brother Llewelyn thinks this foolish. John Cowper knows 'Lulu' is wrong and tells his diary so and John Cowper is right.

*September 1987*

# As Jimmy Durante Said

Recently I wrote of some breakdowns of our car in France which, as soon as I saw it in print, annoyed me because of all it left out. There was no attempt to describe the special dismay when a hitherto trust-worthy car, laden with luggage and miles from home, just stops. And, when mended, a few miles further on stops again. *Swish* go the other cars past, while you sit, and think. Instead, I gave the impression of a professorial type who sat by the roadside savouring *The New Oxford Book of Victorian Verse* while rude mechanicals took spanners to his roadster. Not so, not so. Above all I failed to describe the kind of facial expression it seems necessary to adopt, half-cringeing, half-insistent, with a precisely measured hint of pathos, in order to attract the attention of indifferent mechanics. I wore it so often, and so long, I am still not certain whether my face has returned to normal.

All these things were left out because of difficulty: difficulty of tone, of choice, of detail; laziness, therefore, and fear of being boring. But the best story-tellers, whom I revere, are reckless with their energy and they override fear. When it works the result is glorious. Too often their partner (alas) cries out, 'Get on with it! Come to the point!', whereas the point is in the details, in the journey, not the arrival.

As Jimmy Durante was fond of saying, 'It ain't what you do, it's the way that you do it.' It is a frustration to hear a good story-teller cut short by an impatient audience. I prefer stories, true ones, to chat or gossip, any day. Which is why I want to tell a story here, at second-hand, because it seems too good to lose.

Peter Kane Dufault, the American poet, came over a couple of weeks ago on the QE2 and he usually has a good tale to tell. Last time he crossed on a Polish ship from which, at some German port, the whole passenger-list defected; still a record.

He described the bingo-culture on board, the non-stop entertain-ment, the blue-rinsed American passengers and the surprising ones: the Chicago police-chief involved in the Peace Movement. Then came Amateur Entertainment Night, hesitant joke-tellers, titters, 'Give 'em a big hand!' Peter had been busking for Greenpeace and was delighted to put on his kilt and play his bagpipes, the star of the show. Next, a gaunt, tall man stood up, deep-sunk eyes, stiff brush of white hair, ears sticking out from his narrow head – 'looked like Andrew Jackson' – who gravely announced, in his Kentucky accent,

'Ah-em-goan-to-*dence*-fo-yu.' But first he had to say something so important that he had written it out and would read it. Taking a piece of paper from his pocket, he did so. 'Ah em coming to England with the ashes of my dear wife.' (Restless movement in the audience.) Years before they had passed an idyll on the Blackwater estuary, among the black swans, descendants of the pair brought over from the Holy Land by Richard the Lionheart, she had always wanted to be scattered there … and so on, into a now awed stillness. Yet with such sincerity, and a weird kind of poetry, that Peter, helplessly embarrassed, felt tears coming to his eyes, and continuing to come: 'I had to grab hold of my face to stop it falling off!' Then, with a final word about how his dear wife always loved to watch him dance, he took up the position of a ballroom dancer, one leg elegantly advanced, arms outstretched to hold an imaginary partner – 'My God! He's going to dance with his dead wife!' – signalled to the band and proceeded to waltz round the saloon floor. No one laughed. No child called out, 'What's that funny man doing?' The place was stunned. He finished his dance, bowed, and departed, no one daring to applaud.

Peter did not know if anyone had been as moved as he was, but it turned out that they had been, though they did not know what to make of it.

What is extraordinary is that a man could do something so inappropriate and tasteless, yet make it work because of sincerity and lack of fear. It ain't what you do, it's the way that you do it.

At the railway station in London he tapped Peter on the shoulder. 'Ah understand yu wah kind enough to be moved by mah pohfomance', and he presented Peter with the precious piece of paper.

*October 1987*

# Asides to Himself

Not long ago I casually remarked that Coleridge used the word 'empathy', and a polite reader has asked me where. In his *Notebooks*, of course, I said to myself, and I have been back to them to find it, but they are so vast and enthralling I have been continually distracted by the man himself: 'I would glide down the rivulet of quiet life, a Trout' makes me laugh, and his remark, 'Something inherently mean in action', he enlarges to the extent of suspecting God of vulgarity for so busily creating the world – 'but that I conceive that Thought with him Creates.' 'Better to do nothing than nothings.'

What about this, for anyone autobiographically inclined, as we all are, who becomes increasingly embarrassed by the use of the first person singular?

> With what anxiety every fashionable author avoids the word I –
> now he transforms himself into a third person – 'the present writer'
> – now multiplies and swells himself into a 'we' – and all this is the
> watchfulness of guilt. Conscious that the said I is perpetually
> intruding on his mind and that it monopolises his heart, he is prud-
> ishly solicitous that it may not escape his lips.
>
> This disinterestedness of phrase is in general commensurate
> with selfishness of feeling: men old and hackneyed in the ways of
> the world are scrupulous avoiders of Egotism.

You know at once that this is true, you think of the garrulous self-involvement of the young, and the hooded eyes, judicial detachment of their elders, who can be the true monsters of self-regard.

In fact that last quotation does not come from the *Notebooks* at all, but from Coleridge's introduction to his poems quoted in the Notes to the *Notebooks*. They are by Kathleen Coburn who, as a young scholar from Canada, in the 1930s, tracked down the *Notebooks* to the house of Lord Coleridge – 'Old Sam was only a poet, you know, never did anything practical that was any use to anybody, actually not thought much of in the family, a bit of a disgrace in fact, taking drugs and not looking after his wife and children' – who somehow managed to charm their guardian as indeed he was charming to her, and found herself, in her own phrase, doing a sort of breaststroke through the layers of Coleridge manuscripts in a piled-up alcove. She spent the rest of her life sorting them out, and her account of this, *In Pursuit of*

*Coleridge*, is as joyous a tale of literary detective-work as is ever likely to be written.

The result of her labours was published in 1957 and has held me in thrall ever since I came across them. I could wish I had not been asked that question about 'empathy' because I am lost in them again, lost to the world and those about me: 'mem: not to adulterise my time by absenting myself from my wife.'

It is their unselfconsciousness that enthrals, for it is that of a man intensely observant of himself. 'He knew not what to do – something, he felt, must be done – he rose, drew his writing-desk suddenly before him – sate down, took the pen – & found that he knew not what to do. Octob. 30 1800.' There are suggested essays topics: 'On the art of prolonging life – by getting up in the morning.' Sudden coinages delighted in, 'My heart seraglios a whole host of joys.' Memoranda of brow-clearing commonsense:

> Never to lose an opportunity of reasoning against the head-dimming, heart-damping Principle of Judging a work by its Defects, not its Beauties. *Every* work must have the former – we know it a priori – but every work has not the latter & he, therefore, who discovers them, tells you something that you could not with certainty or even with probability have anticipated.

There is self-knowledge: 'There are two sorts of talkative fellows and I, S.T. Coleridge, am the latter.' The first uses too many words, the latter too many images – 'till I break against the shore of my hearer's Patience, or have my concentricals dashed to nothing by a snore.' It can be painful, 'O me! that being what I have been I should be what I am!' But Coburn has him elsewhere put the matter straight: 'By what I *have* done am I to be judged. What I might have done is a matter for my own conscience.'

A matter for mine is that there is, so far, no sign of the word 'empathy'.

*October 1987*

# Speaking and Writing

When amateurs are asked to join professionals, in order to look into a public matter and opine, they soon find that the evidence presented by interested parties is so wildly contradictory, so filled with antagonisms and mutually exclusive convictions, they begin to wonder how any democratic decision is ever arrived at. In our case, for nearly a year now, the task has been to discover what we think, in the light of what hundreds of other individuals and associations think, about how much knowledge of their own language children should be taught at school. I am not going into the arguments for and against such knowledge (in case anyone is beginning to fidget) but would like to remark on a strange fact the investigation has thrown up: the extraordinary inertness of the language, in nine cases out of ten, used by professors and theorists of language, when they write about it.

The amateur is in danger when he steps on to professional ground, but so are the professionals, who invited him. He is liable to gasp, and point. For it has slowly become clear that this deadness, dowdiness and abstraction is, to some extent, intentional; it derives from an idea that is historically mistaken and surely pernicious in the classroom. The idea (I shall use the italics such writers often resort to, expecting, as well they might, a lazy or inattentive reader), *that there is an essential difference between the spoken and the written language.* This seems to me disastrous. Anyone who writes as he or she would never dream of speaking is bound to produce something which pays too little attention to the meaning, associations and rhythms of words. It is to forget the listener, now asleep, or likely to wake and say, 'What do you *mean?*' In other words to forget that all writing is a form of conversation.

Of course, they are in a difficulty. They have somehow to make it clear to pupils and teachers that written English should usually be Standard English, should not (usually) contain slang or dialect, if it wishes to be generally understood. Speakers of non-Standard English therefore have to be taught a slightly more formal language to write in. But for this formality to be fossilised into a sharp distinction between speaking and writing is to inhibit some children into incapacity, and to produce adults with a prose-style so weird it is hard to believe a human being is behind it.

Teachers often tell children to go away and write things 'in your own words'. But when it comes to the serious stuff, examinations, 'job applications', the distinction between writing and speech seems too often reinforced. It is as though this is done in obedience to some unwritten law. Indeed, the law is quite the reverse. A history of English poetry could be written (poetry not being a 'sub-group' of writing, but its most verbally sensitive and organised manifestation) in terms of the way poets, roughly every 50 years, or less, wrest the language of their immediate predecessors away from an artificiality into which it has inevitably descended, back into some sort of relation with the speech of their own day.

C.H. Sisson, in a book which should be compulsory reading for anyone interested in the matter, *English Poetry 1900-1950*, makes this point, not with the sense that it is an original contribution, but as something that has to be said again and again, so quickly is it forgotten:

> ... when one looks back from a sufficient distance one manages to discern a sort of loose common character which can be attributed to the literature of a period. This is because there is a general, completely inartificial conversation among contemporaries of which what remains as the literature is, in some sense, the finest expression...

Poetry, he knows, is what tends to move most quickly away from this source of strength, to readers' approval. He quotes Lord Chesterfield: 'Prose, as you know, is the language of conversation; it is what you, and everybody, speaks and writes ... But poetry is a more noble and sublime way of expressing one's thoughts.' (Sisson adds, growling: 'The dog returns to his vomit.') He is right, it is a hopeless way of thinking about poetry. But it is interesting to see that Chesterfield seems to make no distinction between what everybody speaks and what everybody writes.

*December 1987*

# Gaudeamus Igitur

If we prudently thought we might need to stay the night, we were each allotted an undergraduate's room. Mine had a single pin-up on the wall, a head and shoulders of a woman who looked familiar. Puzzling who she could be, I climbed into my unaccustomed dinner-jacket *(fl.* 1951), smug that it still fitted, more or less. It was Greer Garson! What was she doing on a student's wall in 1988? It began to rain outside. The Senior Common Room, where we were all to meet, was some distance away. I spotted the lad's umbrella on top of his cupboard and pinched it guiltily. Still thinking about Greer Garson and her presence on the wall, also worrying about the umbrella, sure I would mislay it during the course of the evening, I set off across the garden. A tall, angular figure, unknown to me, fell into step alongside, and I confided to him my anxieties about the umbrella. He had worries about his own. 'The porter at the Athenaeum insisted it was mine. "Oh yes, milord, that's yours all right." It isn't.' Not since a man in America thrust his card at me that bore the superscription, 'The Last of the Big Spenders!' has so much information about status been compressed into so small a space. I wondered if the whole evening was going to be like that, the Merton Gaudy, a rejoicing, at which survivors of various past intakes were invited to meet again: was it to be a trading in self-importances?

Not at all. We seemed automatically to regress into undergraduate self-depreciation and pretence-gloom: 'Hello Richard, what are you up to these days?' 'Law.' (Pronounced with melancholy, as though this the dreariest of servitudes.) 'Actually, the bugger's a judge.' 'You a judge?' 'Yer.'

At dinner I sat in front of a large silver-lidded mug presented by a Mr Tufnaile in 1700. Where have all the memorable surnames gone; Christian names too, for that matter? Where are the Chideock Titchbornes *de nos jours*? I have trouble remembering names (I was in bad trouble this evening, with people I hadn't seen for thirty years) but surely I could never forget Titchborne, or Tufnaile?

After a while things became a little blurred, as I intended that they should, and only fragments of the evening reached me. 'Certain amount of anti-Papist prejudice in Chadwick's *Reformation*.' 'Yes, he's sound on that score.' This exchange made me feel I was really back in Oxford: an argument, half-jocular, moved fast-forward, the antagonists just touching horn-tips, then turning away, amused. As they turned I heard someone else, distant, say, 'He couldn't stand beards. Said they were effeminate.'

Everyone seemed to be behaving as they always had. After the dinner, back in the Common Room, a sort of baying began in one corner, reminiscent of the sound that used to come from Boat Club Suppers, which I never attended, but you did not have to be there to hear it. Likewise it was doubtless typical that I and a couple of companions of those years were the last to leave. One of them had rescued the umbrella.

In the morning I stood in the familiar garden and wondered why I had come, glad that I had. I looked at this tree and that bit of lawn and dutifully said, 'There such and such happened, here so and so remarked...', waiting for the waves of nostalgia to hit me, but they didn't, and they never do. Oxford in this respect seems to me the ideal, fantasy courtesan: intelligent, beautiful, willing to give you all her attention while you want it, then turning to your successor without regret or reproach and with equal warmth. While I was there I felt Oxford belonged to me. The moment I left, it seemed proper that it now belonged to others. It may sound odd, but this inspires a special kind of gratitude.

At breakfast in Hall I was joined by my umbrella-companion of the previous evening. Around us were suggestions that the speaker at the dinner had not been audible to all, and it was canvassed whether this was the fault of the PA system or that its very presence was to blame, tempting the speaker to rely on it. 'Largest audience I ever addressed without PA was eight hundred,' said the umbrella-man. 'They all heard.' In my blearily generous state, induced by the Gaudy, it occurred to me that a man with so much self-esteem, round the clock, had the greatest cause for rejoicing of us all.

*April 1988*

# Jeux d'esprit

Samuel Butler (the author of *Erewhon*) was an orderly man. From early in his life he carried a notebook, in which he wrote down ideas as they occurred to him. These he indexed and, in 1891, made it a rule to spend an hour every morning re-editing these notes, and keeping the index up to date. I could not emulate such organisation, but I have always wished that I could keep a notebook. The trouble in my case is that whenever I do carry one, and something to write with, it has the same effect on my thoughts as going out with fieldglasses to look at birds; they always choose that occasion to be elsewhere. Nevertheless, inspired by his example, the other day I decided to try again.

I happened to be staying on the coast, in the house of a man, once mentally vigorous, whose mind is now nearly a blank. Earlier on that day I had telephoned from the room in which his wife had died; above her fireplace there were still her photographs of her children and grandchildren, of herself, as a particularly striking girl, of her father, whom she never knew, in uniform, killed in the first world war.

The steps down to the beach are ones that I have taken hundreds of times with my children, now grown-up, their childhood gone, at least from me. Even the trees and bushes we had known had been blown over last year, or cut back, and the second-war gun-emplacement, half-way down, had had its roof taken off to stop people using it as a lavatory. In other words, the air was full of the past, full of changes, decay, regret, mortality and, as always, a sense of the horrors elsewhere. There was no doubt that it was full of these things, but it was also full of a sense of something else, quite different. What?

It was a calm, clear day. The chalk cliffs, the chalky sea, combined together in tones of pearl, and over all there was a haze, a thin wash of lemon-yellow. The seagulls flew at the off-white cliffs, caught the updraught and turned, again and again. A patch of orange seaweed attached to the breakwater swirled round and round, tugged by the sea, but it clung on. There wasn't Arnold's melancholy roar, there was the sound, almost inaudible, and it is the wrong word, of a vast, inclusive humour; the kind we hear, or think we hear, in Mozart, even at his most serious. There was a sense, in James Michie's phrase, of 'hazy as foothills, possible laughter'. (Anyone who comes across that insufficiently-known collection, called, and rightly so, *Possible Laughter*, is in for a treat.) The day, in other words, filled to the brim as it was with a sense of various kinds of loss and disaster, was blessed. There was no doubt of this. I remembered Samuel Butler's note: 'To love God is to have good health, good looks, good sense, experience, a kindly nature and a fair balance of cash in hand.' True enough: the obfuscating imp of complacence is never far off, but there was no place for him here.

But how was this sense to be expressed? In the tiny world of writing and publishing poems, in which I do not play any significant part, I have so often been sat on, and dismissed, for including jokes and word-plays in serious poems, that I have come to believe the others are right: a thing is either serious or it is not. Yet, secretly, I am unrepentant. I remembered – sitting on the sea-wall among the soft colours, gulls above, the defiant seaweed in the water below – a television producer, years ago, who came into my dressing-room with a book of my poems, read out the lines, 'What is a soul/But a big wish in a small fool', slammed the book shut and said: 'How can I read on, when I come across a line like that!' But I liked the line. I still do. (I was about to go before camera and deliver an 18 minute 30 second lecture, live, before an audience, on the connection between Norman Mailer and Coleridge. I have long since forgotten what it was, if I ever knew, but his indignation didn't help.)

The trouble with humour is that it is exclusive, not only of seriousness but of intimacy. It is self-defensive. But what about the humour of this morning, which included everything, fearful and otherwise? I liked including jokes in poems, but they had to include, not exclude. Including-jokes, that is what was needed. I reached for the virgin notebook at last. To me that hyphen was important.

*April 1988*

# Tazzie at Last

When you try to prepare yourself for a long trip to another continent altogether, where you hope to present a clean sheet ready to receive new impressions, it is difficult to throw away all the naggings of arguments you are trying to leave behind. So it was that I sat on an immensely long Qantas flight to Melbourne, trying to think what I was going to Australia for, and how I was to set about it, but in reality still arguing with Doris Lessing, interviewed on British television the week before. It seemed to me that both her interviewers, Claire Tomalin and Brian Aldiss, were asking her the wrong questions and letting her get away with murder. It wouldn't have mattered except that they seemed to regard her as some sort of teacher for our times and what she said seemed to me dangerously near nonsense. She is a friend of mine, although I haven't seen her for years, and I kept leaping out of my seat in front of the television set and protesting to her. I was still protesting, though seated, on the aeroplane.

She said, 'Being reasonable has nothing to do with being a writer', but it does, it has everything to do with it. A writer can stretch the boundaries of the reasonable, but must always remain within them, has to, can't help it, or is otherwise talking nonsense. Wendy Cope later quoted her remark as something that is 'bound to come in useful some time', and that is precisely the point: the claim that a writer has the right to be unreasonable has been used to defend bad work by every phoney artist since whatever we call modernism began. There are those who bow themselves humbly before the claim and take whatever the artist throws at them, but the majority turn away from art, and from poetry, on the grounds that they cannot understand it and that therefore it has nothing to do with them. This is disastrous. You then begin to have a whole culture cut off from the best expression of itself.

But she said odder things, unchallenged. That she believed in 'the little people', goblins, was acceptable by comparison. She feared that young people were returning to 'the conventions'. What is wrong with that? There are dead conventions, well discarded, but surely there are others which are expressions of the accumulated wisdom of the race? The loss of these can bring on madness, chaos, the kind which she deplores. She also said that writers had no business describing 'good people. We must keep away from them.' Why? Because it is difficult? Nor did she find any place for religion in her world view; it was never mentioned. Politics were out, so 'the little people' were in, with never a pause between.

It wasn't good enough, so I raged on my aeroplane, the screen creepily showing our advance across Arabia: 'Ground Speed 620 mph, outside temperature –52 degrees centigrade.' Ah that's the Persian Gulf we're over now. It was announced that a light 'continental' breakfast would be served, over Asia. Which 'continent'? Odd that an Australian voice could take for granted that continental meant European. Perhaps I was beginning to forget Doris. The two people next to me had their fingers lovingly entwined. They were both middle-aged women. They at least were not returning to the conventions, dead or alive.

In Melbourne it was Anzac Day and the grizzled veterans marched through silent crowds, chatting to each other as their medals clanked from safety-pins. In the pubs afterwards they ordered beer in jugs. 'Another juggie, Brucie!', and I felt at home.

At dawn, the other side of the Bass Strait, Tasmania rose up like Ireland, like Carlow: unfrightening wooded hills and moulded green fields leading up to them. 'There's Tazzie!' was the cry.

The Queen was visiting Launceston when I arrived. 'Your Queen's in town todye,' said the Diggers in the Royal Oak. 'I know,' I said camply. 'She will follow me round.'

They stood me a juggie for that.

*May 1988*


# Before Breakfast


*New Norfolk*

Was it Lewis Carroll who described someone who could believe twelve impossible things before breakfast? Was it twelve? Was it 'incredible' rather than impossible? Questions that could be answered in a second at home, but not so easily in New Norfolk, Tasmania, by the Derwent River, although some culturally surprising things are offered for breakfast, by the Amaroo Motel – 'Steak and Egg', 'Lamb Chops and Egg', 'Spaghetti on Toast'.

Motels seem usually to be designed in an inward-looking square. If you do not wish to be observed like a goldfish in a bowl, you have to keep your curtains drawn and live by dim electric light.

Most of yesterday was spent visiting the almost-island of Port Arthur, the notorious penal settlement that some men killed themselves rather than stay inside, and it turned out to be, as every visitor has remarked, a green dell charmingly built over with pink brick and yellow sandstone buildings of elegant design. The historian in charge told me the first impossible, or incredible, thing that I have been pondering on before breakfast today. I mentioned to him the extraordinary frenzy in Australia (or at least in Tasmania) for genealogy, family history. In every library, hordes are punching the controls of microfilm machines with the obsessive excitement of fruit-machine junkies in Las Vegas. He told me that the genealogical societies are funded, discreetly, by the Mormons whose purpose it is, worldwide, to trace everybody back to Adam and Eve. *Can* that be true? And how can I find out, continuously travelling on as I am? At nightfall I pulled in here, off the main road, because it was the first place that I had seen in hours where one could stay.

After a gloomy pause, with curtains drawn, under a dim bulb, I went out to see the town, which was said to he at the top of a dark silent hill lined with one-storey houses. Sure enough it was, the 'main drag', I had been told, a single neon strip of one-storey shops, all shut, except two, both of these run by Greeks ('New Australians!' I had heard said with disapproval in Melbourne; 'New Australians' I had heard with enthusiasm in Launceston. 'They've transformed, dressed up that damned Presbyterian wowser town!') After a large glass of Cascade – you have to ask for a large glass, or a 'pot', which turns out to be about half a pint, or you are given a 'glass', which is not much bigger than a large whisky – I returned glumly down the dark hill thinking about Australian beer, which I enjoy. There are usually four here – Boag, Cascade, Fosters and Castlemaine – all from identical taps, to my palate tasting identical; but much importance is attached to your choice by the barman, as though he fears you might throw the wrong one in his face.

So, back to the dead motel. A sign said 'Restaurant', and lo! of all unlikely things there was a bald Irishman from Westmeath sitting, legs apart, in front of a log-burning stove. 'I run this place. Used to run the worst pub in Australia, in North East Tasmania – population 28. You couldn't commit a sin there if you tried.' A bearded American in the paper-milling business is boring us with his boasting. I ask two silent loggers if they are cutting down too many trees in Tasmania. They look at me with Australian directness, with the Australian pause, and say together 'Yes.' It goes to Japan, as woodchippings. They store it in plastic bags and sink it into the sea. What? Yes, and bury it under the roads, against a rainy day when there is no more wood in the world. Millions upon millions of tons. So, one more incredible and impossible thing to think about before this morning's breakfast, and, presumably, to believe. Anyway, the bearded American says it is true and begins to be unpleasant in general about the Japanese. 'Ah well, they were little divils during the war,' says the Westmeath gnome. One of the silent loggers pauses, fork to mouth: 'The Australian government has sold the Australian war cemetery at Gallipoli to the Japanese as a tourist attraction.' What! 'Heard it on TV last week. Nearly fell out of my chair.' 'Why didn't anyone complain?' 'No one knew until we heard it.'

Surely I can find out if that impossible thing is to be believed before tomorrow's breakfast. (It wasn't.)

*June 1988*

# In Search of a Public Drink

*Masterton*

To the category of unnoticed local facts belongs the absence of pubs in huge swathes of New Zealand cities. Pubs, that is to say, not dens.

The other day, for the second time in my two weeks in this country, I was reduced to eating a lunchtime take-away salad sandwich as I walked the pavement because of an inability to find anywhere I could sit and eat it, indoors, over a glass of beer. It was in downtown Wellington where it would have been possible hugely to lunch, but I did not want that because I was burrowing rather hopelessly in the library archives and that needed all the clear-headedness I could muster. I did see a pub at last, a splendid florid Victorian creation with the words 'Royal Albion' picked out in stone on its decorated forehead. It had been newly and tastefully painted, was the sort of place you would be pleased to come across in Putney, or Chiswick, and I approached it gladly. The door was shut, and it was an oddly *discreet* sort of door also newly refurbished, which set off all sorts of distant subliminal warning signals. There was a bell-push and above the bell the one word, discreetly displayed 'MASSAGE' ... There are times when a hatred of this part of the twentieth century can rise up and overwhelm you, a tidal wave.

The native trees of New Zealand seem, for the large part, evergreen, non-deciduous. There are poplars and willows, these at least I can recognise, bare of leaves at this season, but in the forests and the hillside clumps there are fir-like trees and yew-like trees (of great girth) and beautiful pohutukawa trees with grey bark and Nikau palms and lighter coloured shrubs like the Toro, so that hillsides are variegated and herbaceous – a Grand Hotel garden in Torquay. They look especially striking against the cropped light-green background of the smooth hills which have their own distinctiveness because they are both smooth and rippled, like the sea, or the skin of an elephant. So groined and rounded and moulded are they that you think of an over-enthusiastic plaster relief map or of grassed-over spoil heaps from old workings, which in fact is what they are, being volcanic. But very green and smooth, mile after dozens of miles of them, up and down, occasionally whitened by concentrations of particularly cuddly-looking sheep, Romneys, the kind that even have curly fleece over their faces, through which they peer. In Tasmania there was much wild life dead at the side of the road – wallabies, possums, feral cats, wombats (a kind of small brown-furred pig), even, in S.E. Tasmania a South-Eastern Quoll, a cat-like marsupial, light brown, with beautiful powder-puff sized white spots symmetrically arranged. A native, now reduced to that corner of the land, it seemed particularly bad luck that that particular animal should have been hit by a rare passing truck.

In New Zealand there is no such carnage. Only a live hedgehog, spines down, inspecting the road centre; fawn Australian harriers and white-backed magpies. I had discovered in the library that this was my grandfather's patch as a Crown Land's Ranger making sure big estates didn't swallow up small ones. A lonely place on horseback, single white painted houses, miles apart, even today.

Back in Masterton I asked where I could get a glass of beer, feeling like a wino in the Waterloo Road, fearful of being given a Temperance Tract. 'Well in 58 years I've never asked myself that! I drink it at home.'

*June 1988*

# The Great Australian Pause

On television, when someone is interviewed on the screen who is a
long way away, there is sometimes a blank-faced pause, a beat of two,
before he replies to a question. This is the time it takes for the end of
the question to bounce off the satellite. It looks odd, because it seems
to be a part of our politeness to reply at once; a silence suggests that
we think it a silly or impertinent question.

You learn this time-lag when you try telephoning via satellite.
When you speak you hear a faint echo of your last words. The person
on the other end has begun to reply, hears your echo and stops,
thinking you haven't finished. But if you allow a beat of two the result
is bizarre, as well as passionless: 'The dog died-died,' one, two,
'When? – When?', one, two. The pause makes personal communication almost impossible, although probably it is all right for the
transmission of facts. It is as though, in order to make human contact,
we verbally have to tread on each other's heels. If we leave a gap, odd
little doubts can creep in.

At all events, that seems to be the case in England; not so in
Australia. I first noticed this in England, among Australian friends.
When I finished speaking they paused, before they replied, as though
what I had said was being sifted for rubbish-content, or trawled for
Pommie ironies. Then I began to suspect they were just not very
bright. It was only when I reached Australia that I realised this pause
was a national characteristic; that, far from being rude, it was their
form of politeness. They wish to make sure that you have entirely
finished before they speak. It is as though they had invented a way,
perhaps made necessary by the vastnesses of their country, of
communicating, as though by satellite, long before the things were
ever fired into the sky. It can be worrying, if you are not used to it.
For this silence is preceded, it is important to understand, by an apparently blank and earnest attention. There is no recourse to those
fidgeting signals of agreement, demurrals, nose-scratchings, lobe-
pullings, crossing and uncrossing of knees. They would regard these
as attention-seeking, rude, and they are extremely polite people. They
sit passive, as though in class, thinking their own thoughts. It is terri-
fying. I had not realised how much we in Britain take part in a
conversation when not speaking. Without that encouragement,
unless you are self-obsessed, you begin to falter.

When I returned home I eagerly examined the conversation-style of Richie Benaud, the great Australian cricketer, when he appeared on television. No, his replies came without a pause. But then, he has been here a long time, perhaps too long, and has been affected by our decadent ways. Certainly the coiffure of that fair dinkum Aussie – who once diddled out a whole English Test side by pretending a pitch was taking spin when it was not – has gained in complexity and is now reminiscent of that of Quentin Crisp.

But that is by the way. Not all Australians employ the satellite-pause, but enough to attract my attention. Perhaps our wildlife has affected us, we are made jumpy by the nervous ways of our sparrows, the speed of our mice; whereas Australians are unconsciously calmed by the slow wing-flap of black swans, made still and patient by walla-bies' sleepy eyes.

Nevertheless, I would never have dared to generalise in this way if the whole business of the Australian pause was not ritualised, formalised on Australian radio; with, to the English ear and imagina-tion, disconcerting results. Imagine a pause of two slow beats after a politician has answered a question, before the interviewer asks the next one. Imagine it, and you will soon hear, in nearly audible English, that the interviewer is silently calling him a liar. Imagine a pause of two beats, or more, after a recorded report from some distant trouble-spot. To our imaginations comes a picture of the producer desperately signalling, behind his glass panel, 'Wrong report!' Or the presenter, microphone switched off, 'Who sent *that* loon out there?'

Perhaps they are right. Perhaps we fill the dangerous gaps too quickly, hysterically, which is why they suspect us of effeminacy. But relations between the sexes, in Australia, require another chapter.

*June 1988*

# Varieties and Sports

Follow my heart my dancing feet,
Dance as blithe as my heart can beat.
Only can dancing understand
What a heavenly way we pass
Treading the green and golden land,
Daffodillies and grass.

That sort of stuff could go on forever, and it almost does; it is
Lascelles Abercrombie, in 'Ryton Firs', which takes up the first six
pages of Sir Edward Marsh's *Georgian Poetry 1920-22*. It has been a
commonplace to sneer at 'the Georgians' for fifty years but it is an
eyeopener to be reminded how dire some of them were – big names
of the time, like Abercrombie, Gibson, Drinkwater. They grit their
teeth and insist on a cheeriness to be found in the rural scene that fills
the reader's heart with dole. The trouble is, he doubts if they knew
much about the rural scene; they were never wet, or cold, or muddy,
except by choice. When John Drinkwater writes (in *Poems 1908-14*, it
seemed only fair to look at him in bulk):

The chestnut cones were in the lanes,
Blushing, and eyed with ebony.
And young oak-apples lovingly
Clung to their stems with rosy veins …

you wonder if he knows that oak-apples are canker. Possibly he does
but the suspicion is fatal, sown in other poems: 'And every soft-lipped
breeze/Makes music for the Grafton men/In comfortable trees.'
Had he spoken to any 'Grafton men'? *Every* breeze? Drinkwater says,
of Thomas Hardy, 'He serves us best who sings but as he sees', but
Drinkwater hardly seems to see, or at least make the reader see,
anything distinct at all.

The curse of this sort of writing is that it has poisoned attempts by
non-countrymen to describe country events. (A real countryman is
too busy trying to make things grow to have time.) About any rural
report there still hangs a taint.

Nevertheless, the other day, outside my window, there took place
a unique event which I would like to describe. 'Ah,' says the reader,
rightly suspicious, 'outside, at a remove, why is he not in the middle

of things?' If I had been out in the middle the things would not have happened, which is the point.

I heard a susurrus, a loud disturbance of air, guessed it was wing-beats, but there were no accompanying twitterings, and it was unusually loud. I looked out, onto a patch of grass surrounded by ragged elders and littered with brown leaves; some of these moved, and were brown birds, a large flock, on the ground, of about five or six dozen. They flit about in crowds at this time of the year, but you never get close to them because they fly away. Now, perhaps because of a reflection on the window, it was obvious that they could not see me, as they pecked among the leaves, turning them over, approaching, until a selection of them was only two or three feet away. Then it became clear that they were not brown birds at all, but highly coloured, and varied. The majority were greenfinches, and seemed fairly uniform in plumage. But one goldfinch, instead of a white bar along the top of its tail, had perfect marquetry squares, black and white, neat and clear as a brand-new chequer-board, which none of the other goldfinches had. Also there were two birds markedly different from the others, with parallel stripes on top of their heads, rose-coloured throats, like linnets, and the rest of their plumage a varied tawny, from dark to light, as though it was highlighted. These I saw very clearly, for one of them even hopped onto the sill. I watched as long as I could and then became impatient to look this one up in a bird book, left the room to find the book and, of course, they flew away. It was not in the book, or any bird like it.

Ornithologists first defined the appearance of bird-species by killing individuals. W.H. Hudson sent bird-skins to London from the Argentine. Now I suppose they occasionally net them, to have a closer look. But very few, surely, have had the opportunity to stand, as it were, in the midst of a bird-flock, and observe how many sports and varieties there are within the same species. I have used that room, most days and seasons, for about fifteen years, and have never seen such a flock, so patient and close. It may be another fifteen years before it happens again, so I thought I would mention it.

*July 1988*

# Good Sense on the March

Last year we looked out at the noon-dark and the rain, listened to the weather forecasts, and gave ourselves permission to stay at home. Thus another annual twenty-odd miles of the River Severn remained unwalked by us. This year we looked out at the darkness and rain, then grimly at each other, packed into haversacks as many complete changes of clothing as our backs could bear, and drove to Shrewsbury through an early morning dark as dusk.

It was only raining lightly, but there are pleasanter things than wading through waist-high grass when it is wet. It is amazing how much moisture the stuff retains, and transfers; if you lay down in it you would drown. There was an additional hazard: my companion revealed a sensible suspicion of young bulls, and farmers along the Shropshire Severn seem to be going in for beef cattle this year. It was no use my telling him, as the heavy herds gathered speed towards us, that they were only curious, that the prevailing bovine disease is boredom. In mid-explanation I would hear a splash behind me, and a kind of sigh, as he found the ditch he had taken refuge in was both deeper and wetter than he had thought. From there I would hear him explaining patiently that although I was probably right, it was also possible that one among the herd might have got it genetically wrong, and was a hard case, a troublemaker from birth. With praiseworthy determination he pursued his way, dripping, round the backs of the hedges through nettles and brambles and bogs and wire, from which he eventually emerged to join me in the next cattle-free field; where I sat smoking, I hoped, a not too nonchalant pipe. For I, with a greater dislike of nettles and bogs, chose to test my theory by walking through the inquisitive beasts, not nearly as confident as I hoped they thought I was. So far, they have not let me down.

After such a catalogue, who can believe we enjoyed it? But we did, two of the unheartiest of men. It is oak country, some of them vast and therefore ancient. It was honeysuckle time, and we saw king-fishers, whose heads and wings are shadowy, almost unseen, so that a blurred creature seems to be dragging behind it a brilliant opaline ball. Or, as Laurie the painter suggested, parallels from natural forms being inadequate, you would have to turn to the metallic finishes on certain kinds of car. We saw a fox and heard the melodious gargle of curlews and, that night, met a man in a tiny pub in lost Melverley, on the Welsh border, who told us there was no wild life left along the Severn, it had all been eaten by white mink released from a mink farm by Animal Rights people. We tried to tell him about the kingfishers and the curlews but he was not a good listener, our friend. If into any small pocket he allowed in his seamless monologue (to draw breath) we inserted our tentative demurrals, he always replied, 'That's right, there's nothing. Ask anyone here', and continued to pluck our sleeves.

He launched into wilder flights. 'Tell me why no ship has crossed the middle of the Bay of Biscay! Tell me! It couldn't. Whirlpools. The Niagara Falls could power the whole of Africa. They do. They divert them at night.' He was not much madder than most of us. Poets, painters, politicians, all we crave is a bit of attention for our views. He had clearly been denied this, and our exhausted late-night *politesse* had gone to his head; the dam burst and he flowed, a surreal poet. In Laurie this Ancient Mariner had found his Wedding Guest. He told us the best way to go next day, and was right. He told us about the wooden church at the bottom of the lane, he had made a model of it out of clothes-pegs. 'That church. What would happen if you turned it upside down? You'd have a man-of-war!'

In the morning we visited it, said to be the oldest wooden church in England, secret, by the little River Vyrnwy. Inside it is like the inside of an old ship.

That day the sun shone, the warblers sang, and because of him we found a clear path. Up to now this stretch had contained too much enforced map-consultation. Now, in Montgomeryshire, we could see our path clear ahead for subsequent years. It is called that again, Montgomery, officially rescued from the blanket region 'Powys'. Good sense is on the march.

*July 1988*

# England, our England

I have seen rows of empty beer cans swept off tables by beer-bellies on the cross-channel ferry. I have seen ancient hedges grubbed up to the sound of Radio One. I have heard teachers deplore the ignorance of their pupils yet fiercely defend the ways they teach. I have heard students declare that rhythm in poetry (and prose) is irrelevant. I have endured Muzak in old public houses. All these things have I seen and heard, and more, but I never despaired of England until, like a djinn through the floorboards, Harry Carpenter appeared on the dais at the presentation ceremony after the Open Championship of Golf.

You did not have to be interested in golf, as I am not, to realise that for the last hour or so something extraordinary had taken place. It was the last round of the championship and the leader, a white from Zimbabwe, a comparative unknown called Nick Price, had kept his lead for three rounds. Many famous golfers were at his heels, Faldo, Lyle, Ballesteros, waiting for him to crack, but he did not, and it was Lyle and Faldo who faded. Then Ballesteros began to play even more perfectly than Price.

There are sporting occasions that seem to demand over-writing, the use of words like 'visitation', 'accesses of grace', the sorts of things a sceptical age finds hard to believe can happen to spiritual geniuses, saints, who have spent their lives practising for such moments; but in sportsmen we can see it happen, count it, measure it in inches, and then we marvel because we know something strange is going on. It came upon McEnroe a few years ago in a Wimbledon final. You could see him become startled and withdraw into himself, to watch, because he realised he was no longer playing tennis; tennis, at last, was being played through him.

This is not at all far-fetched. Ask McEnroe. If he could do every time what he did then, if he could predict when it was going to happen, then he would. But he can't; he can only wait, and practise, and it may never come again.

So it was with Ballesteros. Although he continued joking with his caddy and the crowd, that was on the surface only; you could see that he was watching himself, his moment had come. He played one bad shot and was astounded, began to gesture, argue, consult his distance-card, examine his club; this was an aberration from a sequence the Goddess had planned. What accident had deranged it?

At the same time another kind of dream was going on. Nick Price was not in the grip of any such *daemon*. He was merely brilliant and entirely brave. Faced with the miraculous – Ballesteros said afterwards that it was the best round he had ever played – Price kept level. He was only beaten at the last hole. And that, after being faced with an opponent's round of six under par, which equalled the course record, which was played under the colossal pressure of the closing stages of a great championship.

When the Spaniard went up to receive his prize he brushed aside congratulations, for the moment thanked no one, but as though still in the grip of his visitation, like one only partly come back from wherever he had been, he gave his beaten opponent a long Iberian stare, and spoke, oblivious of everyone else: 'Nick played like a champion. It is a pity there can only be one champion. Nick, if you play like that again you will be a champion soon.' This was miles from being politely generous to an opponent. It was News from Elsewhere. It brought a lump to the throat. He alone knew the extent of the miracle Price had had to endure, the depth of courage and concentration that had been required nearly to match such play. It was a private moment, in public, and the crowd was still, awed. Into the silence, as if from some fiendish trap-door, popped Harry Carpenter, pushing aside Price and officials, his microphone thrust into 'Seve's' serious face, and, using the familiar diminutive of his Christian name, he asked him what it felt like to be champion again …

You cannot *teach* Carpenter, or the BBC, what is inappropriate and therefore vulgar. It has to come out of a general background of sensitivity and decency, as did the remarks of the Spaniard, Ballesteros. That is the reason for the despair.

*July 1988*

# The Melodious Warbler

Facts are all we can know for certain but there are few things that we can be certain are facts. When writing for publication it is best to avoid them, if possible, because the world is full of the fact-maddened, pens poised, eagerly (angrily) waiting to tell us the Battle of Hastings was not fought there at all, and how dare we say so. An example of our uneasy relationship with facts, their fascination and our impatience with their limitations, is exploited by the new paper *Sunday Sport*, which goes in for headlines like 'Space Alien Turns My Son Into An Olive' and 'Hitler Was A Woman'.

Facts can be bad for us. The need for religions (all religions) is suggested to us by our natures and becomes suggestive; our next need is to turn these hints into facts and at that point we start to kill each other. I have spent the last year investigating the fact of 'Irishness' – which is a fact, it has affected the course of history – and have become dazed by the impossibility of finding out, for sure, wherein it exists. It seems that our lives, on many important levels, are not lived in the realms of fact at all.

But it is a fact, and a rare one, that on the first Saturday of this August the sun shone from a clear sky. So I rose unwontedly early, for conscience' sake, to do some work on the 'Irishness' book, because I intended to take the rest of the day off, enjoying the sun and following the course of the current Test Match against the West Indies, because that would contain an unfolding series of harmless and incontrovertible facts. The ball-by-ball radio commentary is a shameless orgy of them. People ring in to ask if it is a fact that, if the ball lodges in the visor of a batsman's helmet after he has hit it, and a fielder plucks it out, the batsman is caught. This then becomes the subject of a radio debate, perhaps daylong, and there is much reference to the 'laws' of cricket – laws, not rules, which makes them sound immutable. Because of this particularly rainy summer the commentary has become a little hysterical. They have had to keep up hours of chat in case interrupted play begins again, and now, when there is play, they find it an interruption of their chat. Brian Johnson, even when much was going on, told a story about a gull and a buoy and gave us his rendition of 'If you were the only gull in the world and I was the only buoy'; meanwhile the bowler Marshall was destroying England and it was left to the West Indian commentator, Tony Cozier, to keep his eye on the fact. As I listened to this pleasant rubbish I tried to imagine myself as a hard-pressed social worker, or as Mr Paul Foot, intelligently devoted to revolution; I even managed to imagine myself as an Irishman, and realised how maddening, insular, backward-looking, I might find it. Meanwhile I sat, nearly guilt-free, in the shade of a buddleia.

In the tall bush was a movement. I had, without much hope of ever having to use them, some field-glasses and through them I saw that it was a warbler. I knew this for certain because of boyhood instruction by the legendary Spud Murphy who taught me all I know about birds, which is about a tenth of what he knew. It was a bird of striking elegance; thin pointed beak, streak above the eye, but surprisingly yellow-breasted for an English warbler, a very pale, sorbet-yellow. It hopped closer, to a branch above my head; it seemed to be made fearless by the warblings of Brian Johnson on the transistor. I watched it through the glasses, visually so near it could have been on my thumb; watched it preen (its feathers, below the yellow, a milky white), remarked the slenderness of its grey-black legs, its lightness, for it stood within the bush on a green shoot that the weight of my little finger would have bent, but under the bird it remained straight. At last it flew away and, its photograph clear in my mind, I went to the house to consult the *Hamlyn Guide*, which is the best. Unmistakably there it was, a Melodious Warbler, *Hippolais polyglotta*, 'common in gardens' (in France) but unknown in Britain. If it were known here it would have a less silly name. How difficult it is to be certain of a fact. Someone in the house asked if I had seen a strange elegant bird. It is my only confirmation. August is not a month for birdsong – 'faster, with fewer discordant notes than that of the Icterine', which would have been a kind of proof – but from this Melodious one, not a dicky-bird.

*August 1988*

# Necessity the Mother

Someone not Irish has said that I know nothing about Ireland. What he probably does not know is how much I agree with him. In fact there come moments of vertigo when, as you learn about any subject, there dawns upon you the impossibility of knowing anything for sure, because you find that almost all of what is important has been invented. I remember, for example, being greatly impressed by a book called *The Allegory of Love*, by C.S. Lewis, which convincingly argued that much of the sentiment we attach to sexual relations, and regard as instinctive, was invented by the Provençal troubadours. If this was the case, I thought, I was grateful to them. For without their inventiveness I would have missed a great deal.

Much the same gratefulness, I suppose, has led me to value religious ritual, and public ceremonial (within reason), which are obviously inventions, but most of us need them, because without them most of us become dismayed. This protectiveness towards outward show – or theatre, if you prefer – is thought to belong to the 'Right'; whereas the 'Left' see it as their duty to strip away such tinsel in order to reveal the forked creature (and forked tongue) underneath. This can also be useful, but if carried to the ultimate it can leave people with nothing in common but grievance, digestion and death, which is too stark for most. Nor does it quite ring true. Invention is necessary but, even so, dismay can enter in. Recently in New Zealand I was in the library of a Bishop's Palace (or Bishop's House as it is properly called there). Next day there was to be some high-level ecclesiastical conference and on chairs in the library were laid out mitres and copes and, if I remember rightly, even a cardinal's hat. In the mote-filtered light they looked very tawdry. It occurred to me that I might as well be in the prop room of a repertory production of one of Jean Genet's transvestite plays, and was there any difference? Such questions can make you sweat.

But to get back to Ireland. It is true I was brought up on a theatrical notion of oppressed, laughing Ireland, passionately devout with a clear stream of poetry running through. True, my Irish writer-friends viewed this sceptically, but their country, and they themselves, triumphantly justified this perception. Now I discover some of it was an invention, by Daniel Corkery, in a book called *The Hidden Ireland*, in which he 'used literary evidence to sustain a picture of unrelieved poverty and oppression'. The present Professor of Modern Irish History at Trinity College, Dublin, Louis Cullen, has now published a pamphlet suggesting (proving?) that some of the complaining Irish bards themselves owned land; nor was the religious demarcation at all clear.

The most perfect example of Irish self-invention (which is not to say that the English do not invent themselves, we all do, daily, out of necessity) occurred in Australia, and is charted in a marvellous book, *The Irish in Australia*, by Professor Patrick O'Farrell (note the name) of New South Wales. A very few of the rebels of 1798 were sent to Australia, the vast majority of Irish were sent there for petty criminal offences. By 1855 a newspaper is asserting that *all* Irish Australians were spiritually descended from the 'politicals'. 'The only radiance that illumines the darkness of Australia's early history was reflected by bright Irish names – the glorious names of the patriots of '98.' In 1905 Cardinal Moran (some sort of uncle of mine, I fear) had gone even further in fantasy, claiming that 'the great body of the people were genuine Martyrs. Hatred of the Faith was the motive of those who forced them into rebellion, and they freely died for their Faith.'

Mind you, it must be remembered what insufferable bigotry the Irish were up against in Australia. A newspaper in 1850 describes 'a set of ignorant creatures whose whole knowledge of household duties barely reaches to distinguishing the inside from the outside of a potato, and whose chief employment, hitherto, has consisted in trotting across a bog to fetch back a runaway pig'. As Professor O'Farrell drily remarks, 'that is a masterly conflation of the then (and now) standard insults – dirt, stupidity, potatoes, bogs and pigs.'

Necessity is the mother of self-invention.

*August 1988*

# Aphoristic Assistance

It is difficult to read a page of aphorisms without feeling beaten about the head; it is their nature to have a bullying quality. C.H. Sisson has translated a few hundred of the *Maximes et Réflexions* of Vauvenargues (fl.1740). Because of their brevity and apparent discontinuity, these have the usual effect, a sensation of being tapped on the skull by the edge of a ruler, but they are the calm conclusions of a wise man. C.H. Sisson is himself an aphorist, unsleepingly at war with folly, but he buries his acerbities in continuous prose, from which they must be extracted. About his subject, for example, he begins by saying – watch the little clause, slipped in, after the semi-colon: 'Vauvenargues is hardly the most fashionable of writers; he has a further distinction, that there never was a time when his work was fashionable ...' The son of a nobleman who spent most of his adult life as an army officer – 'milieux not particularly favoured by the lore of the twentieth century'. The asides of Sisson are as savourable as the propositions he translates.

Vauvenargues, therefore, was a soldier, suffered from ill-health, and was unsuccessful; three conditions which make him sympathetic. Voltaire detected his quality, perhaps a little enviously, and did not help him as he might have done. ('84. It is rare to get much out of men one has need of.') Vauvenargues' genius is for psychological observation: '328. Through weakness, and through fear of being regarded with scorn, men dissimulate their dearest, most constant, and sometimes their most virtuous, inclinations.' He puts his finger, almost unintentionally, on the question that baffles most contemporary novelists, and is the reason why their invented characters so seldom earn their livings convincingly: '334. A talent and a taste for writing is supposed to be ridiculous in a man of the world. The question I put to reasonable people is: What do people who don't write do?'

Attractive though Vauvenargues is, he is formidable, as is C. H. Sisson, and the reader inclined to argue with either feels in need of a hand to hold. What a marvellous discovery, therefore, soon to be published in *The Chesterton Review*, is a book of aphorisms, *Platitudes in the Making*, 1911, by Holbrook Jackson, in which Jackson's worldly wisdom is genially demolished in gothically handwritten annotations by GKC himself.

To read both together has the pleasure of watching a sporting replay on television. We frown, puzzled, at Jackson's 'Negations without affirmations are worthless', and our brows are cleared by Chesterton's cheerful commentary, 'and impossible'. While we hesitate before Jackson's 'Treat the crowd as if you knew best: its units as if they did', Chesterton waves it away altogether: '(Be careful. You might end in the Cabinet.)' Here is some Jackson, with GKC in brackets: 'Theology and religion are not the same thing. When the churches are controlled by the theologians religious people stay away.' '(Theology is simply that part of religion that requires brains.)' 'Desire to please God is never disinterested.' '(Well, I should hope not!)' 'We are more inclined to regret our virtues than our vices; but only the very honest will admit this.' '(I don't regret any virtues except those I have lost.)'

Chesterton becomes impatient when Jackson deserves it. 'Every custom was once an eccentricity; every idea was once an absurdity.' '(No, no, no. Some ideas were always absurdities. This is one of them.)' He sometimes nearly agrees with him: 'Woman is not undeveloped man; but man is.' '(Witty. Five marks.)' 'To drink to forget is to abuse drink.' '(Thoroughly sound. One should drink to remember.)'

But Jackson is a lightweight. It would be good to read Chesterton's annotations of Vauvenargues, whose profounder eye is also fixed on this world. It arrives like a shock, therefore, when Vauvenargues reminds us suddenly: 'Newton, Pascal, Bossuet, Racine, Fénelon, that is to say the most enlightened men in the world in the most philosophic of all centuries, and in their prime, when their minds were at their best, believed in Jesus Christ; and the great Condé, dying, used to repeat these noble words: "Yes, we shall see God as he is, *sicuti est, facie ad faciem.*" '

*November 1988*

# The Subjective School

On my first morning ever in New York, confronted by a surprising neo-classical building, I asked a man waiting at an intersection what it was. He told me, and I no longer remember his reply, but I do remember he was wearing a smart tweed overcoat and a neat little trilby.

The lights at the intersection changed to 'Walk' and I set off quickly, because the man I had asked seemed disposed for conversation. I had him down as a lonely bachelor, a Clifton Webb-type, taking his morning constitutional along Fifth Avenue, hoping for someone to chat to. But I was looking forward to a brilliant Fall morning spent alone, taking in a strange city. I heard him quickening his step behind me; I could hardly break into a run, so he drew alongside.

How he opened the conversation is lost to me, but I am clear that after five blocks we were talking about poetry. It was long ago, but not all that long, and I must have been much younger than I feel now, because I do not remember being at all surprised that within a few minutes, in the United States for the first time in my life, I was walking down Fifth Avenue deep in conversation with a stranger. I suppose it just seemed a possibly typical New York experience. (It isn't.) However, I did want to look around me more than such an encounter made possible. I enjoyed it, but I chafed. By about 46th Street he asked me what I thought of the poetry of John Ashbery, and I said I couldn't understand it. He stopped dead: 'Neither can I!' he said. 'But they go *on* about it.' This is always an awkward moment. For all I knew, his favourite poet was Ella Wheeler Wilcox; just at that time I did not want to know, nor did I want to add fuel to his possible Philistinism, anti-Modernism. But what I had said was the truth, so far as it went, and, probably to cover the moment, for still he stood, I pulled out a cigarette. I certainly pulled out a box of 'England's Glory' matches, at which his eyes grew round. 'Excuse me, sir, but what are those'?' I presented him with the box, for which his thanks were extravagant, and there we parted. All day I went without a match, no one sold them. It was only by evening I had discovered that when you buy a pack of cigarettes they give a *book* of the things.

That, as I say, was long ago, and since then I have tried Ashbery again, and he sends me to sleep. That is not a judgement, or if it is it belongs to the Subjective School of criticism. I may be wrong about the poetry hut I am not wrong about the sleep. Now, all these years later, James Fenton has caused a storm in the US by confessing in the *New York Review of Books* that at times, when reading Ashbery for review, 'I actually thought I was going to burst into tears of boredom … I was approaching the book under a certain misconception, that it was asking to be, well, *read*.'

It must be a real storm because an American, Marjorie Perloff, is given seven whole-page columns in the recent *Times Literary Supplement* to put the Ashbery, and American, case. It is more than an academic row: it is an argument about the use of language – its usefulness – and suggests that the American sensibility is going in a different direction from ours, that the gap will become awesome, the Atlantic a salt estranging sea. Her point is that poetry has to be expressive of a *new* sensibility. She quotes some lines of Clark Coolidge, as an example:

> past of blow
> blimp one home
> blister copper as sap but one
> due from ice at tennis
> around a cent wind
> cynosure
> any of a central able carp

'For the American critic a poem is always already emblematic and exemplary of its time and place … For the British critic … the poem is first and foremost a poem more or less well written …'. I do not want to add fuel to anybody's Philistinism, anti-Modernism; but why 'critic', why not 'reader'? If I am sure of anything it is that poetry should not be written with critics in mind. My sympathies are with that reader in his tweed coat and trilby, grateful – it is too pat, but it is irresistible – for 'England's Glory'.

*February 1989*

# Aloof to the Ludicrous

Blows can fall that make it impossible to read, for many months, because all but the greatest books are seen to be silly, and even among those there are some that fail the test. But if you come across a book that you can read, at such a time, and pick it up again after thirty years and find it just as companionable and helpful, it seems only grateful to name the writer and the book: W.B. Yeats and his prose *Autobiographies*.

This was surprising at the time, and is so still. Perhaps he consoles because he is a sort of alchemist, or at least he blows gold-dust over all he describes, places, friends, enemies, so that they shine clearly. Nothing and no one is diminished. He can even give a hypochondriacal uncle the status of a character out of an ancient comedy:

> Sometimes when I pitted my cheerfulness against his gloom over the breakfast-table, maintaining that neither his talent nor his memory nor his health were running to the dregs, he would rout me with the sentence, 'How very old I shall be in twenty years.'

If he so aggrandises his friends and relations, weaving them into a mythology, he is gilding himself also, as some have pointed out, but his gold reflects also on us, confirms a faith that there is, after all, a splendour in life.

*Autobiographies* is several books, written over many years; *Reveries over Childhood and Youth* (1914), memories of the Nineties in London and Paris, of Irish politics, reflections, journals; themes disappear and emerge again in other contexts, to be further elaborated with anecdote and speculation.

The people Yeats talks of are now antiques, but he knew everybody and gives each an individual shine. Of Wilde:

> If he did dedicate every story in *A House of Pomegranates* to a lady of title, it was but to show he was Jack and the social ladder his pantomime beanstalk.

Of Aubrey Beardsley:

> I think his conversion to Catholicism was sincere… and yet perhaps I am mistaken, perhaps it was merely his recognition that historical Christianity had dwindled to a box of toys and he thought it might be amusing to empty the whole box on the counterpane.

He tells us of William Morris, the amiable blunderer,

> saying to the only unconverted man at a socialist picnic: 'I was brought up a gentleman and now as you can see associate with all sorts.'

Of the exasperating George Moore, writing for the Abbey Theatre, attempting to imitate Yeats's style:

> He made the dying Diarmuid say to Finn: 'I will kick you down the stairway to the stars.'

These excerpts are meant to show Yeats's liveliness of mind, not his bitchiness, for he revered these men, with the exception of Moore, who amused him, and therefore Moore too becomes grand, a Humour in some classic comedy.

Who accuses Yeats of being a poseur misses the point; you could turn it round and find in him the inspiration for an almost Boy Scout self-renewal. If he shrank from company he made himself enter it, if he suspected himself of diffidence he attended public meetings and made himself speak at them, to learn composure. He was able so to re-create himself because he believed in something outside himself, the revival of the soul of Ireland, without violence. This helped him – which is a laugh, he, the self-proclaimed 'king of the cats' – to believe that he was without personal ambition. Soon he was a leader founding committees, speaking all over the place.

> I knew that I was shy and timid… yet here I was delightedly talking to strange people every day. It was many years before I understood that I had surrendered myself to the chief temptation of the artist, creation without toil.

His remark about Beardsley's Catholicism is a reminder that Yeats appears almost ignorant of Christianity. His adored father was a vigorous unbeliever, and he barely mentions his mother. Yet,

> I was unlike others of my generation in one thing only. I am very religious…

This causes him not to dabble in, but scrabble almost humourlessly among, 'the ancient mysteries', aloof to the ludicrous.

> If you burnt a flower to ashes and put the ashes under, I think, the receiver of an air-pump, and stood the receiver in the moonlight for so many nights, the ghost of the flower would appear hovering over the ashes. I got together a committee which performed this experiment without results.

He quotes Lady Gregory saying to him,

> I have longed to turn Catholic, that I might be nearer to the people, but you have taught me that paganism brings me nearer still

which is silly enough to hold some truth. He endearingly worries about the gap between his self in poems and his daily self and evolves the theory of the antiself which sounds like Jekyll and Hyde. More sensibly, he concludes,

> Whatever happens I must go on, that there be a man behind the lines already written

– somehow he must live up to his poems. He hesitates over an old carved chest that contains his cabbalistic symbols (a real chest? an imagined one?) and wonders if he would not be better with the simple faith of a peasant. But he knew little of that faith or simplicity and the ignorance kept him from the religious squabbles of Ireland, the hesitation became the argument with himself that is his poetry. Do I make him sound daft? I find him magnificent.

His asides about writers can make you jump, and laugh. Of George Eliot:

> She seemed to have a distrust or a distaste for all in life that gives one a springing foot.

Perhaps it is his wholesale loathing of rational materialism, even at its highest-minded, which I found so inspiring, and still do. If it paradoxically sent him in pursuit of the materialising immaterial – which is to say, spooks – it also led him to detest realism, to mutter bitterly between his teeth, after a first encounter with Ibsen's *Ghosts*, 'Art is art because it is not nature'; helped him see through Shaw at once, yet recognise his value:

> I listened to *Arms and the Man* with admiration and hatred. It seemed to me inorganic, logical straightness, not the crooked path of life... Yet I delighted in Shaw, the formidable man. He could hit my enemies and the enemies of all I loved, as I could never hit... For years to come I was to wonder, whenever Shaw became my topic, whether the cock crowed for my blame or for my praise.

He may absurdly have tried at one time to become an alchemist, but out of his own base metal he made a style able to convey the gold, the glow, which he saw on the surface of the world, which gives the reader a 'springing foot'.

*October 1989*

# Saying It How It Is

These days publishers bring out lives of almost everybody, however marginal. Maybe readers buy them because they like to be assured of finding a beginning, middle and end. For desperate biographers there ought to be founded an Anecdote Bank. A recent review (of a biography) of the poet Allen Ginsberg has reminded me of two remarks I heard him make in the 1960s, which I offer to that Bank.

It was at the International Festival of Spoleto, in 1967, of which he was one of the stars. John Berryman was another, in a strange way drunk and not drunk at the same time, nearly incapable, but coherent. It was always Ginsberg who looked after him, cutting up his food, feeding him. ('*Il est une Soeur de la Charité,*' whispered Octavio Paz.)

One morning I walked with the robed, bearded, beaded Ginsberg, who had been frisked for drugs on arrival, his room searched, under constant police surveillance, as though his very presence was a threat. In fact he said he was using neither drugs nor alcohol, and the way he played guardian angel to Berryman's *âme damnée* was beautiful to see. I mentioned this, and he made an impatient exclamation (first anecdote): 'Why are these academic poets so goddam *intemperate*?' It was true; a remarkable number of the academically respectable American poets of the time – Berryman, Lowell, Roethke, there were others – seemed bent on self-destruction, for whatever reason; whereas here was the popular demon of the time, clean as a whistle and polite to boot. (Berryman was spectacularly rude.)

When he heard me read my poems (second anecdote), Ginsberg did a mime of being sent up the wall, resumed the lotus position and said, 'If you've got something to say why not say it how it is?' My response, probably unspoken, was double: 'Oh, if only I could!' and, 'How far will just saying it, Ginsberg, get you in the end? Anyway you don't.' I also permitted myself an unkind prophetic vision of the last of 'the best minds' of Ginsberg's generation jumping howling off a high building and survivor Allen, now sombre-suited, on the pavement applauding. But it was impossible not to like him. He had found something fresh, which suited the time; it had become a fashion, which he rode, but at least he had found it.

'Say it how it is', that Sixties recipe of hope, sincerity, and mess; wiping out past literature, its forms, obliquities, allusions. Obliterating the past itself perhaps, for can we ever be sure we can 'say it as it *was*'?

Yet it is a beautiful ambition.

To say it how it is must presumably be the aim of a journal, the reason for its dailyness. In his *Journals* Philip Toynbee, too, dips into the anecdote-pile. Concerned that he may be writing too intimately about his wife, he remembers Thomas Mann's wife complaining that she appeared too nakedly in her husband's work, and Mann replying, 'The more intimate, the more universal.'

Toynbee's aim, like Ginsberg's, was kindness and truth, but no more than Ginsberg ('Hebraic-Melvillian bardic breath') could he wholly abandon art. 'What is presented here [the first journal, *Part of a Journey*] remains a frank and intimate record of my daily life over a period of two years; but this does not mean that it is wholly spontaneous; still less that I have "told all" ... the order in which ideas came to me was not necessarily the *best* order.'

Toynbee was not an obviously Sixties figure, but he fitted obediently into the fashionable rebellions of most other decades: communist in the Thirties and Forties, nuclear disarmer in the Fifties, communard in the Seventies. Then he became clinically depressed. (He describes his final cancer as child's play compared to depression.) Within a couple of months of being cured (he hoped) of that depression he began what was to become *Part of a Journey*, a book which turns into a dogged search to possess the sort of loving kindness Ginsberg was able to show. Then, more explicitly, by means of meditation, prayer, and an almost frenzied reading of devotional literature, it becomes a search for God or, more precisely, for an intellectual justification of his intuition – 'There must be more to it than this.' In the end he decided that he must be 'the apostle to spiritual dolts', and there does seem in him a strange belief that the kind of truth he sought was to be found in religious books. But then he was the sort of man who had only to look at his cat, Bubbles, to then have to promise himself to buy the definitive book on cats.

In short, as Auden said of Yeats, he was silly like us, but shafts of self-mockery lighten every page. These take on the fascination of narrative because, unknown to himself, complaining, laughing, with many backslidings, he does seem to be turning into a saintly man. After the disintegration of the commune, his home, Barn House, was in a great mess:

> As I was starting the fearsome task of clearing out the big front flowerbed at BH Phil came up and offered me a whetstone for my hook. Then he stood watching me work, with the full intensity of his shaggy earnestness. I gestured, as if whimsically, at a particularly tall clump of docks and thistle; and Phil thought it over for

some time before saying, 'If you mean you want me to do some *work*, Philip, I'm afraid I can't because I'm just going up to meditate with Rose.'

It says something for the efficacy of Philip's own meditations that he is able, after a while 'through the grace of God' to regard this as 'hilarious'.

'Gardened for a full hour with only a single thought of God (God Wot!)'. Does that give the flavour, of earnestness and self-consciousness? 'Beer is indeed the greatest help – apart from S. Perhaps my whole journey has been to find a God who will be an adequate beer-substitute.' These are from the second hook, *End of a Journey* (not his title) in which he finds he has cancer. In notes he did not live to revise he charts his dying. These are some of the best (as Ginsberg would expect). At first reading, I hastened to the end eagerly – we all like middles and ends. But at the second I kept postponing it, could not bear to part with him, a man still watching himself when he is being taken home for the last time. 'As I left, Mr T came out of his office and said: "He has been an inspiration to the whole ward – to all of us, doctors and staff as well." I wanted to say Go on! Go on! in case any of the family had missed it!'

Perhaps, instead of biographies, publishers should be commissioning journals. But saying it as it is, and then selecting, is not as easy as Toynbee makes it look.

*February 1990*

# Shoes Covered for Occasions

The poet Pearse Hutchinson, old friend, Dubliner, has long been sceptical of my tales of the pleasant experiences that Ireland always affords; he feels he knows the place too well. It seemed a good idea to take him to the west, and prove my point. I had been lent a cottage in Mayo, long disused, and I wanted to leave Dublin first thing in the morning so that we could reach it in daylight, find how to warm the place up. Then I remembered that Pearse likes to sidle gingerly into the day, so in Dublin I telephoned to book us a staging-post, and immediately began one of the pleasant experiences, with Directory Enquiries. 'D'you mean you got *through*?' was the chorus when I returned to tell my tale. I had indeed. 'Could you tell me the number of the Anglers' Arms at Headford, County Mayo?' 'Of course I can – except it isn't in Mayo, it's in Galway. A lovely place.' 'You know it!' 'It's one of my favourite watering-holes when I'm visiting my brother Matt in the west. You'll have a great time. The new people there have done a fine job with the renovations.' That word cast me down a little, for it is always bad news when connected with a pub, but I was enchanted by the personal note, characteristic of my experience of Ireland, although I suppose it may be a reason why people get the engaged tone. Anyway, when I told the story, Pearse's face took on its usual expression of courteously suspended disbelief.

On our way to supper we passed a notice: 'SHOES COVERED FOR WEDDINGS'. Pearse and I stared up at it, puzzled, and one of our group said gently: 'It's for people with not too much money', as though fearful that I was about to make an English Marie Antoinette remark, and wonder why they did not just buy new shoes. It was good to be reminded how much poorer Ireland is than England.

Reminded, also, of how settled it is, compared to England. In the car driving west Pearse's talk was always of people, and these were given a locality – 'a Limerick man', 'a Cork man', even 'a west-Cork man' – and such origins were held to explain, in some part, their characters and behaviour. By late afternoon we had crossed the Shannon, and were certainly in a particular place, the skies widened, the fields were bordered with walls of black boulders, with white lichen on them. When the sky is seen through the gaps between the boulders these walls are like intricate lace. The cottage, on a lake, nestled, it seemed, in its own cloud of variegated birds, but it would be too difficult to warm up in time; besides, Pearse had arranged for us to read our poems to the Yeats Society in Sligo, so, at least to my regret, next day, we left the Anglers' Rest and pressed on. In Sligo we were talked to, pleasantly, by strangers in the street, Pearse's disbelief diminishing by the minute. Also, you can talk easily about Christianity in Ireland. Someone at the Yeats Society said that it was all right to love Creation, since Vatican II, because it is God's; 'the vale of tears' side is now played down. Many of us have had no difficulty with this, but it was a reminder of the importance, and danger, of words. A misplaced emphasis can ruin a life. The later Church Fathers recognised this and developed a principle of *oeconomia* (economy of precise formulations) and Christ was notably economical when he was allowed to be; it is easy to hear his impatience with the demands on him to be too narrowly specific, of which, more later.

We heard neighbouring Leitrim called the Cinderella of Irish counties, be-laked but little visited, and so poor, 'the snipe fly over it upside down', because they know they will see nothing below worth eating, so we made our way into it. At Dromkeeran – 'slope of the rowan trees', Pearse speaks Irish – the snipe would have known there would have been no food in the pub we stopped at, but would have been wrong, for somewhere from a private kitchen a sandwich was produced, for which payment was refused, and that was before Pearse had found out he knew the barman's cousin. This young man bade us Godspeed to Ballinamore (just down the road) with such an unselfconscious Syngesong of eloquence, so lengthy, so well constructed, that we both sat for a while silent in the car, wondering if we could trust our ears. 'Can you remember *exactly* what he said?' I asked Pearse. 'I wish to God I could,' he replied. In the Ballinamore hotel a princely girl climbed two flights of stairs to ask the newly arrived visitors whether she could bring them a cup of tea. Our progress, for so it seemed to have become, was much punctuated by such princely girls, bold-eyed – so long as 'bold' does not suggest an invitation, which was certainly not there.

But Tommy Sheridan, presiding over the bar opposite did not see this quality in the younger generation. He genially pronounced them useless. 'The young fellas, if they had to look after themselves they'd even burn the shaving-water! And the girls are no better. They may have qualifications as long as your arm, but they'd serve a dishcloth for a dinner!'

Sceptical Pearse, after a last, lengthy encounter with a woman from whom he was buying me some homemade pickle, was convinced at last. He had been told the people of Leitrim were the pleasantest in Ireland, and he found them so. There and elsewhere, he agreed, we had had nothing but good experiences. But back in Dublin, before our poetry-reading, someone said Jane Grigson had died. This shook me; she was a friend and neighbour and I had meant to ring her before I left for Ireland. 'Oh yes,' boomed the voice, 'it's been a great week for literary deaths. Rosamond Lehmann is dead too.' My mother-in-law, a central part of my emotional furniture, to say the least. The evening passed somehow, we cut the trip short and I flew home.

There I came upon something that has nagged at me since: a matter of words. Her obituary described Rosamond as a Christian. Rosamond believed many things but whether the word Christian could be elasticated to include them all, and whether she would want it to be, is doubtful. There was the same discomfort at Jane Grigson's funeral. She was not a Christian; she told me so, when inconsolable at Geoffrey's death. But the devout priest, a friend of hers, claimed that because she was brave and generous – which she was – hers was a 'Christian soul'. Well, maybe, but I had an uneasy feeling that in both cases shoes were being hurriedly crammed on feet they did not fit, shoes two thoughtful women had chosen not to wear while they were alive; or, at best, willy-nilly, a sense of Shoes Covered for Funerals.

*April 1990*

# Eavesdropping on Language

In a book of essays by different hands, *Newman after a Hundred Years* (OUP), the Warden of Merton College, Oxford, J.M. Roberts, argues in lively fashion that in Newman's *The Idea of a University*, even Newman's *language*, in the sense of the presuppositions behind the words, has become irrelevant, in practical terms near to meaningless, in a 'pluralistic' society. Even so, Roberts comes down heavily on Newman's side in one respect, and reiterates the warning we hear booming from every quarter: 'We have never needed more in this country Newman's emphasis on the importance in education of writing and good language.'

You stumble across evidence of this need everywhere, but you only have to dip a toe into the educational pool to find an impassioned and influential body of theorists who do not believe in the correction of writing, spelling, vocabulary, and who, when the results of their theory can be seen to be disastrous, and somebody suggests doing something about it, are awesome in their wrath. So, resignedly, when you pass a shop-window with a printed notice in it, 'The Management apoligises ...' you think, sadly, 'Oh, what does it matter, if the sense is clear?', and pass on, trying to rid yourself of the further, nagging question, 'If that doesn't matter, what does?'

On the radio you hear so many odd usages you wonder whether the language itself is changing (of course it is – but so fast?). There seems to be a problem about which preposition goes with which verb. Can you say, 'equal with'? Perhaps you can, but it sounds strange to me. I once even thought of writing these things down as they occurred, but dismissed the idea as only befitting a grisly buffer who is determined to believe it is not he, but the world, that is going to pot. As a result of not writing them down I forget them at once, delighted to, but some have stuck, mostly from cricket commentaries. Trevor Bailey used to smack his lips over the 'solidarity' of Geoffrey Boycott's batting. My sympathies are with Bailey's instinct, because 'solidity' is an unpleasant, mincing word, whereas 'solidarity' you can flick neatly round your palate and your teeth, almost hear it rattle against the boundary-board. Solidarity with his team is precisely what Boycott lacked; he was described the other day as the most selfish batsman who ever buckled on a pad. (Once, when he was losing the chance of winning a game by playing for himself, Botham called him for an impossible run. Uncharacteristically, Boycott obeyed and, as they passed, demanded to know what Botham thought he was doing. 'Running you out, you bastard!') More topically, a new commentator, the Lancashire David Lloyd, insists on calling Atherton a 'singular' batsman. His colleagues have decided that he must mean 'single-minded' and they leave it at that. Perhaps it is a Lancastrianism.

Still on cricket: at Lord's these days what used to be called the tannoy and is now called the Public Address System addresses the public constantly and tannoyingly, puffing the books of cricketers and commentators, reminding us that behind the Pavilion is 'the most unique cricketing museum' … (At Luton Airport the PA asked Mr So-and-So to come to the ticket desk 'in personage'.)

But these are ragged thoughts about verbal untidiness in a month which is itself untidy. My dislike of the English August is as deep-rooted as it is daft. In nature it is a month in which most things have finished growing and now look tangled and exhausted. Trees become thin on top, you can see the sky through them, like a scalp. This is not the natural autumnal change, but one that makes you wonder if the trees are in fact dying; it is an uneasy month. However, there has been one change in the direction of tidiness and it is beautiful. There used to be haystacks and strawstacks, then there were straw bales, then straw was collected into swiss rolls in black plastic bags. Now there is a new machine that rolls up the straw after the combine harvester and places round it, automatically, a thin transparent membrane which glows a slightly lighter colour than the straw. So now the hill-sides are littered with these neat cylinders in two tones of gold, and lie on a third tone, the stubble, and the fields are like the background of a de Chirico painting.

August is also untidy as regards work; a time for visiting and being visited. Even while visiting it is impossible not to eavesdrop on language. On St Michael's Mount last week a small girl asked her mother what a monk was, and our ears swivelled towards the reply like radar saucers: 'A kind of man nun – who says prayers – does good things.' Not bad. Another mother, gently, to a galloping son, 'You are not being patient.' This stopped him in mid-galumph, his head angled, thinking. It is a rather tricky concept. I doubt whether I would have put it like that, semi-positively, but it worked. Maybe we only learn how to bring up children in, as it were, August, when the growing is done, the tangles in place, and their next step is to grow thin on top.

As for being visited, I hope I am sociable enough, but find daylong chat so difficult that after visitors are gone I sometimes feel like writing to them, to apologise. Encouraging, therefore, to find a note from Newman to one of his novices:

> It is strange to write you a note about nothing; but such is my fate just now and for some time, that, since I have nothing to say to you, I must either be silent or unseasonable. Many is the time I have stood over the fire at breakfast or looked at you in Recreation, hunting for something to talk about.

Altogether, I have in August a sense of time being wasted; neurotic, no doubt, and perhaps it is not so. 'Time … worships language, and forgives' (sang Auden in his Yeats poem, though he later cut the verse out),

> Everyone by whom it lives.
> Time that with this strange excuse
> Pardons Kipling and his views
> And will pardon Paul Claudel,
> Pardons him for writing well.

All this went from the poem, as it is now printed, presumably because Auden came to disagree with himself. A pity; it seems *almost* a waste of time to remember lines that no longer, officially, exist.

But Cardinal Newman, Warden Roberts, maestro Auden, are right about language. In his *Commonplace Book* E.M. Forster copied a sentence from a letter sent him by J.R. Ackerley:

> The days potter by here much the same: sometimes the sad sound of their ticking feet gets into my ears as they disappear into history, carrying nothing in their delicate hands but a yawn.

(Can Ackerley have been talking about August?) After writing this down Forster adds: 'Can the day which produced such a sentence be lost?'

*September 1990*

# The Courtesy of Naming

Farmers don't go in for gates in County Mayo. Or rather (no part of Ireland is quite the same as another, and no part of a part) they do not often have them on the near-islands of Inishard, Inishmaine and Inishcogue, on the shores of Lough Mask. They were full islands once, probably within historical memory, and perhaps are again when the lake is high because the dark little hazel-woods are lined zig-zag with a surprising wrack of dried lake-weed and bleached timber. The absence of field gates is puzzling, the small fields enclosed with no break by those single-layered walls of round or roundish stones, the kind you can see through when they are against the sky. How do they let the animals in, never mind the sky? Also, they are difficult to climb over because unsteady; the top stones wobble and fall, with a noise that echoes across the quiet islands. These are easy to replace, and that is the answer, I daresay. When you want to get anything in or out you take down a bit of wall, and build it up again behind you, or behind the sheep.

Not only is that tide-wrack zig-zag; so are the walls and the wood and the shore with long inlets and lagoons at different angles, so it is easy in that small space to become entirely lost. Then you are confronted either by impassable water, or bog, or a tangle of trees and brambles apparently undisturbed since the Ice Age. Or so it seems, though you come across roofless overgrown cottages – Captain Boycott's house is just across the way; you can see its smoking chimneys through the trees. But then you come across all sorts of things, inscrutable now, but post-Ice Age: sweathouses, with triangular stone entrances still intact and usable, were there anybody still around to use them; and the standing stones of the fort of a King of Connacht before Saint Cormac came to build his abbey in the sixth century. These stones have almost vanished under briars and elders, but it is an affecting place when you tear your way through to it, commanding a wide prospect of his bare kingdom. Cormac's abbey is there, well-tended, with the usual National Monument gravel on the ground between its roofless walls; but that too has an astonishing habit of popping up unexpectedly when you thought you were far from it, and appearing distantly, on another shore, when you thought you were about to reach it.

For these reasons it needs no explanation that Irish folklore is full of *pucas*, fairies, and why people believed in them, or half-believed. It is not just the shifting Atlantic light, making a mountain lour like a North Welsh slate quarry one moment, and beckon like the Garden of Eden when you next glimpse it from between the branches of those small, low woods; it is not only the fact that the place is constantly changing before your eyes. It is the woods themselves, full of green light and quiet, littered with the débris of some volcanic explosion, pocked and squared-off rocks like the remains of ancient buildings, covered so deeply with sphagnum moss you can sink your hand in it up to the wrist. Between these are paths, which are not quite paths – but what could have made them? Only an unusually individualistic sheep, and that some time ago, for it is not certain that they are paths, yet they seem to be. You do not believe it, of course, but when you lose sight and sound of your companion – probably pausing, lost in wonder at having come across another stretch of water that shouldn't be there at all – you are oddly relieved when you hear again the rustle, and the voice, and you both involuntarily speak in whispers. This is surely why every nook and cranny in rural Ireland is securely named. It is a form of reassurance, a way of making the place keep still.

Not that Ireland, any more than anywhere else, is keeping still. A boyish-looking and cheerful TV columnist in the *Sunday Independent* decides, long after Yeats, that Romantic Ireland's dead and gone, because the future lies in big farms, run as businesses:

> What are we going to do with the whole country, then, since nothing we produce (or very little, on the positive side the Germans like our fillet steaks) is much required by anyone? Surely there is something we can grow … carrots? parsnips? cabbages? Maybe they have enough of everything. Maybe it's farmhouse holidays they are looking for.

Young as he is he remembers the mill and maltings and bacon-factory of his Enniscorthy boyhood and, Irish-fashion, relishes the latter's name – 'Buttles Barley-fed Bacon'.

> These did not close because of falling profits, they closed because of the takeovers, large conglomerates seeking larger monopolies; they are a thing of the past, pre-1992 Ireland. What's to be done with the whole country? Offers on a postcard only please.

This is the mood of Ireland, but the naming goes on; it is like the building of a round-stone wall, a definition, not an exclusion. Perhaps it has always been necessary in the eery, shifting countryside. The blind poet Raftery manages four names in four lines of his Song of County Mayo:

It is in Claremorris I'll stop the first evening,
At Balla beneath it I'll first take the floor;
I'll go to Kiltimagh and have a month's peace there,
And that's not two miles from Ballinamore.

(A poet in Dublin recommended the Claremorris bacon, 'the best in Ireland'. The 'To Let' notices were up on the bacon-factory before we reached it.)

Nobody knows what will survive or not, anywhere, but the new Penguin *Contemporary Irish Poetry* is stuffed with names, of both people and places, and an extraordinary number of the poems begin with one, in the title or the first line. 'It is December in Wicklow ...', 'Bartley Costello ...', 'I think of that meadow off down in Coyne's', 'A Disused Shed in Co. Wexford'. You begin to understand that this persistent naming is a form of courtesy, like replacing a stone in a wall. It is a way of arresting, not history, but dissolution; it is clear-eyed, and saves the reader that weary unassisted climb into the psyche of the poet that is so often required elsewhere. By means of names they get the particular world into their lines – even those most prosaic of letters, 'EEC'.

In that borrowed house on Inishard I made the acquaintance of *Flashman* (he had the experience of an Apache sweathouse) and of John Mortimer's *Clinging to the Wreckage*. Both Good Reads, but so is the Penguin *Contemporary Irish Poetry*. Contemporary Ireland is in it, which still includes, because of generations of naming, Cormac and Raftery and ex-bacon-factories.

*October 1990*

# A Touch of the Tassos

James Fenton conducts a little poetry class in the review section of the *Independent on Sunday*. Each week he takes a single poem, or part of a poem, and talks about it. An idea as simple as *Desert Island Discs*, it is surprising that no one thought of it before. A Sunday or two ago he produced a poem of his own and held it up to the light. He confessed as he did so that, in his view, you cannot revise a poem, you can only tinker with it, because you are permanently stuck with the sound and the idea that made you want to write the poem in the first place. In his case it was the sound of a four-beat line in a certain metre, about the falling-away of love. Given this matter and rhythm to play with he found himself blocked, or at least impeded, by the memory of Shakespeare at one end – 'Fear no more the heat of the sun', and Auden at the other – 'Lay your sleeping head my love'. Whether he succeeds in wriggling away from these echoes towards something of his own he leaves the reader to decide.

Such a workshop glimpse provides one explanation of 'writer's block'. Any writer, whether of verse or prose, knows that if you begin at the wrong point you find yourself having to swerve round unsuspected obstacles until you lose your way altogether and find yourself stuck in the sand. Fear of this sometimes makes it impossible to set out at all, because once sand is reached all tinkering is useless. What is needed is revision and that is like trying to fit caterpillar-tracks to wheels, sand-embedded, intended for the road you have somehow lost. Fenton cites the case of Tasso, revising his epic for traces of heresy, and becoming so obsessed that, fearful he would end by tearing to pieces his own poem, 'men in white doublets came and carried him away'.

But in 1900 Yeats confided to his friend Æ (George Russell) that his idea of happiness was to spend the rest of his life rewriting the poems he had already written. It is easy to understand what he meant, but our loss would have been great, because we now know that he had barely begun. The story comes from George Moore's irresistible autobiography, *Ave, Salve, Vale*, a wonderful book in many ways, but one which inadvertently contains an example of why writers sometimes stare in panic out of the window. As if fear of engulfing sand were not enough, there is also the consciousness of the appalling significance of apparently trivial detail; a misplaced comma or, in this case, apostrophe, can not only wreck a sentence, it can wreck a writer, as we may see. Unfortunately, the passage is long and has to be cut, but nothing is omitted that could save it from its final, last-word wreckage.

Moore tells us that while he was writing *Esther Waters* it became his habit 'to gossip with my laundress after breakfast, a pious woman of the Nonconformist type, like Esther herself'. He wants to know what she thinks of the Parnell-O'Shea divorce case, but he cannot keep her attention away from the recent murder of a baby. Surely, says Moore, she doesn't think the two cases parallel, divorce and murder?

Don't you think so, sir? And I can still see her rolling her apron about her arms. It comes to the same thing in the end, sir, for when one party goes away from the other party, the party that's left behind dies.

Her view of life interested me; the importance of desertion is greater among the lower classes than it is among the upper...

You can't seriously maintain, Mrs Millar, that adultery is as great a crime as murder?

Still winding her coarse apron round her arms, she stood looking at me, her eyes perplexed and ambiguous...

You know your bible, Mrs Millar? You know the story of the woman of Samaria? And you remember that Christ forbade the people to stone her, and told her to sin no more? Mrs Millar, you can't deny that Christ said that, and you a Christian woman.

Yes, sir, he did say that; but you must remember he was only a bachelor.

I think I fell back in my chair and looked at my laundress in amazement, until she began to wonder what was the matter, and she must have wondered more when I told her she had said something I should never forget.

But what I said is true, isn't it? she answered shyly.

Yes, it's quite true, only nobody ever thought of it before, Mrs Millar! It's true that the married man who brings home his wages at the end of the week is the one that understands life, and you are quite right to condone Christ's laxity in not pronouncing a fuller condemnation. You are quite right. The bachelor may not attain to any full comprehension of the 'ome.

Oh, George Moore, that aitch so fatally dropped! Liberated, 'modern', George Moore, apostle of sexual freedom, lover of Manet and Monet, you were, after all, of your time, caught in the trammels of class, unable to resist that wink towards the gentle reader, past Mrs Millar, that conspiratorial "ome'. Even in the midst of your admiration it fell upon you, like a tic. You nearly knew this, nearly. Irish-born you had fled Ireland, because you regarded 'Irishness' as a form of disease. But the Boer War revolted you, the complacent cruelty of England, and you fled back to Ireland, half-crazed according to your own account, to sit in Druidic souterrains with Æ, invoking the ghosts of Etain and Midir. Anything, to get away from English pride of race and class. You even, amazed at yourself and hypnotised by your beloved Yeats, found yourself writing a play about Diarmuid and Grania in French, to be translated into English by Lady Gregory, by Taidgh O'Donaghue into Irish, then back into English from the Irish, again by Lady Gregory, 'for Yeats to put his style upon'. This four-fold removal was intended to cleanse the language of its associations, was an attempt, precisely, to get away from that time-bound, class-bound, tic of a wink at the reader, that dreadful "ome'. If only you had been afflicted by even a touch of the Tassos at that point, had removed that damning blob, that point of condescension. But that would not have been tinkering, that would have needed revision, Tasso-sized, of your whole view of the world, the world you struggled to change; it would have required new tracks, new bogie-wheels, a new vehicle altogether, which might have brought you safely among us, because, although we have not much to boast of, we are wiser in that respect, or hope we are.

*December 1990*


# The Real MacCaig


Brian Inglis, one-time editor of *The Spectator*, genially reproached me because last month this column began with an account of James Fenton's poetry teach-in – which did not interest him at all – and then went on to discuss George Moore, a writer who interests him very much. This he might have missed, because put off by the beginning. Should there not have been a headline telling him what was the real subject of the piece? Well, a declaratory headline might be a good idea, if only to save Mr Inglis from wasting his time, if there is any single subject to declare, but his remark set me reflecting on the bogusness of one-subject writing. The most apparently forthright article is deceiving us about the way the mind works. It may concern, say, the excellence and utility of Mr Rupert Murdoch. He is good for reasons, a, b, c. Those who do not think so are wrong for reasons, x, y, z. QED. We know where we stand, we move on, perhaps to be battered about the ears by the next open-and-shut and cocksure list of opinions. But we know at the back of our minds that we are not being told the whole truth, that the writer is inevitably writing about himself, his history, even about his relationship with Mr Murdoch, although he does not say so. He is also affected by his domestic circumstances, and by what is happening around him as he writes. He cannot be expected to explain all this every time but his directness is illusory. G.K. Chesterton long ago suggested that the portentousness of such journalism would be greatly reduced if the writer were forced to confess where he was writing it; if, for example, under the title, 'Will Australia adopt Bimetallism?' we could read, 'Top of an Omnibus', it would be more honest. More honest, also, is the sidelong approach, suggestion of less than complete certainty, an attempt to make connections between apparently disparate things, not only because this is fun but because it is the way our minds work, or should work, and to make such connections is perhaps why we were placed in this vale of tears in the first place. It is a form of poetry, and one with which Auberon Waugh would presumably have no truck.

His name comes in here because he has long been campaigning against obscurity in modern verse, and he may find it obscure because poetry is usually trying to do two or three things at the same time and to suggest (not insist upon) a connection between them. It cannot be skim-read for content because it can change course, come in one door and leave by another. Annoying.

To support his case he has published an *Anthology of Real Poetry*, verses published in the *Literary Review*, which he edits. In his Introduction he dismisses 'the modern movement' (inaugurated, he suggests, by T.S. Eliot) as a cul-de-sac, and its imitators as 'a disgrace to English literature'. But there are no imitators, not in England, not direct ones. He wants a return to traditional forms, but W.H. Auden boasted that he had employed every traditional form. He wants a return to rhyme, but Louis MacNeice was a superb rhymer. These are both post-Eliot and they have their equivalents today. I am not arguing with him, I agree that most contemporary poetry is bosh – it always is. What I found surprising, going through his anthology, was how unreal it is, and lifeless. I found myself saying, time after time, 'But this isn't a *poem* at all!', and was filled with a gloomy sense that I would have to tell him so, and why; so here goes. Firstly, the verses frequently only contain one subject and are so verbally predictable that as soon as we know what it is we know we are in for no further surprises; secondly, most of the verses contain too many words put in to satisfy the mechanical tyranny of the scansion and the beat often falls on the wrong, flat word; thirdly, and this was perhaps inevitable after the firstly and secondly, too many of them degenerate into facetiousness.

But Auberon Waugh is right. Form in poetry is important; hard to imagine a single contemporary poet, worthy of the name, who would disagree with him. The trouble is, it is not as simple (or single) a subject as he seems to imagine.

Take the worrying case of Norman MacCaig. It is equally hard to imagine any of his contemporaries not agreeing that he is a good poet. Seamus Heaney has suggested that of living poets in English MacCaig is his favourite. He has recently become 80 and, to mark the occasion, his publishers have reissued and enlarged and rearranged *Collected Poems*. If you work your way through this volume you become aware that, in any usual sense of the word 'form', MacCaig is slowly abandoning it, *and becoming better and better*. This is worrying, even frightening, because others may imitate, without his ear and eye. He makes it look easy. Asked how long it took him to write a poem he answered, looking sidelong, 'Two cigarettes', but he is a sly, Edinburgh man, fond of teasing. Or it could be true.

### Cock Before Dawn

Those dabbling hens I ferociously love
sag on their perches, half deflated.
I'll have none of it. I'm regimental. A plumbline
goes from my head to my toes. I burnish
the dark with my breast.

Lucifer's my blood brother. When I spread my wings
I'm crystal battlements and thunderbolts. I tread the earth
By pretending not to.
The West and the East are measured from me ...
It's time I crowed. The sun will be waiting.

If any should say that has only one subject, a cock, does it not also make us cringe, at our own illusion of centrality?

Absence of form has liberated the poetic bits of himself; he sees, he writes down, and leaves the rest out. It is like the freedom of the old Matisse, with his masterly coloured cut-outs. Possibly this lack of conventional form gains its strength from our knowledge that form exists elsewhere, and its absence here is a comment, a kind of form; a justifiable trick because it gives him a sketcher's quick wrist. However, it raises an impossible question: it is poetry – but is it a poem? Perhaps the difference is between oil-paint and crayon, I don't know. His poems are short and, collected, draw strength from each other; but that, too, is fair, because a long poem is only bits joined together; as somebody said, a long poem is a contradiction in terms.

*January 1991*

# Alienation a Way of Life

Holed up in a house on the outskirts of Boston, the two battle-buddies, English and American (well, each of us had, at different times, worn uniform and had heard shots fired), sat transfixed by CNN on television. The Gulf war was reaching its climax, the land attack was going in, and we could not get enough of it. I, hypnotised by the strange format – when one of the deadpan newscasters said 'CNN continues', that meant it didn't, it stopped for a commercial break – he, drinking in as much as he could because his own house, whither we were headed next day, did not have a television set, never mind Cable Network News. Even then, a few hours into the visit, I sensed that his interest in the war, that mirrored my own, was unusual among his countrymen. True, when CNN took a longer break than usual and we went for a walk, there were yellow ribbons round the telegraph posts and an unusual number of flags about. I never did get to the bottom of those yellow ribbons. Peter thought they had some-thing to do with prostitutes and the Civil War, others that they derived from a popular song. It seemed an instant tradition, shakily founded, but its message was clear: sympathy with 'our boys' in the desert. As for the flags, he shrugged; people showing that they were patriotic? More likely, he growled, they were saying, to unflagged houses, 'Why aren't you as patriotic as *me*?'

My own preoccupation, which I had brought with me from England, was that Americans should stop talking about 'our' forces and talk more about United Nations' ones and, above all, should not crow over the likely victory because that would only make them more hated than they already were and that, for the future of the Middle East, was a Bad Thing. 'What the hell? They're going to hate us whatever we do.'

That reply confirmed something I had already suspected. There for ten days, self-committed to an orgy of visitor's generalisations – a longer stay, and too many contradictory messages would be heard – I decided it meant that Americans had given up any hope of being understood by the outside world, or of understanding it themselves, and had therefore made up their minds to take as little notice of it as possible. That was day one, and nothing that followed in the next nine days gave me any reason to change that view.

Indeed, on the last of the ten days, I was in a bar in Princeton, New Jersey, opposite the University. It was lunchtime, the place was crowded, the television set was on, President Bush was announcing the ceasefire (I think) and not one single person was watching or listening. I could not hear what he was saying so I walked to the loudspeaker of the set and still I could not hear. I took a careful look round, checking, making sure my generalisation had a right to be so firmly in place; no doubt about it, not a single person of the 80 or so there was taking the smallest notice of the President. (For three or four days previously, in New York, as I crossed the lobby of the hotel, I had been aware that CNN was permanently on a large screen in the bar. There was Stormin' Norman, there was that staring-eyed Marine General, there were the whole *dramatis personae* of the televised presentation of the Gulf war which had so fascinated me and my upstate friend, *and the sound was turned off.*)

Upstate New York is like England, like the west country, only there is more of it, range upon range of wooded hills, with smooth pastures between, and creeks. A few hundred yards down the road from us John Cowper Powys wrote *A Glastonbury Romance* in the cottage he scandalised locals by calling 'Phudd Bottom'. He had reason, because it is almost buried at the foot of an eminence called Phudd Hill, near the top of which he thought he detected Indian graves, piles of stones, against which he was in the habit of leaning his forehead, asking their forgiveness. Around Phudd Hill we could learn little of the progress of the war, certainly not from the few locals, but eventually, on a hissing radio, we heard that President Bush was to give a press conference so we stayed tuned. Would he crow? My battle-buddy,

Democrat, poet, listened with his head on the table, cradled in his arms, not daring to look at me. His opinion of his President was rock-bottom – 'He crawled up the inside of the pipe', and, a keen constitutionalist, he was doubtful of the legality of Bush's commitment of forces to the Gulf. Bush was modest, natural, giving credit to the allies, showing sympathy for the Iraqi people, in human, non-pompous terms. You had no sense at all of his aides biting their fingernails, fearful he would depart from their brief, as you had with his predecessor. He trusted himself to feel the right things and therefore to say the right things, and he did. 'Jeez!' said Peter, his face raised from his arms, 'he was brought up as a Christian and a gentleman *and some of it rubbed off.*'

I wondered at the time if there was anyone but me to whom he could have said that, at least in that way. There seems a loneliness in Americans (the habit of generalisation, once indulged, becomes addictive). I had lunch in New York with another writer-friend and he talked of the stifling conformism of American society. He told me that Oxford in the early 1950s, after his own Ivy League university, opened his eyes. This made me open mine, because if he found Oxford at that time liberating what can his American university have been like? Certainly Princeton had seemed overly quiet – on the campus, if not in that bar. After lunch we walked in Central Park, along Fifth Avenue. It was a Sunday and the park was closed to traffic and half New York was jogging, cycling (very fast, head down), roller-skating (ditto), all clad in more or less identical day-glo trainers, knee-pads, helmets, all going in the same direction and all wearing Walkmans. (We happened to be wearing tweed jackets and some of the cyclists wobbled dangerously at the sight of our weird attire.)

I like the place; it is unanxious, because alienation is accepted, made a way of life. I could not live there because there is a hole in the town that no one outside it can think of, the wrecked upper West Side, Harlem, breakdown, Aids, crack. How do they manage, if there are things they dare not think of, talk of? The answer to that is the last discovery/generalisation of the trip, and worth another attack of italicisation. In four different places we found four very different people who confessed they spent several evenings a week at Alcoholics Anonymous, and *they did not have a drink problem.* It just made them feel good, they went to it as to a sacrament, a communion. The religious instinct will out, somehow.

*April 1991*

# Sir Victor and Seán

Just re-issued in paperback is V.S. Pritchett's *Dublin*. Even those who have no interest in the town, or in Ireland, cannot fail to be entertained, so well-observed it is, so intelligent and sympathetic. He first went there as a journalist in 1922, a 21-year-old who found himself 'in a marvellously eloquent city', and stayed there for two years learning his story-teller's art from people like Frank O'Connor and Seán O'Faoláin. He went back often, and in 1967 wrote *Dublin*, with knowledgeable love. There is one passage, however, when even he seems to lose his admirable balance, in a way that tells us more about a certain kind of Englishness than about Ireland:

> I have seen men running anxiously, prayer book in hand, to mass, with an expression on their faces that one sees nowadays perhaps only on the faces of elderly Welsh Baptists. The habit of making the sign of the cross as you pass a church or convent is still common in Dublin – I have seen a young man in running shoes, practising for some race, pause to cross himself as he ran past Haddington Church; and bus conductors pause, as they hand you your ticket, to do the same if they catch sight of the cross out of the corner of their eye as the bus sways past. It requires an art to clip a ticket, take the money, cross yourself and keep your balance all at the same time. Taxi-drivers, as in Spain, will take their hands off the wheel to do the same... At Westland Row Station, early in the morning, the male passengers pop quickly into the church next door for a few minutes on the way to the office. Is the Dubliner a very cautious man or woman? Is he constantly insuring himself? Or is it evidence of the dramatic, anxious inner nature of Puritan or Jansenist religion? I think the last.

The questions are surprising, but what is disappointing is the detached amusement, sense of the quaint – despite the mention of Spain. The fact is that everyday acknowledgement of the supernatural is commonplace just about everywhere *except* England. In Bali the people put a handful of rice beside a statue, before they eat, as casually and abstractedly as you would put out a saucer of milk for a cat – or as people cross themselves in a Dublin street. Ivor Gurney, than whom no poet is more English, noticed the difference in France, in 1916: 'They are very devout, and feel their religion much more nearly than *les Anglais*.'

He came to the conclusion that

The truth is, as Hardy says, the English fall back on stoic fatalism; and whatever it is they believe, it is not Christianity. They go to church, and desire something spiritual, but it is nothing the churches give them. They are fine, but self-reliant, not relying on God.

Whether this is true or not the point is that the English do not find themselves odd in this respect; it is the others who are odd. This can create a gap, a possibility of historical and cultural misunderstanding (to put it at its mildest) with the rest of the world, in this case with Ireland, that can make the son of a British policeman, John Whelan, almost an exact contemporary of Pritchett's, call himself Seán O'Faoláin.

It is a despairing recognition of the gap, put in linguistic terms. It says, if we cannot hear each other, let us each be free to make our own noise. Not that O'Faoláin was an eager crosser of himself in the street. He soon came up against the clergy and most of his books were banned. But that is another part of the same story, which is not simply told.

In *An Irish Journey*, O'Faoláin finds himself in Castlecomer and remembers 'J.K.L.', who is still remembered – James, Bishop of Kildare and Leighlin, one of the priests who gave the Irish back their dignity.

He would come here dressed in his episcopal robes, and, clasping his crozier, he would face these dark-eyed, frieze-coated men of Leix, maybe as many as 8,000 of them, and he would harangue them in the open (no Catholic churches in those days – only mud hovels) until the sweat poured off him. His methods were Hildebrandine. He, too, would have made a king crawl on his knees before him.

Then O'Faoláin, distracted by a picture of a British soldier in his hotel room, remembers his cousin, killed at Arras – so narrow is the gap; but it is deep, because he thinks again of 'J.K.L.'

His predecessor in the see of Kildare and Leighlin lived in the bog in a mud hovel. So did the church cower in the bad century, the 18th, Doyle was of different metal. With his long lean hands he used to tear the thatch from cabins unfit to be churches, and rip the tattered vestments in two, trying to make his clergy realise that the bad century was finished and done with. Poor men, they sometimes sewed up the vestments when he was gone. Once he took a leaking chalice and smashed it flat with a stone…

That was written by a man who was no fawning friend of the clergy, or of the Ireland they were creating. Far from it, but it does show, as the Irish might say, 'a power of history' behind the public Catholic manifestations which so surprised Pritchett. Sometimes it seems that knowledge of that history might help to remove the gap. But the gap has side-effects, it can become institutionalised, economically so. O'Faoláin is measured, secular, funny, until he reaches the Six Counties and then he is enraged, in terms of ordinary justice. By the Government of Ireland Act, establishing the Six Counties, it is laid down that no one shall 'give a preference, privilege or advantage, or impose any disability or disadvantage on account of religious belief'. Seán O'Faoláin then quotes the public utterances of the Government of the Six Counties which are in contradiction of this Act. 'Ours is a Protestant Government and I am an Orangeman.' Lord Craigavon, Prime Minister, 1932. 'Many in the audience employ Catholics, but I have not one about my place.' Sir Basil Brooke, Minister for Agriculture, 1933. 'Neither Communism nor Romanism will ever receive any quarter from us.' Rev. J. Tolland, M.P. 1936…

No need to go on. We humans are adept at muddle and hatred. But that passage of Pritchett's was saddening, and saddening, also, the thought of a man aged 91 dying, as Seán O'Faoláin died the other day, aware that so little in the North had changed, and that the South was not the one he had hoped for, and fought for.

*May 1991*

# This Demi-Paradise

The outstanding image from recent events in Moscow is, for me, the deposition of the statue of Dzerzhinsky from outside the Lubianka, seen on television. There was something so graceful and gentle about the winching of the bronze figure from the stabilising spikes of its armature – gentle, lest the ponderous object swing and harm the surrounding crowd – and something irrationally touching in the way the vertical overcoated figure slowly became horizontal, as though happy to be allowed at last to rest, to lie down. Even the stiffness it retained seemed to have dignity; it was almost surprising not to see it bend a little and rearrange its limbs. Of the man himself I knew nothing, except what I was told, that he was founder of the Cheka, precursor of the KGB, outside the headquarters of which, the Lubianka, his statue had stood, and now lay. Here, we have been wiser, decorating our capital with forgotten and equestrian generals, round whom no hostile crowd would be inspired to gather. There was even an affecting innocence, I thought, in putting up a statue of a secret policeman. Behind him, on the television screen, was the Lubianka itself, yellow-painted, classical and handsome. Can it really have been a place of such dread? Of course, of course, but we have undergone so many years of anti-Soviet propaganda it is reasonable to ask that question.

Then I remembered that I had read an eyewitness account of what went on inside it during the 1940s, while I was a schoolboy playing cricket on this 'blessed plot'. It occurs in a book called *The Inhuman Land*, by Jósef Czapski, published by the Polish Cultural Foundation in 1987. I went to look up the passage and found, to my astonishment, that I was re-reading the whole book, although it contains horrors enough, because the general effect of it is mysteriously heartening; there is no touch of cynicism or hopelessness in it, from first to last. It was reviewed in this magazine when it first came out, but from a political viewpoint – the betrayal of Poland to Stalin, both during the war and after – so there was no space in which to analyse the inspiriting, even chirpy, *tone* of the book.

Jósef Czapski was a Pole born in Prague, educated in St Petersburg, a painter who lived in Paris, a lover of music and, generally, a cultivated cosmopolitan European; the kind that most aroused the loathing and suspicion of Stalin, and one who got lucky. Made a prisoner of war by the Russians, he became one of the 400 Polish officers 'fortunate enough to escape the fate of the ten thousand murdered in Katyn and other places'. Strangely, he had had the job in 1918 of searching Russia for five missing Poles; in 1940-41 he was given the job of trying to find the missing thousands. Of course, he had no idea they were already dead.

His search takes him just about everywhere, because the KGB toyed with him, sent him on false scents, but he was a trustful man (what else could he do but trust?), far too busy to go in for Cold War propaganda; all he wants to do is cooperate with his country's 'allies' in order to find the missing prisoners. He is not to know that it is Stalin's secret policy to destroy as many Poles as he can. On his journeys he talks to anyone who will talk to him, reports their stories, and thus his book becomes one long eyewitness account of chaos, confusion and death. He comes across a fellow-officer, an ex-Professor of Mathematics, who has himself been in the condemned cell in the Lubianka.

Czapski is by this time with the Polish Army in Russia and, on his way to a party in the camp, is waiting while his friend shaves. He begins to tell his story:

> I looked at the slender, emaciated body leaning forward in front of the shoddy little mirror – 'How do you come to know in such precise detail how they liquidated those condemned to death?', I asked. 'I shared the condemned cell with a fellow called Luc... For several months he had shared a cell with past members of the NKVD whose job had formerly been the executing of prisoners. They were now, themselves, behind bars, and it was they who explained to Luc the nature of the procedure... Prisoners condemned to death were transported to the Lubianka, marched to the ground floor and locked in one of a number of boxes, all of them opening on to a corridor.'

Their belongings were taken from them and noted – it was all very orderly. If a prisoner was called and told to collect his belongings that was good news, he was only going to get fifteen or twenty-five years' hard labour. If he was told to leave them, that was it.

> He would be led down a long corridor into the basement of the building, escorted by a member of the Prosecutor's staff, a doctor, and the Governor of the gaol. Two men of the NKVD would hold him by the arms while a third shot him in the back of the neck at close range.

So that is what was going on, in that beautiful building, while we were playing cricket in Berkshire.

In due course the man shaving is taken to the Lubianka and, eventually, told to 'leave his belongings'.

'Were you frightened?'

'Not in the least.'

What concerned him was that he would never speak Polish again, and the ignominious nature of his death. Then, suddenly, he is given his possessions back. News of the Sikorski-Stalin agreement has penetrated the Lubianka. *The Inhuman Land* is packed with such stories, too many, too circumstantial to be doubted. Like that of the world-famous scientist, Vavilov, denounced by his subordinate. Lysenko, for 'a bourgeois and ecclesiastical conception of science', and, of course, condemned to death.

As was that extraordinary poet Aleksander Wat, whose poems have just been published by Penguin. He was editor of Poland's leading communist journal, went to the Soviet Union in 1940 as to the Promised Land and was immediately clapped in the Lubianka. There, Czeslaw Milosz says, his interrogators 'tried to make him confess that he was a Trotskyite, a Zionist, and also when the mood struck them, an agent of the Vatican'. In prison he lost track of his deported wife and child and, released under the same amnesty as Czapski and his colleague, his story is different from most; after months of frantic searching in Kazakhstan he miraculously finds them and they are together ever after. He survived to write his best poems in the 1960s – 'A Turtle from Oxford' is in the Penguin, translated by Czeslaw Milosz and Leonard Nathan. His poems have humour, as does Czapski, and what these two Poles underwent makes a reader in John of Gaunt's island feel a provincial – thank God.

*October 1991*

# Fuller's Earth

We should say goodbye to poets gratefully, if they were any good. Out of the muddle of their lives they may have put together some words which could clarify ours. Such a one was, is, Roy Fuller, who died a few weeks ago; and the remarkable thing about him is, that as his focus grew tighter, his range of experience more limited by illness and age, so did his poems get better. His messages from slippered and suburban retirement – he had been by profession a solicitor, Director of the Woolwich – his wry accounts of the evening highball, of putting out the garden chairs on his modest terrace in SE3, became one of the delights, and in an odd way one of the most original recordings, of our times. It was garden chairs that first suggested to me that something interesting was going on. In a fifteen-line poem, 'Great Events' (to be found in his *Consolations*, 1987), he interrupts an observation of his own ageing:

> Damn it, I'll not
> Enshed the garden chairs: thus engineer
>
> Tomorrow's great event – the shock of meeting
> Light-fleeing earwigs when I come to unfold
> The blue or scarlet in yet another noon.

A man who can make something of earwigs hiding in a garden chair deserves watching.

The problem for a writer is always to catch and hold the material in hand; Roy Fuller was doing this, and knew it. 'I try my best with poetry to match/ Everyday's marvellous and varied prose.' It is poetry about being an elderly man, not an old man's poetry – he would be in his mid-seventies when he was writing that – and what clarity and humility it contains is the outcome of a lifetime's writing. Surprisingly, for he was a defiant secularist, he uses as an epigraph to *Consolations* a quotation from John Donne's *Essays in Divinity*; but it is apt.

> Let no smalnesse retard thee; if thou beest not a Cedar to help towards a palace, if thou beest not Amber, Bezoar, nor liquid gold to restore Princes: yet thou art a shrub to shelter a lambe, or to feed a bird; or thou art a plantane, to ease a child's smart; or a grasse to cure a sick dog.

There is much feeding of birds in these late poems, such tits and robins as Blackheath afforded. He even feeds 'Good Boy' vitaminised chocolate drops to dogs tied up outside the supermarket:

> Reason: unclear. It's surely not the sense,
> Retained from indoctrination when a child,
> Of the approach, near death, of Judgement Day.
> Besides in almost every other way
> Old age is famous for its selfishness;
> And it may well be, having lost one's looks,
> One tries to get in even dogs' good books.

I first came across him in the 1950s, in back numbers of *Penguin New Writing* and, though 'he had been heard to babble/"Poets should be intelligible"', he was not always so. But what made him stand out then was what became so attractive thirty years later; his ability suddenly to earth himself in a poem, describing where he is sitting, what he is looking at, why he is thinking what he is.

Such a method has its drawbacks. He later wrote some autobiographies which, though lively in places, sometimes went into such detail about how sailors tied the tiddly-bow round their caps or folded their bell-bottoms that one suspected the mickey was being taken. His poems, too, could bore. He had begun far to the Left, 'fond of Uncle Joe': slowly he found he could no longer believe in all of that, or in anything else, and went on about this. It seems that only when he admitted to himself that he really had no faith in mankind, or even affection for it, that he began to appreciate what was under his nose. There is no paradox in this. He had relieved himself of a strain. Nevertheless, he would have no truck with higher consolations. He asks how could he

> Respect those priestly leaders, arguing
> Whether the Second Person of the Three
> Is equal or subordinate to the First…
>
> I suppose their creed must conquer in the end
> Because it gives the simplest and most complete
> Answer to all men ask in these bad years.

(He concludes, 'Disgusting questions, horrible reply.' You cannot help liking him, nor could you when you met him.) Neat moustache, thick wavy hair as tidy as his suit, the picture of the Man from the Woolwich, with attractive Lancashire vowels. I once sat in on a meeting of the Arts Council Literature panel, of which he was the chairman, and his exasperation was a joy to watch. It was a time of experiment, and money was going to all sorts of things he disliked – concrete poetry, 'happenings', and so on. At last he burst out: 'And how the hell can we make sensible decisions when we have to look at that bloody picture!' Facing us was an over-excited abstract expressionist in puce and orange and pea-green, perhaps the pride of the Arts Council, certainly one of its 'investments'. I was shocked; I thought we artists ought to stick together, but afterwards I found his outburst refreshing. I too had thought the picture a mess, but he had dared to say so. We needed Roy Fuller.

This made greater the pleasure in the success of his last lap. It is time to give a late and representative example. His last book, *Available for Dreams*, 1989, is not all success: there are some obscurities, but also there are clarities. His wife is ill, he fears her death and his own, also fears his bladder trouble. He has to dive into the Gents of a pub and out again. 'The marvellous relief was all/ Too quickly cancelled out by feeling like/ A sparrow flying through a feasting hall.' He feeds the birds and still defies the gods. 'I turn to get some bread to throw: a god/ Typically unreliable, even mad.' His wife has an operation (we infer this, the biography is of his mind), and returns home; his relief and preoccupations are those of

*The Elderly Husband*

Once more a lenient December: is
It really the case that I am spared to try
To burn what fell when she was at death's door?
I hear the usual robin as I rake;
I have to quit the smouldering when the dusk
Announces strangely that it's time for tea:
A quince of summer crunches underfoot:
Below the rot a gold or even green
Sprouting prognosticates the still-far Spring.
I bear a cup to her, then guiltily
Over my own hear Gerald Finzi's work
For cello that illegally I've changed
From air to tape. What gods can possibly
Exist to whom thanks must be breathed for this?

*November 1991*

# Roy the Lion and Unicorn George

In a private letter a distinguished poet defines two kinds of poetry – 'diary entry' poems, and poems that 'create' something. A valid distinction – he much prefers the latter – and what interests me is that two poets have recently died, coevals, within a few weeks of each other, who perfectly illustrate, at the furthest extremes, the two kinds. There is something almost creepily neat in the way these two men, Roy Fuller and George Barker, in their lives as well as in their work, are almost exact contrasts.

Roy Fuller was a solicitor, a nine-to-five man all his working life; he worked for a building society and became a director. It seems clear that it would hardly have occurred to him, as a poet, that a poet should not have a proper job, and he makes it clear in his autobiographies how much he valued and admired his professional colleagues. Not for him the snobbery that the only 'creative' people are artists.

George Barker never had a job at all. Elizabeth Smart, by whom he had four children, said that he was adamant that the only job for a poet was poetry, anything else was a betrayal. How he lived I do not know. Public George gives little away; private Roy wrote his own biography. I have an idea that Graham Greene helped Barker. But there was no artistic snobbery about George Barker either. ('The Gods exacted a price from me and it's too expensive. The song's not worth the money, and vice versa.')

Roy Fuller began as a Marxist, and latterly lapsed, withdrawing into a conscious fogeyism salted with self-parody. George Barker began as a Catholic, and lapsed almost at once. As a young man he sat outside the Brompton Oratory counting the number of women who came out of Mass, and when he saw that this was greater than the number of men, he formally seceded from the Roman Catholic Church. There is self-parody in Barker too, plenty, but that story has always seemed silly; callow, as well as misogynistic, and Barker was a lover of women. At least, he had fifteen children by various of them, although his poetry is often pervaded by sexual disgust. Perhaps it was post-coital:

> Shun, shun the bedroom like a blight:
> Evade, O amorous acolyte
>     That pillow where your heart you bury
> For if the thing were stood upright
>     It would become a cemetery.

Roy Fuller, from the evidence of his poems, was contentedly monogamous, although he does say that he was sure he would die by crashing his car, distracted by the sight of a pretty girl. That is the authentic Fuller note, or Fuller of the last poems; wry, quotidian, concerned with the sweeping of garden leaves, the evening drink, the evening music – and reflections arising therefrom. Some might think them hardly poems at all, mere 'diary entries'. But I think it was Marcel Duchamp who said that whatever artists call art is art; that neverthe-less there remains 'good art' and 'bad art'. As a remark this seems to leave us where we began, but at least we are relieved of itchy anxiety as to whether something is 'art' or not, as in the case of the notorious bricks at the Tate. In the same way the nineteenth century wasted too much ink worrying whether Alexander Pope was a poet or not. Later, a group of toadies asked old Tennyson whether Browning was a poet or not. He made them wait for his reply; indeed, he slept on it. In the morning he said 'Yes', and they were left to interpret his hesitation. (In any age one thing is sadly certain, that poets resent rivals. It would be good to know what Barker and Fuller thought of each other. In this case I have a feeling we might be pleasantly surprised, they are so utterly different. It is affinity that causes anxiety.) Anyway, Fuller is deceptively quiet, domestic, fearful of death, and frequently humorous; Barker is noisy, apocalyptic – is certainly 'creating' some-thing – also fearful of death and, with the authentic note of human dismay beneath the often wildly flippant:

A Cardinal shrank from reading Saint Paul
    For fear of spoiling his style;
I shrink from writing this stuff for fear I'll
    Find there's nothing in it to spoil.
Which might be delightful for you, my dear,
    (Why don't you slip out for a drink?)
But if I weren't scribbling this drivel here,
    Why, bless me, I'd have to think.

And never a man I ever knew
    Could take his head in his hand
And think himself out of the juicy stew
    In which, to the neck, we stand.
Yes, my friend, not only I, but you
    Boil in the cannibal pot,
For the lot of man is a fiery brew,
    So skoal. And don't think a lot.

He is almost impossible to quote, except at length, because he changes mood and tone from stanza to stanza; jokes, prayers, puns, bawdy. He is an aural hypnotist. He hypnotised T.S. Eliot, and a generation younger than Eliot; the stanzas unreel, you doubt if you know what he means and whether he does himself, but you are sorry when he stops. You could call Fuller, by contrast, a miniaturist, but you are equally sorry when his vignettes of suburban life come to an end.

Both men are addressing what is important, searching for some-thing solid, failing to find and continuing to ask. Besides, neither was really 'lapsed'. Fuller, doughtily secular, shrank his politics to what he could manage, the routines of domesticity and age. Barker 'creates' in both senses; badgers a God in whom he does, and does not, believe. Both recognise the human need to praise. Barker quotes Saint Ignatius Loyola – 'We were born to praise, to reverence and to serve.'

Old Catholic, he ponders the problem of Grace, and reckons that despite everything he might have it, or be in a state of it –

> Since Grace is clearly everywhere
> And I am either here or there
> I'm pretty sure I've got my share.

None of their questions were answered, of course. They hardly expected it. Barker wrote 'Epitaph for the Poet':

> The single sleeper lying here
> Is neither lying nor asleep.
> Bend down your nosey parker ear
> And eavesdrop on him. In the deep
> Conundrum of the dirt he speaks
> The one word you will never hear.

There is something heraldic in the way they face each other. Roy a quiet English Lion, perhaps; fabulous George the Unicorn (which he would doubtless call the Eunuch-horn). They face, but do not outface, each other. Room on the shield for both.

*December 1991*

# News of the World

I wonder what the weather is like now in nearly frost-free County Antrim, that purple and green place, one of Europe's best kept secrets? Here in Gloucestershire the news is that it has been freezing hard for three consecutive days, all is white as snow, and when ice-caked sheep lumber painfully to their feet at first light they leave lozenge-shaped blobs of green where they have been lying. There is no wind, the sun shines ineffectively in a gold and blue sky, and sunset, like first light, like Antrim, is green and purple.

We were there a few days ago, in the Province, the Six Counties, and while we were in Belfast there was a small explosion, which was the publication of the *Collected Poems* of John Hewitt, four years after his death. He was an Ulster Protestant, and proud of it, left-wing, with

Catholic friends (which last prevented promotion in his job), and is something of a father-figure to the nest of Ulster singing-birds that came after him, Heaney, Simmons, Paulin, Mahon, and the rest; a remarkable number of good ones. He cleared the ground, enabled them to write, if they wanted to, of their own complicated patch.

As for complexity, and an attempt to remedy it, there was at the same time a bigger explosion, a blockbuster in fact, elsewhere; the arrival of the three, 1,000-paged, volumes, of *The Field Day Anthology of Irish Writing*, all 1500 years of it. This is a national event. There are so many conflicting strands in Irish history and consciousness that the whole length of the material ought to be held up to the light and peered at. Its chief editor is Seamus Deane, poet and academic, himself a Northerner who lives in the South. Years ago, probably before this vast project was envisaged, Deane said, 'Everything, including our politics and our literature, has to be rewritten, i.e. re-read. This will enable new writing, new politics, unblemished by Irishness, but securely Irish.'

Kelt, Briton, Roman, Saxon, Dane and Scot,
Time and this island tied a crazy knot,

says John Hewitt. But there has to be a danger that the selection for such an anthology may limit itself too closely to what is relevant to the disentangling process, which is to say, to writing that is overtly political. It is hard to do this with Saint Patrick, with whom the anthology begins. (Patrick apologises for his clumsy Latin, on the grounds of education interrupted by Irish pirates, who took him as a slave from Britain to Antrim when he was sixteen.) It is easy to do this with Hewitt, who wrote explicitly about Ulster hesitations and prejudices. But discomfort arises, for example, when you discover in Antrim that Louis MacNeice is becoming a kind of cult there, made to be representative of Ulster Protestant duality, poised between Ireland and England. MacNeice was born in Belfast, son of a Church of Ireland clergyman, but left Ireland when he was ten, and ultimately became a Classicist, which surely had as much effect on his detached temperament as a childhood in Belfast and Carrickfergus. It is true that MacNeice sometimes writes about Ireland with ambiguous affection, but his mother died when he was about five, and one of his earliest memories is of hearing his father alternately crying and praying in the room below him; any unease he may express about displacement could as easily be attributed to that as to a sense of interrupted 'Irishness'. His ashes are buried at Carrowdore, in County Down, in his mother's grave, and people go to read his poems in that churchyard, as why should they not?, except that it makes me uncomfortable.

I suppose what I am saying is that I am dead against writers being recruited for any narrow purpose (nor can I detect, so far, that this anthology does this); because then their 'newsworthiness', their newspaper value, is extracted from them, and the rest is thrown away.

Hewitt's Ulster Protestantism, for example, is explicit and refreshing; its history troubles him, but his final attitude could be summed up as – I and my ancestors have been here so long we *are* this country. We made it, and cannot go on forever feeling guilt that we dispossessed the original inhabitants. (Hewitt's cairn is on a hilltop next to 'Ossian's Grave': Oisin, legendary defier of Saint Patrick, who preferred the old, wild ways to the summoning bells of the new religion. But Hewitt was by temperament puritan, he says so... It is indeed a 'crazy knot'.)

Hewitt's 'relevance' is obvious, but he is really at his most lively when he is reporting the daily news, the small natural events of his beloved Glens of Antrim. He knew this was a mistake, as far as his audience went. They wanted more politics, 'the sun was not on the agenda... I found myself alone who had hoped for attention.' But what he is doing, as an artist and 'politically', is asserting his possessive love of his native place.

What makes this exhilarating and authentic is that he cannot understand why he, a Belfast man, must walk muddy lanes, cross boggy fields in order, 'like a tippler', to feel more alive. Why does he have to go

> to taste pine-resined air and mark below
> moss-cumbered boles
> the yellow flowers in spate
> or just to gaze at grass across a gate?

But this is what he most wants to convey, and what is most likely to be left out, if his work is scanned for comments on his times. These are his times, and ours. He sets up, as it were, a bureau of alternative news, or a parallel information service, hot with bulletins from the Glens, and finds himself alone, 'who had hoped for attention'.

The world is changing faster than usual, and we are shaken. The morning newspaper is out of date before it can be used to light a fire. But the natural world changes naturally, in front of our eyes, and this also should be reported. Recently, near here, a bare hedge was like a jeweller's window, scattered with brilliantly coloured necklaces of bryony berries, from pea-green to cricket-ball scarlet, and in lavish clusters. When they can find nothing to climb up, they climb along, attached to nearly invisible grasses, so the colours seem suspended on nothing, poured from a casket, frozen mid-air. An American friend looked at this and gasped, Why didn't we use them for Christmas decoration? I wondered too, but by Christmas they are gone – unreported. The next week the news was that a field was suddenly covered with creeping thistles, the kind that expand horizontally; hardly a blade of grass could emerge. Never was such an infestation. I started to hoick them out with a mattock, extracting long yellow roots, feeling like a mad dentist. Now the grass and the thistles are equally white and cannot be distinguished. It is all news, and I would like to have given more of it, but feared to find myself alone.

*January 1992*

# Landscape with No Figures

Waking to a morning of snow. It is early, but the snow under the trees is already honeycombed with drippings. There is a hissing in the air, near trees, which must be millions of small meltings, but if you stand under the trees there is no moisture on your shoulders, only a slight damp. Where are all the birds? There is a distant, disconsolate rook, even a lark, but that sounds grounded, uncertain. Is this prose 'poetic'? No. Only a report, an experiment, a pleasure.

No one is about. Some mornings there is now a jogger, who goes 'ermph!, ermph!' with each breath, head down. Difficult to say why this is annoying. Sometimes a horse-rider with an enormous protective hat, fastened under the chin with thick straps, so it is only from a scrap of face that there comes some hearty comment on the weather. On the horse's knees are protective leather pads, like those of a hockey goalkeeper. But this morning there is no one.

Five still heifers huddle together by a hedge on a steep slope. You cannot see their breath, so it is not cold; thus the hissing and melting. They do not turn their heads, but roll their eyes to look at you, so you see the whites, but they are not really curious, just patient; they have nothing to eat, no one has visited them yet. One decides to lie, and goes down like a camel, bending its forelegs, rump in the air. There is a loud cracking sound, it has settled itself uncomfortably on the dry branches of a fallen elder tree. Perhaps it is better than lying on snow. They are Herefords, and between their wide-apart eyes they have muddy white curls, strokeable, but they would not permit that.

Further down the slope there is a track of boots: going to the stream and returning from it to the green caravan in the hollow where the hermit lives. Possibly he has gone there to collect water. No one knows how he managed to move the ancient caravan to such a difficult hollow without it falling to pieces. It looks impossible, because the field falls away sharply, is scooped with deep hollows, scattered with tall thorn trees, some of them fallen, many of them barring the way he had to pull the caravan. He must have done it when inspired, in a frenzy for solitude.

The air is murky, with a slight yellow tinge, like an old smoker's white moustache.

Yesterday was bright, with the sudden clarity that can arrive in late February. There was sun, there were shadows, and this was good, it was as though the possibility of contrasts and shadows had been forgotten. There were fieldfares, winter visitors from the north, this is their Mediterranean; well-tailored birds, with elegant sloping shoulders, erect, like Guards officers in plain clothes. When they fly they are neat too, a few wingflaps and then they glide, wings to their sides, swooping, making small parabolas through the air. They walked across the sunny field with quick, military steps, all in the same direction, stopped, then marched again. Until starlings arrived: quarrelling Irregulars, disciplined only in flight; a hundred can change direction as though one bird. When they landed they were scruffy, and waddled; the fieldfares took to the trees and watched, as though in distaste.

At a certain moment, on the other side of the small valley, every bare tree in the sun was covered in plump white blobs, like fruit, a child's drawing of an orchard. And below the trees on the ground were more white blobs, marble pebbles on a shore. Pigeons, made to look white by the sun. Extraordinary, an infestation; from schooldays the memory is that pigeons seldom lay more than two eggs, do no more than replace themselves. (A book says they do this twice or three times a year.) What will become of the crops? When they took off the flock stretched for half a mile.

A rabbit clumsily stumbles towards a hedge. Blind. Myxomatosis. So what will be done to the pigeons? Shot, they fetch less than the cost of a cartridge.

Back home there is a crash. Because the sun made them unusually transparent, or because the sun made them glare, a sparrowhawk had flown into a window. It lay still, its yellow eyes open, the same colour as its horny yellow legs. We picked it up, warm, and laid it on a place it could fly away from, should it recover. But slowly its eyes closed. That was yesterday, it is still there, with its long spade-like tail it uses to balance on in the air, and its white breast patterned in shallow crescents, each round feather-end tipped with milky brown. It will have to be buried. Unnatural; but after all it was we who were in the way, who deceived it, and even in death it is a kingly presence.

A few days before there was an air-frost, rime, about three feet above the ground. The fields below were green and soft but, waist-high, the bushes and trees became perfect white, as though there had been a great blizzard. It happened during the night and there must have been a steady wind, because the ice on the leaves and branches had been flattened, extended, and all one way. So everything had attached to it a white and spiny extension, irregular, semi-transparent, like the fins on a fish. This frost continued for several days, the air was still and stayed the colour of milk; green fields, coloured hedge-bottoms and, above, everything locked in finny extensions of white ice. Then a watery sun came through and there were cracks, pops, pistol-shots, even the roof kept going bang as though things were being dropped on it. Almost simultaneously came hissing, sliding noises, every tree shedding its load of ice till each stood free and shining wet in its own personal drift, while all around was green. This had never happened before, not quite like that. Nothing like that ever happens in quite the same way.

Now, today, the soft hiss of melting has turned to aggressive splashings and pourings. The snow has nearly gone. Time to bury the sparrowhawk. It has opened its eyes again, but it is cold; every line of its body demands a regal interment.

*March 1992*

# The Music of What Happens

England loses the final of the cricket World Cup, our footballers look ordinary against Czechoslovakia, our election sounds even more petty and provincial than usual, so perhaps we are becoming a second-rate country, as many say we are, and does it matter? I find myself increasingly inclined to praise what is, like an old and saintly vicar (which I am not), noticing, for example, what an extraordinary number of wild violets there are this year, hidden everywhere, and feeling defiant in my pleasure.

In his new book, *The Last of England,* Ted Walker, Sussex born and bred, true Englishman if ever one existed, bids a furious goodbye to the England he knew. Now, in his local village, after the hurricane,

> the Highways Department have planted not an English tree but some copper-leafed exotic which would look nice in a stock-broker's garden in Putney. It is surrounded in the square by 56 items of street furniture…

He lists them, and throws in

> container-trucks longer than a terrace of farmworkers' cottages… male reps in white fleet Fords, all coat-hangers and portable phones…

and so on. 'In another five years the village would be a thoroughly hellish place.' Well, quite right, and indignation can be appropriate, but whenever I feel myself tempted towards it I am halted, and forti-fied, by the admonishing finger of Geoffrey Grigson.

The Grigsons, Geoffrey and Jane, lived in a rambling farmhouse just below the Marlborough Downs. No man would have been quicker to spot and celebrate a hiding violet than Grigson. Nor did any man more indulge himself in lethal angers and indignations. However, the truth was, this beautiful old farmhouse, since he came to live in it, had become surrounded on three sides by new houses that overlooked it, on the other side was an increasingly busy road and – this is the point – I never heard him mention this or even appear to notice it. For all I know he battered down the Planning Officer's door before the first new foundation was laid, but I doubt it. I never dared ask him, because I thought I could see his eyes narrow danger-ously at the question, and hear his reply, that if he lived there why should not others? In other words, like Finn McCool, he thought the best sound in the world was 'the music of what happens'.

I came across Finn's oriental-sounding philosophy while at work on *A Literary Companion to Ireland*, a job that is giving rise to alternate bouts of exhilaration and hair-tearing despair. If you approach it topographically, in terms of literary associations with place, you find in Ireland as many laminations of reference and writing as would make a hull for an ocean-going yacht, and these so tightly glued one on top of the other that to prise them apart, in order to present matters in some kind of decent sequence, would take the strength of the legendary strongman, Finn McCool himself. But when my courage flags I again remember Grigson, and his *Englishman's Flora*, a different kind of book but surely as onerous, and when I think the job not worth doing I remember his enthusiasm for the old, exhaustive guide-book to Northumberland, Tomlinson's, which he revered as a classic precisely because there were so many connections made in it.

The trouble is the difficulty of being sure about anything Irish. Possibly Finn McCool never said what he did. Of course he didn't; he never existed. But perhaps that sly old pixie, James Stephens, just made it up, in his *Irish Fairy Stories*, and it has no old text to confirm it. Finn (or Fionn, we are even dealing in two languages, and some-times five or six variations of transliterated proper names) asks his warrior-band what is the best sound in the world. The cuckoo calling from a tree, says Ossian (or Oisin), the ring of a spear on a shield, says stout-hearted Oscar (or Osgar), the laugh of a gleeful girl, says another. 'They are good sounds all,' said Finn. 'Tell us, chief,' one ventured, what do you think?'

'The music of what happens,' said the great Finn, 'that is the finest music in the world.'

I tried that story on two English women, both of whom said, 'Yuk!' The second, in Ireland, and with evident lack of admiration, added, 'But that's just how Irish Catholics think!'

No one could be more Protestant by instinct than Geoffrey Grigson (his father was a vicar), although he had no religion, nor more English (at least, Cornish), but, blow us all down, in the midst of researches into the literary associations of Donegal, who is to be found by the dim light of an oil-lamp, beside a smoking peat fire in darkest Donegal, and listening to the tales of a *shanachie*, an Irish story-teller, but the man himself, your Geoffrey? I should have thought he would have loathed all that, but not at all:

If I had to choose between living my life under the Saint Bridget shapes of Donegal [they were stuck in the thatch] or else on one of the streets of Swindon or Sheffield, the choice would not be difficult. I would sooner inherit my stories and also manufacture them for myself than have them manufactured by Mr Rank.

Then he is off to the limestone wilderness of the Burren in Clare, and to monastic Skellig Michael. It is all in his *Country Writings*. He is a fingerpost, always pointing in useful directions.

Donegal also yields, among others, William Allingham, derided in England for the whimsy of 'Up the airy mountain, /Down the rushy glen, / We dare not go a-hunting,/For fear of little men', a poem beloved at the time. But of his *Laurence Bloomfield* Turgenev said he had never understood Ireland till he read it. Allingham was a celebrity-hunter, but a humble one. His *Letters* consists of letters sent *to* him, by just about every Victorian literary figure. But his *Diary* is a treasure-trove. He called on people like Tennyson and Carlyle and they asked him to call again and again, until they were intimates. Tennyson confided:

> 'I could not eat my dinner if I did not believe in Immortality. If I didn't believe in that, I'd go down immediately and jump off Richmond Bridge.' Then to me, rather shortly, 'Why do you laugh?' I murmured that there was something ludicrous in the image of his jumping off Richmond Bridge. 'Well,' he rejoined, 'in such a case I'd as soon make a comic end as a tragic.'

I only have an old library copy of the *Diary* and I was looking through a Belfast bookseller's catalogue to see if there was available a recent edition of this almost unknown treasure, and the hair stood up on my neck, there really did seem to be a tune to the music of what happens. There was one, edited and with an introduction, by Geoffrey Grigson.

*April 1992*

# Oldtimer's Disease

*Toronto*

During the first few days here I was visited by an unfamiliar panic, a physical one. I do not know if there were, in fact, heart-flutters, impediments to breathing, but I was able at last to imagine what such things could be like. My first, philosopher's, reaction was, 'Ah well, P.J. … you've had a good innings…', but this was quickly succeeded by something much nearer real panic, when I thought, 'My God, I don't want to keel over *here*!'

I wondered if it was lack of exercise. The hotel room was temptingly comfortable, our duties were mostly in the evening, and perhaps I had spent too long just sitting there, reading, or looking out of the window at Lake Ontario. At breakfast I heard a man announce to his companions that he had just had a swim in the hotel pool. He looked chipper enough, the opposite of how I felt, so after lunch I went down to the shopping mall in the hotel basement to buy some swimming-trunks. There were none there that I fancied, but the salesman was so engagingly drunk, so obviously delighted to have a customer, that I was too cowardly to disappoint him, not even when he announced that the sober shorts I was about to purchase would, when wet, reveal an unknown but amusing pattern. 'Go *on*,' he slurred, noticing my hesitation, 'have fun.'

Public pools are difficult to enjoy if you have suffered compulsory swimming at school, nor is it particularly pleasant to emerge from the water and find your loins decorated with large Disneyland frogs. So I decided to put up with the heart-flutters and suffocations, if that is what they were, until, one day, I had an idea. I turned off the air-conditioning. Problem solved.

This may sound naïve, but I had barely taken in that the air-conditioning was switched on, because I associate it with heat outside, and in Toronto the wind was blowing from the frozen north. What do they condition the air with, what chemical? No point in asking any of our group, no one would know and, if they did, I would be no wiser.

We are in Toronto as a gathering of poets, summoned to read our work at the Harbourfront Festival. As we are whirled about, crammed into the backs of limousines, to be generously fed and watered, a different restaurant each night, then crammed again to be taken to read by the lake, or to listen, then levitated afterwards to the 21st floor to be fed and watered some more, I begin to feel we are an entirely self-referring group, cut off from the world. A convention of mother-of-pearl salesmen, say: purveyors of a minor luxury for which there is decreasing demand. As a result we are gentle and considerate with each other, as though we share a private grief. If we had been a convention of air-conditioning salesmen we would be more confident of our place in the world, and I could have found out what mysterious poison caused me to hear the wingbeats of the unwelcome Angel.

Our hotel, appropriately, is on the harbour front, which is reclaimed land. Behind it, also on reclaimed land, Mies van der Rohe built a black skyscraper in the 1960s, for a bank. Other banks did not like being overlooked so they built taller ones next to it, a San Gimigniano competition; or they are like those clustered towers in the Mani, built close together so they could shoot into each other.

To reach the pre-1960s town you have to thread your way through this huddle of competitive beauties – green, blue, black, white, gold – all their windows opaque and glinting, giving no indication of human muddle inside. The gold one is indeed covered with gold leaf, which you might think grotesque until you see the subtlety of its colour-changes as the light shifts. It has even turned out to be an economy; because of its golden skin the owners have to spend less on heating (and air-conditioning).

If you persevere past this blinded opulence – those blank windows are eery – you come to Cabbage Town, human-scale and pleasant, built by the Irish after the Famine, and Chinatown, where every hanging shop-sign is in Chinese characters, as far as the eye can see, and you can turn down other two-storeyed streets and hear just about every known language spoken on the pavements, and the people seem at home and at ease.

These readings are an annual event and when a group of us is taken in a bus to see Niagara we are told that more poets have seen Niagara than any other natural phenomenon. Before entering the cloistral catacombs below the Falls, in order to stand behind them, we are issued with hooded plastic gowns, daffodil yellow, with no sleeves, so beneath them we monkishly fold our arms. The noise of falling water is deafening as is the crackling of our plastic garments, so we do not speak. The striplighting in the tunnels is white and bright and reflects the yellow of our habits into our hooded faces. We become a line of Capuchin friars, none of whom is long for this world.

Next day the Americans arrive, mostly male, all of surpassing beauty, which gives rise to the nettled question: in the United States, if you are beautiful, do you feel compelled to become a poet? Or (in America) do you become beautiful by following that strange calling? Mark Strand, for example, this year's equivalent of America's Poet Laureate, looks like Robert Redford, with long elegant limbs. Scottish Douglas Dunn is short in stature and is driven to hiss at Irish Michael Longley. 'Let's go into Mark Strand's bedroom tonight and *steal his legs*!'

There is one American protest-poet who seems to have brought with her her own feminist claque. They whoop and cheer and leave noisily when she finishes. She is followed by Peter Levi, in his three-piece English suit, and I fear for him, but he manages the transition to his own elegiac cadences with such delicate courtesy, and courage, that my heart swells with pride in the Home Team. Afterwards I discover that American, Canadian, Slovenian, Polish hearts swelled also.

Levi and the American W.S. Merwin and I have lunch next day by the water and, admiring their contrasting good looks, I reflect what a strange trio of sixtysomethings we make, eating our oysters in a deserted café by the windswept lake, quoting the Mabinogion and Theocritus. Occasionally we pause and stab the air, because the wind seems unaccountably to have swept away the name of a book, or of our dearest friend, and we look at each other with bleak sympathy. 'Back home,' says Merwin, turning the dread thought into a kindly joke, lingering on the first syllable so the word becomes a near-dactyl, 'back home we call it "Oldtimer's Disease".'

*May 1992*


# Daring to Trespass


It is silly, as well as vain (in both senses), to argue against an unsympathetic response. But there was recently published a review of a collection of literary 'consolations' – which I put together, but is the work of a couple of hundred other people over a period of about three thousand years – which raises such a gloomy prospect that it is worth arguing about.

In the course of the review Carol Rumens usefully, and danger-ously, defines one attitude to the role of literature. She says that the very idea of consolation, 'trespasses against the view that literature's job is to disturb rather than to reassure us'.

Clearly, some people believe this, but can it be true, or true enough? Leaving aside for the moment that word 'reassure', which is a big one, and pausing briefly at the word 'trespass' – as though the view she mentions is permanently walled-off, and no other view is permitted entry – let us focus on the word 'disturb'. Is the meaning of it 'rekindle' (Leopardi's word), or 'animate' (Matthew Arnold's)? Does it mean 'inspire', 'elevate', 'instruct', 'enliven', or even 'amuse' ? I fear not, I fear it means disturb in the sense that a burglar disturbs us in the middle of the night, or an icicle pang of remorse disturbs us in the middle of the day. Is literature to be restricted to that, with notices round it saying, Trespassers will be Prosecuted?

For years now the word 'disturbing' used approvingly on a dust-jacket has meant that we will put down the book not so much disturbed as demoralised, possibly feeling sick as well. When did this become literature's 'job'? It is not only fatuous, it is far too easy. Saul Bellow's Herzog dances with fury at this over-simplification:

> You must sacrifice your poor, squawking, niggardly individuality – which may be nothing anyway (from an analytic point of view) but a persistent mania, or (from a Marxian point of view) a stinking little bourgeois property – to historical necessity. And to truth. And truth is true only as it brings down more disgrace and dreariness upon human beings, so that if it shows anything but evil it is an illusion, and not truth.

Rumens would not think that, for sure. But as for 'historical neces-sity' and 'bourgeois property', she does allow a political note to creep in. She says, 'the notion of literary consolation implies privilege.' Tell that to the author of the Book of Job, William Blake, Walt Whitman, Van Gogh; indeed, to anyone who refuses to be paralysed by such a conception. It is true that if we have just had our legs blown off, or are starving, literature, art, is small beer. But art is created *from* the world, and in *despite* of the world, and *for* the world, all of it. It is a measure of our human capacity, a kind of defiance, it is all we have to reassure us about ourselves. And there we come to Rumens's other word, 'reassure', which, she says (she does not say that she agrees with them) some hold that it is not the job of literature to do.

Geoffrey Grigson has a piece about fires reported on television. One season, he decides, you could have gained from TV the impression that the whole of England was ablaze. It was like a series of pictures of hell. Grigson's bump of complacence was unnoticeable, so was his religious bump. But, reminded of hell, he is reminded of old pictures of the Last Judgement, and he remembers that in such pictures there a Heaven is depicted as well as a Hell. There is a balance:

> We are not each of us – I don't just speak as a writer – called upon by decency or moral imagination or necessity or the inescapable facts or the universal weight and posture of things, to suppose all the time that we are having to wade, companions of Thomas the Rhymer in the old ballad, through red blude to the knee... we need to see the detestable and the enjoyable with equal vision.

Of course, any book written specifically to reassure us (unless written by 'the pencil of the Holy Ghost', in Bacon's delightful phrase) would soon be seen to have designs on us. But any truthful expression of experience can enliven us, reassure us with a sense of shared humanity. It must be the whole of experience, however, not just the dreary part of it, although that need not be omitted, because we share that too.

After all, what was literature from its beginnings? It would be possible to say that it began from a perceived need for reassurance and continuity. Tales of the history of the tribe, to give social cohesion; praise of princes, for the same reason; lament, which is a form of social consolation; attempts to placate the gods. The whole endeavour aimed at giving stability to society and significance to experience and, even inadvertently, suggesting a wider possibility to necessarily cramped lives.

> Forth pilgrim forth! Forth beast out of thy stall!
> Know thy countrie, look up, thank God of all,
> Hold the high way, and let thy ghost thee lead,
> And truth shall thee deliver, it is no drede.

So Geoffrey Chaucer, and there perhaps is the rub, or nub. This is post-Christian England and now we are left with only the gloomy anxiety about whether something is 'privileged' or not. But our roots are still in the Judaeo-Christian soil, and the word still is, 'Peace I leave with you; my peace I give to you.' Because mere disturbance clouds the judgement. No one could interpret it as an invitation to chubby-cheeked slumber. ('I say unto all, Watch.') But this is not a plea for one sort of orthodoxy; this is a vehement rejection of a much narrower one that seems to have crept over us, like a fog. It is strangely exclusive. It has built a wall round itself on which are fixed cannons to repel trespassers with cannonballs called, Complacence! Reaction! Philistinism! It is not because of this that most of us live most of the time in a state of physical and metaphysical dread, it is because we are human. 'Literature's job is to disturb us, rather than reassure us.' Surely wrong. Literature's job is harder work. It has to do both, and other things as well. It can even make us laugh, and has to risk being laughed at. Its job is to climb over the wall, dare to commit trespass.

Serendipity, or Tiny Miracles Department. The reader will have to believe this, because it is true. After drafting the above, and banging on, probably too long, about the words 'disturb' and 'reassure', I idly picked a book from the table, by a poet new to me, M.R. Peacock and found that she says it all quicker. She finishes her elegy to Philip Larkin:

> You never took a stand or tried to staunch
> The draining out of hope, or begged a cure.
> Odd how wry private truths of one who's gone
> Disturb and reassure.

*July 1992*


# Same Difference?

Is there still such a thing as national identity? Let us hope so, because it adds to the gaiety of nations: But what about those that speak, more or less, the same language? There are certainly signs that Australia is developing a distinctive literature, packed with things specifically Australian, but what about Ireland, which also has a language of its own? It would be a pity to lose Ireland, as an enlivener of English, and because present trends are too close to see properly, we have to go back a couple of generations to guess what preoccupations may have filtered down.

Take Catholic Oliver St John Gogarty, for example, surgeon, poet, wit, Anglophile, who never seems able to leave the question of national identity alone, and take theosophist Æ (George Russell), poet, mystic, dipthong and influential creator of Ireland's new sense of itself.

Gogarty ends an autobiography, *As I Was Going Down Sackville Street* with a picnic in the Wicklow hills high above Dublin, and in an un-English way he makes the occasion fabulous, his guests godlings and their wit Olympian. But underneath the wit other things are going on, all of them to do with newly independent Ireland's sense of identity (the book was published in 1936).

One of the company suggests that the true anthem of Ireland should not be 'The Soldier's Song' but 'Johnny, I Hardly Knew Ye', which expresses the astonishment of a woman at the return of her soldier, because so many bits of him are missing:

Where are the legs with which you run?
Hurroo! Hurroo!
Where are the legs with which you run?
Hurroo!
Where are the legs with which you run
When you went to shoulder the gun?
Begob, yer dancing days are done.
Johnny, I hardly knew ye.

The point of the picnicker's preference for that jaunty, charnel realism is that it is *Irish*, because Ireland lost its wars and more of its soldiers returned literally legless. As a consequence, others, out of frustration, doubtless made themselves metaphorically so, but that is a myth about present-day Ireland; there is no more drunkenness there than elsewhere. Once, when astonished by the hectic over-crowding of a hotel bar late at night I was given a reason for it. 'We like to *meet* each other. In England you get stocious alone in front of the TV.'

Certainly Gogarty sees to it that his guests' glasses are filled, and one of them, caught up in the habit of self-mockery that contains national self-pity, pretends he imagines that song seen in a vision on a wall in Patmos by a member of the Hermetic Society (a swipe at Æ, who was a member of that Society. He and Gogarty were friends – but Ireland is a small country.) He offers to translate that vision and, 'having applied himself to his tumbler', comes up with this:

Alas, for the going of Swiftness, for the feet of the running of thee,
When thou wentest among the swords, and the shoutings of
                                                captains made shrill,
Woe is me for the pleasant places! Yea, one shall say of thy glee
'It is not!' And as for delight, the feet of thy dancing are still.

This is funny stuff, the sub-Swinburne parody presses the vulgar life out of the Irish song, but the improviser goes on to say that this is what is happening

> to the irrepressible spirit of our land. Dulling first, then deadening it, then covering its grave with a formal foreign urn.

In other words a genteel *foreign* spirit (still English?) is suffocating what is lively and defiant and *Irish*. All this is quite a lot to be going on below the surface of a couple of jokes.

Gogarty is urbane, representative of Irish quick-mindedness. Æ is not. He lived in a world of spirits, saw visions, and painted them. He would hardly have thrived in England, not with a funny name like that, for a start. Yet he, theosophist from Ulster, played a large part in fashioning the consciousness of the Irish Free State. It is an extraordinary story, and was begun by his fellow esoteric, the Diaghilev of the Irish Revival, its casting-director, W.B. Yeats.

At the turn of the century Irish tenant farmers became able to buy their tenancies – the beginning of the end of the Anglo-Irish Ascendancy – and needed to be taught how to market the produce which was now their own. Sir Horace Plunkett set up an agency to teach them, and needed an assistant. The young Yeats, remembering that his druidical friend kept the accounts at his place of work, suggested his name. So it was that mystical Æ found himself bicycling round Ireland lecturing rural committees and, even, founding agricultural banks. Later, as an editor, this dreamer who thought every community should have a Soul – 'all our political ideals are symbols of spiritual destinies' – became an international influence. Nobody quite understood what his spiritual beliefs were, but that he believed in them was so manifest it gave him authority. At the height of the Civil War in Ireland, the Head of the Irish Free State, Michael Collins, came secretly to consult Æ at Gogarty's house. Catholic Collins let the magnificent talk of 'spiritual bodies' and 'psychical powers' wash over him for a while and then to Gogarty's consternation produced a notebook and pencil (revealing, as he did so, a large revolver strapped to his thigh – he was killed a few weeks later) and said sharply, 'Your point, Mr Russell?'

Æ had breakfast with Lloyd George. He was summoned to the US to advise Henry Wallace, the Secretary of Commerce. He helped shape Catholic Ireland with a philosophy derived from the *Upanishads*, the Tibetan Book of the Dead and Madame Blavatsky.

He lashed his country:

It is the essentially irreligious spirit of Ireland which has come to regard love as an unnecessary emotion and the mingling of sexes as dangerous ... a woman who has a natural delight in awakening love in men is the priestess of a divinity ... We praise the virtue of our women ... one wonders was there temptation?

He defends Catholic Ireland against Kipling, who had written, 'We know the hells declared/ For such as serve not Rome.' Æ replied:

I am a heretic judged by their standards, a heretic who has written and made public his heresies, and I have never suffered in friendship or found my heresies an obstacle in life.

This pagan assistant in the birth of a new Irish national confidence should be given the last word on the subject of national difference:

I have met the hundred per cent Irish and the hundred per cent English and the hundred per cent American and I have always wondered why these perfect embodiments of their nation were the most perfectly intolerable people ...

*June 1993*


# Midsummer's Day Impatience


'I sometimes storm about the lanes, wondering what I am doing in this cow-parsley desert.' I found that I had scrawled that on the telephone-pad the other day. The mood has possibly passed, but I still remember it, though the expression of it is already out of date. Today, Midsummer's Day, the cow-parsley has gone, and been replaced by hogweed. 'How unimaginative of the Creator to replace one white flower with another,' I said in the car. 'Not at all,' came from the passenger seat. 'Infinitely subtle. Different architecture.'

I have just been peering at the stuff, and that is right. Hogweed is altogether a sturdier, no-nonsense affair: coarse, in the way all things grow cruder and more assertive as summer progresses, the leaves on trees thicker, stickier, the insects more annoying. Hogweed is a tubular, cantilever construction which, instead of nodding its white face demurely at the passer-by, shoves its flower, which is off-white, flat as plate towards the sky.

As for the Creator, Coleridge thought everything that is meant by nature – wind, sea, light, darkness, natural shapes – is a form of God's language to us; should He exist, it is difficult to see what other He would choose. Nevertheless, it is easy to become impatient with this because it is nearly just out of ear-shot, like a radio in another room, and we crave to be distracted from those indecipherable cadences, which is one of the reasons why we gather together in towns. So, news from the country – which this is going to be – should not be regarded as a communiqué from some privileged refugee. It takes nerve to stay here, what with that murmur going on as through a wall, and some-times the nerve cracks, as it must have done when I complained about the cow-parsley desert.

In fact I love living here, a parasite – no tractor, cowshed, gun – watching the farmer make the place. On one side of our modest strip he has planted linseed, on the other side rape. The rape is now bright yellow, the linseed is green until the sun comes out and then its flowers open, blue, as though the sun had painted the hillside with a brush, and we become a tiny green peninsula between two large slabs of colour, lavender-blue and chrome-yellow, thanks to Brussels, I suppose. It is not even necessary to know anything about it. I picked one of the blue linseed flowers and crushed it, half-wondering whether I would smell cricket-bat oil, but smelt nothing. W.B. Yeats mentions a linnet in one of his poems and as a boy I was so impressed I looked it up. I have since discovered that he noticed hardly anything at all of that kind, just used them as stage properties, 'props' to prop his meaning, and very effective. There are two birds on the electric wire twittering tunelessly; they have pink throats. I know they are linnets, courtesy of Yeats. I thought linnets sang well; perhaps not at the end of June, or not today.

You notice things, perhaps they are not worth noticing, but it takes time to get your eye in, and notice them at all. I notice there is a plague of slugs. Last night I counted 23 on the grass in a small radius round my feet.

Once, with a friend I watched some cows munching meditatively and felt 'peace come dropping slow' – Yeats, miserable, got the idea while watching a ping-pong ball balanced on a jet of water in the window of a London sports shop – and I said, expecting agreement, 'Don't you get peace from them?' No,' he answered, shortly. Served me right. Another time, with a companion, we came upon a holly hedge entirely shrouded in white, dew-spangled cobwebs, shining. 'Look!' I said, and the companion obediently stopped and stared at the hedge. After a while he politely murmured, 'Look at what?' It is not that I am more observant; it is just that I have been here longer. It takes time. Many of the newcomers fight a fierce battle with grass, making a bald sward, puttering up and down and driving their neighbours mad with the sound of their sit-upon mowers. Many of them are retired, it is something to do and the silence can be frightening if you are not used to it. I let the grass grow, cutting paths through it, and not always collecting the clippings (which I dare say is the reason for the plague of slugs).

We have one foxglove. Foxgloves made Katherine Mansfield think of the Lawrences, Frieda and D.H.:

> 'And how beautiful they are against whitewash!' cry the Lawrences.
>
> As is their custom, when they love anything, they make a sort of Festa. With foxgloves everywhere. And then they sit in the middle of them like blissful prisoners, dining in an encampment of Indian Braves.

We have only one, but it seems enough, like one good word in a poem. More might make me nervous. We went to a party in Dorset in one of the most beautiful gardens in England; it was made by a painter-friend, it took twenty years and I love it, but I think to sit among such graceful, coloured ingenuity would make me anxious, make me feel there was something else to be done.

Even in a non-garden anxieties, forebodings, remain; the usual ones. And strange things can happen. The other day, standing by the foxglove, and perhaps deploring the cow-parsley desert I found myself in, there was an engine roar that grew so huge that I involuntarily cowered. A helicopter, a big one, shining red like a glossy pillar-box, kept coming at me, as though it was going to crash.

Deafeningly, it hovered just above my head, then it did a right-angle turn so that I thought its rotor-blades would hit the field maple near the foxglove, and roared off, maybe twenty feet above the ground, leaving me sorely shaken. Now what, or who, was that?

The 'real' world hovers. The radio says I should concern myself with an unappealing minister who has given a watch to an absconding tycoon. The reporter is almost frothing with excitement. To each his own interest. It is not that I am 'above the battle' but am risking remaining apart from it, listening, and unintentionally making a cliché count. I suppose what is good about this place is that it is a window of non-opportunity. I am grateful that the playing-fields round here (the light plays on them) are not level, and that nowhere, for miles, are there goal-posts to be moved.

*July 1993*

# Looking About and About Looking

Finished: three years' work on *Ireland: A Literary Companion*. It is not a dictionary; it is a journey through Ireland, north and south, relating writers to places they came from, or wrote about, and quoting them; quoting from visitors also. However, Ireland has been a talkative place for 2,000 years – not a *dun* or *rath* without its attendant songs and stories, carefully copied down over the centuries – so the book swelled to nearly twice its agreed length. The publishers flinched, but decently allowed half the overspill. Therefore, teeth clenched, enough was cut out of it to go, in bulk, to the making of a decent-sized novel, and the cut version was delivered. It is still half as large again as any other in John Murray's series of literary companions, so now they are thinking of removing it from the series, printing it in a larger format, and could I, they gently suggest, think of a new title for this now isolated work?

At this point it is necessary to bring in Austin Clarke. He is a poet much admired in Ireland, who died in 1974, under-represented in this vast tome, partly because he was difficult to fit in topographically, but also, more importantly, because he uses so many coinages, word-plays, puns, that he gives me a headache. There are such double and triple meanings under the surface that his lines snag on them. Or so it seems to my Anglicised ears. But this is exactly what good Irish judges admire in him. They find that it reflects the way the bards played with words in Irish; Clarke is continuing a tradition, brilliantly.

I do not know Irish and I must take on trust the tradition. However, what am I to make of it when, casting about for a title that will include all the dissonant voices of the past which the book contains, there comes into my mind this suggestion for a title – *The Ould Sods?*

Terrible. Worse, when I have thrown away that idea as fast as it came, and think of the other aspect of the work, the topographical, and remember all the delightful journeys we made down sunken lanes, like corridors of green, I want to call it – *The Emerald Aisles*. The infection of Gaeldom, if that is what it is, seems ineradicable from the bloodstream. Better to stop altogether, and stop blaming Clarke for his Gaelicism, if it is incurable, and praise him instead for being a man who 'looked about' him.

The phrase is popular here, because of a letter thanking this column for, says the writer, 'reminding me to look about me, which otherwise I'm afraid I sometimes forget to do'. No thanks could be more gratifying, and so, waiting for an early-morning bus in London, near 'The Man in the Moon' – the next pub along is called 'The World's End'; our fathers were better at titles than we are, who can only come up with the facetious, like 'The Frog and Firkin' – on my way, among other destinations, to tell the publisher that I can arrive at no title for the hypertrophied work other than the wholly ludicrous, I reminded myself to 'look about' me and remark, not for the first time, that at this particular bus-stop people seem to have abandoned the notion of queueing. I station myself old-fashionedly by the pole while they drift up and huddle in doorways, ahead of me. A longish bus journey in London is one of the delights of the town, but you have to be in the right mood to enjoy it, to 'look about', and this apparently purposeful drift into positions of advantage is disturbing. Am I going to have to stick up for my rights?

It has happened, but not this time. So I settled myself on the crowded top deck, wiped the window with my sleeve, and prepared to enjoy the flamboyant intricacy of some of the drain pipes on buildings in Sloane Street. I forget who it was who advised me always to look above the shopfronts, and that I would be amazed at the variety of architecture that survives. May he be forever blessed. Without him I might never have noticed the extraordinary pagoda-like little projections, turrets, that Victorians liked to put near the tops of tall buildings, not room in them even for a poet invented by Max Beerbohm to swing a quill. There are particularly good examples where Oxford Street crosses the Tottenham Court Road ... Then I realised that on the whole of that steaming top deck I was the only one looking out of the window.

Surely one of the great pleasures? Suspended, safe, voyeuristic in the sense of observing without responsibility, what could be more pleasant? But my fellow passengers preferred to read their newspapers or stare into space. Some of them happened to be unusually good-looking girls, who all wore heavy men's boots. One beauty gazed adoringly into the face of her companion, who fidgetted, jerking his neck; you almost expected to see him run his finger round the inside of his collar. So, outside, a world; inside, a world. It was a pity the journey had to come to an end.

The rest of the time I have only the country to stare at, but you have to be quick because it changes faster than Oxford Street. At the end of January not much seems to be happening but there is expectancy in the air, blackbirds try out a note or two, hesitate, then stop. Yesterday was clear, and a distant high field, its stubble the shade and texture of a brindled pelt, lion-coloured, was being ploughed. The hilltop looked flat but the new, dark furrows seemed to undulate because of the unseen contours of the field. Nearer at hand (outside the bus, inside the bus) a quince tree suddenly filled with round pink fruit – Pickwickian birds, flat hair like tango dancers, parted in the middle, with long split tails like evening coats. Today you can see nothing at all, except mist, and everything drips. You have to look about you while you can.

Inside, the house fills with books of contemporary poetry, because of my job, sent by publishers, sometimes sent by poets, sometimes just picked up. Naturally, some of it is no good, or does not appeal, but what can you do with it? You cannot throw away somebody's life-blood. Meanwhile the shelves groan, and, after a given trial-time, I have taken to carrying the volumes I know I will never open again up the stairs and into a kind of lumber-room. I always do this apologetically, and last week I found myself saying to a poet – to a book I was taking upstairs (never mind, others praise him, so he is all right) – 'I'm afraid you're going to join The Dud Poets' Society'. It was only then that I remembered Robin Williams's energetic performance in a film of nearly that name. If I go on unconsciously making (dud) jokes in the manner of Austin Clarke – and he has always remained indisputably *down*stairs – it is time I gave him another chance. He was certainly the man to look out of the window of a bus, and he probably could not help the punning anyway. The *gael* bloweth where it listeth.

*February 1994*

# Fairy Tales of New York

The building was dilapidated. Through the window the bar looked dark and dirty, but outside was an ill-written chalked notice, 'Rooms vacant', and I knew I would have to stay there. I was in search of the 'real' rural America and had had enough of featureless roadside motels. So I went in and booked a room and, ridiculously, it is one of the actions of which I am most proud, because I was scared. On the landing, stuck on with Scotch tape, were handwritten warnings about no liquor in the room, and no women. The room itself, with its high wooden bedstead, was just the place to unbuckle your gun-belt after peering, standing carefully to one side, down on the street below. A room, also, where I might be visited by the dark-eyed daughter of the proprietor, Linda Darnell maybe, because she detected in this stranger a mystery and refinement denied to the crudities of the saloon below – later she would interpose her taut white blouse between me and the bully's bullet and die, lipstick intact, in my arms.

In fact everyone was kind, even avuncular, in that place, which turned out to be a stop-over for truck-drivers. The trouble was that I could find nothing whatsoever to do in the evenings.

This was long ago, and I was there, in Upstate New York, to see if I could find the equivalent of an English country lane. By day I haunted the woods. Everyone slumped on stools in that crepuscular bar – and they barely ever spoke – had grunted at me to avoid the woods; it was the first days of the cross-bow hunter season and they shot anything that moved. This was daunting, as were the notices pinned to nearly every tree fiercely warning against trespass. It was not at all like England, and in the evening, the township so deserted it might have been uninhabited, we silently watched television in the bar.

It was baseball, the World Series, and at one stage the excited commentator burbled, 'This isn't just the championship of the world, it's the championship of the *universe!*' Reflecting on the untruth of this, and the general lack of communication I had observed around me, I decided then, and have remained convinced, that the United States is the most parochial and in-turned country in the world (in the *universe*) and therefore, if you can say such a thing about a continent, the most insular.

No other Great Power has had to travel so little, or meet so few strangers, in order to be Great. The Greeks, Romans, Spaniards,

British had to move across the world, and settle for long periods. Other histories, languages, customs, *games*, impinged on them willy-nilly. Two weeks ago in New York City the signs advertising the soccer World Cup were on A4 size paper on the occasional lamp-post and had an apologetic air, as though for a village fête. In our newspapers are brief accounts of American baseball, football, golf. In American newspapers there is nothing like that. Indeed, in the *New York Times*, a massively old-fashioned and genteel paper – there were worries in it about the amount of methane produced by cows *belching*, as though, out of gentility, they had got hold of the matter by the wrong end – it was difficult to notice any interest in the outside world at all.

Perhaps the US did not need to go to the world because the world came to the US? At the time of writing it is early days in the soccer World Cup, but the stadiums cannot be crowded only by visitors. The impression is one of American Italians, Germans, Irish, 'Hispanics' rushing to support their various original countries while the rest of the nation looks on puzzled, perhaps annoyed. The US team is doing well at the moment and maybe that will make a difference because Americans believe they only like winners, but is that true?

Almost all American ideas about themselves seem to the visitor to be wrong, perhaps because Americans so seldom measure their behaviour against that of others. They like to think of New York as 'tough' but in beautiful June weather it was a joyous place to be (at least in Manhattan) and less threatening than London or Paris. People dress well and individually, to match their personalities and purses, and the social strata are not too topographically isolated; you can move a block from the gloss of Madison Avenue, say, and find a different world, but not necessarily a dangerous one. They like to think of New York as brash, thrusting, but the courtesy is old-fashioned, people in buses offer their seats to the elderly. They like to think that New York is up-to-the-minute, but between the shining skyscrapers, on lower buildings, are those extraordinary water-towers clad in weathered wood, like wine-vats in Tuscany. True, their courtesies are sometimes technologically advanced. At bus-stops the press of a button causes the bus to tilt alarmingly towards the sidewalk, to allow the disabled on.

But they are unused to visitors, to non-Americans. No one thinks to tell you, for example, that you have to buy your bus-tokens from a machine in the *subway*. Everywhere advertised at fast-food places are 'Heroes', 'Submarines', 'Torpedoes' but to ask what they are is to invite a stare. (Maybe they are kinds of hot-dog?) It was the same in the country. Seeing a large bird with a russet breast I asked what it was. 'A robin.' 'A *robin?*' 'Yes, goddamit, a robin!'

Because I did in the end find a country lane, and a poet who lived at the end of it, Peter Kane Dufault. Now he has retired to a hut deeper in the woods where he ponders, to good purpose, the State of the Union. But even he forgot to tell us about poison ivy. We visited him by Amtrak, a slow rail journey along the Hudson. Once there, in the Berkshire Hills, we visitors walked bare-ankled through meadows, stumbled on a sleeping fawn, saw turkey-vultures overhead, and strolled dirt-roads so busy with vast yellow swallowtails it was like picking our way through traffic. All this 100 miles from New York. We had admired poison ivy which looks like seedling trees. But surely everybody knows about things American – Heroes, Submarines, poison ivy? How long before the rash starts? 'Couple o' days.' Is it bad?' 'Awful.' Jewel-weed was the antidote, so we rubbed ourselves with that.

Other things were more familiar. Amtrak back to the city was two hours late. In fact it never arrived, the later train came first and we boarded that. No one seemed to mind, there was a cheerful buzz in the railcar. The food was good and everyone, everyone, carefully put their paper cups and cartons and cans – America still produces an astonishing quantity of disposables – in the trash-slot. An old-fashioned country.

*July 1994*

# Authentic Hero

If your Life tends towards Letters as, in a zig-zag fashion, mine has done, when enough time has passed you notice it contains an involuntary and unconscious tribalism. I'm not sure if that is the right word but I am talking about a discovery recently made, which startled me. Jon Stallworthy, in his biography of the poet Louis MacNeice, lists the real names of the people mentioned in MacNeice's long 'Autumn Sequel', hitherto hidden under pseudonyms, and I am astonished to see that I knew a high proportion of them, and in unconnected circumstances.

René Cutforth, for example, I met when he was BBC War Correspondent in Korea and I was a National Serviceman briefly in charge of journalists there; we wandered the streets of a wholly deserted Seoul, a ghostly experience. In one house a child's half-finished homework lay neatly open on the table; it was like Pompei without the lava. Even MacNeice's first and beloved schoolmaster, Littleton Powys, I feel I knew, because he was the revered brother of my own revered John Cowper Powys. The Greek painter Ghika I came across elsewhere... and so on. And so what? Most of the others were connected with the BBC, for which my father worked, so I suppose I came across them through him.

The point for me is that I find MacNeice's world was also partly mine, and I had not known this. Also, the fascination for me, and one of the great interests of the biography, is that it describes a kind of life I observed not so very long ago – the boozy, clubby, pubby, seedily intelligent world of the BBC Radio Features Department, a world to which I youthfully yearned to belong – and it has wholly disappeared, like Babylon, or the Beaker people. That crew of beaker-imbibing, chain-smoking, woolly-tied and free-ish spirits is no more. It was a world disintegrating even while I envied it – though I still permit myself a silly surprise whenever I see pictures of present-day Seoul, with its pullulating skyscrapers.

I am also surprised to be reminded how much I owe to MacNeice, that his work has affected my life (even the way he looked and publicly behaved has, I think, influenced me), and I feel I ought to examine this a little by way of tribute.

If you aspire to 'be a poet' (secretly you want to write good poems, but you are uncertain about that, so it is the glamour of 'poethood' that draws you) it is always a thrill to meet your first, famous, authen-ticated bard, whose work you admire. I only met MacNeice a few times and he was a figure of genuine romance to me: I liked the way he dressed, carelessly but well, his Irishness and the way he figura-tively stood apart – the two may have been connected; some trick of the set of his eyes which made them seem always to contain amuse-ment; I liked his shyness. There came a day when I entered late into the crowded pub and he confessed to me that he had run out of things to say to his companions and would I come with him to Lord's? We sat in the Mound stand – I must have been nineteen or twenty – and I searched for something brilliant to say to my lion-companion, my Hero. Eventually I turned to him but, probably fortunately, had no need to deliver because the lunchtime session in the pub had proved too much; he was asleep.

The odd thing about my admiration, which continues, is that from the first it contained an exasperation. Not with his apparent facility with packed, flowing lines and clean-cut images, which still fills me with awe; it was with something else that seemed to me facile: his tendency to underpin his colour, rhythm, detail, relish, and give it a factitious depth, by referring at the end to the dissolution of all things, to mutability, death, For example, 'The Gone-tomorrow' begins delightfully:

Two years high, by the world wide,
It scatters pebbles on every side,
It takes two hands to cake or cup,
It pulls the tails of puss and pup.

And the blaze of whins, the smell of turf,
The squelch of mud, the belch of surf,
The slop of porridge, the squawk of gulls,
Enter that smallest of small skulls.

Nothing could convey infancy quicker or more pictorially than, 'It takes two hands to cake and cup', and the second verse is pure MacNeice, all the five senses deployed. But he has to go on: 'Which some day, skull and nothing more/Will lie in a box on a foreign shore …' and we *know* that. Although, not until reading his biography did I know how many demon sadnesses, some from infancy, inhabited MacNeice. He was not being glib after all: he was being himself. He was always authentic.

Even if a reader is unaware of the shadows below the surface-glitter of Macneice, any irritation he might feel is surely overcome by the richness and variousness of daily living that MacNeice manages to cram into his lines, and his technical mastery, which is not just showing off, is part of the meaning of the poem. It is not even necessary to notice it, you just feel comfortable that he is in control. I have read his 'Didymus' several times, but have only just noticed that one section plays a difficult game with internal rhymes – 'sea … see, climb … clime' and so forth: he was a master.

The radio features he wrote for the BBC I suppose I must re-read, but I always found the form pretentious – narrator intoning, bogus sound-effects – wind in the rigging a Swannee whistle, the Legions' feet marching in a sand-tray. He thought it brought poetry to Everyman. He caught his last cold preparing one of these programmes, unnecessarily down a pot-hole. It was called *Person from Porlock*, the famous interrupter of Coleridge, and MacNeice's life had been full of interruptions, not all of them his fault, and he chafed. Asking for extra, unpaid leave from the BBC he reminded his boss that he was

> an (for want of a better word) artist – which means that I can do some hackwork all of the time, and all hackwork some of the time but not all hackwork all of the time.

He was 56 when he died and I hope he didn't want to catch that cold. His ashes are buried in his mother's grave in Co. Down. As a child he had believed that his birth had caused his mother's break-down and death, when he was aged seven, and 'the bad dreams came'. Someone has placed on his grave his own lines:

> This man with the shy smile has left behind
> Something that was intact.

This suits him, but it gives a cold shock to realise that the lines come from a late, good poem called 'The Suicide'.

*March 1995*

# Gussie Finknottle, Reporting

Was it Christianity or cowardice? I gently took to task a fellow-contributor for seeming to dismiss too lightly the Penal Laws imposed on the Catholic Irish in the eighteenth century. He is a relentless demythologiser of Ireland's past and present, but this seemed to be going too far. I called the Rev. Sydney Smith to my aid, 'the Smith of Smiths', who wrote firmly about the matter in the beginning of the nineteenth century; thus I bantered and tut-tutted, with Smith's teasing support, thought my duty done and the record adjusted.

On print-day the alerted author complained from across the Irish Sea. He asked for the right of reply, and at that my heart sank deep. I agreed to withdraw my article. Cowardice? Boredom, I think, and a sense that it was my Christian duty to protect readers from too prolonged a rerun of Ireland's ills. Even Winston Churchill's nerve broke when faced with that: 'Not Oliver Cromwell again, please Mr de Valera!'

Thus silenced I was reduced to what my household calls 'giving him a look'. The accusation is that I content myself too easily with a sudden chill in the eye, a pursed lip, which they say nobody notices anyway. But confrontation seems at the root of most of the world's ills, as the New Testament says it is, which I suppose is where Christianity comes into this.

Nevertheless, this avoidance of 'unpleasantness' seems a bit timid, and I have been examining my conscience. Certainly urban life leads us too far in the direction of self-defence. An otherwise pacific friend presented his credit-card in a shop and the assistant mused, 'That's a funny name…' 'And you have most peculiar ears but I haven't mentioned it!' roared my hair-trigger friend, at what I would have regarded as a clumsy attempt at matiness.

If I avoid 'unpleasantness', what would I defend loudly and publicly? I should say it was the personal discovery of what truly interests: the fruitful demythologising of one's own responses, the attempt to distinguish the genuine from the conditioned. It can take a lifetime. John Cowper Powys said that his life divided in two. Up to the age of 40,

> I struggled desperately to evoke and to arrange my feelings according to what I admired in my favourite books, but during the second half of my life I struggled to find out what my real feelings were …

He too chided himself, half-heartedly, for his human appeasements, his propitiation of others (slyly admitting the layer of self-protection these gave him). However, 'real feelings'? Powys would have approved of my preoccupation of the last weeks: this Spring, whenever opportunity presented itself, I have spent time peering into a nearby water-trough, startled by the life that is in it, the involuntary, unconditioned fascination, and by the length of time it takes to really notice this.

To a passer-by I must look cracked. The stone sides of the trough are about two feet high, and to get close to the smooth surface of the water and shadow it, the better to see inside it, you have to kneel, and bend low over it, like a worshipper. Slowly you realise that below the first surface is another one, restlessly moving and flicking the watercress stalks: tadpoles, in that small area countless thousands. (Powys worried about these. His Diaries have just been published, and he describes carrying them each day from drying puddles to distant, deeper ones.) But there is something else in those troughs. What looks like a yellowish watercress stalk curls into a circle, moves, and is a newt, yellow-flecked, with bulging golden eyes, a salamander, enormous in that context, ten times tadpole size. It has four legs with four fingers, and uses them like oars, feathering them and pressing them to its sides when, after long stillness, it speeds through the water. Presumably devouring tadpoles, but it is too quick for this to be seen, and the tadpoles seem quite fearless, frisking round the newts. It is like a wartime film. Jack Hawkins, John Mills, chatting on the bridge of the battleship, caps at an angle, dashing white polo-necked jersies under their uniform jackets, while underneath – Cut to Exterior U-Boat, bubble-surrounded, and then, Cut to Interior U-Boat, Conrad Veidt at the periscope; Danger from the Depths.

Maybe too elaborate a simile – Jack Hawkins makes an unlikely tadpole – but it suggests the lurking threat the newts seem to represent, their stillness, their sudden stabbing progress. They are strangely sinuous, seem able to scratch their eyeballs with their long thin tails. I proclaim my unwonted interest in them, and defend it. I now understand Wooster's newt-fancying friend Gussie Finknottle, and defend him too. When I ask somebody else to look they say, 'Oh, yes' politely, prepared to look and turn away, but they bend closer, transfixed. One went to fetch his distant friends.

In an odd way this kneeling to stare at a surface, and the gradual perception of what is happening underneath it, is like an act of worship, and brings to mind the extraordinary exhibition of Spanish still lifes that is on at the National Gallery.

These were painted over a period of 200 years, and the earliest are a devoted description of surface, that of cabbages, onions, fowls shot for the larder, all hanging on strings against a background entirely black. So minute and accurate is the observation that it becomes devotional, and it is no surprise to learn that the best of these early painters, Cotán, became a Carthusian lay-brother. It is as though, for him, it is the surface of the created world that he cannot praise enough. Then, as time passes, in later paintings people and narrative begin to appear. In Velasquez's 'Christ in the house of Martha and Mary' the story is reflected in a mirror, the point is the foreground kitchen objects and emotions. Then, when you come to Goya, a pile of dead bream (their profiles remarkably like that of the Duke of Wellington – Spanish revenge?) stares out at the world through glazing eyes, as though still experiencing the shock of their suffocation. The two centuries tell the story of our development, from early certainty, when to number the feathers of a dead bird was photographic praise enough; to drama, uncertainty, moralising, to a horror at what we do to the world, and at the finality of death, which includes our own. I found myself drawn back to the earlier, confident ones by Cotán, in which 'confrontation' takes on a larger meaning: to stand before a cabbage and really take it in, take it on, becomes a spiritual act; this, to the world, is 'giving it a look' positively. The attraction to earlier certainties may be cowardice, may be Christian, but I wish someone could remind me who it was said, 'description is revelation'.

*May 1995*


# 'Kilvert was here'


When you pick up a book called *The River Wye* and come upon the sentence, 'they are grand folk, the people of Llangurig' you know it is going to be no good, celebrating an unreal 'changelessness'. Books of sour observation of change are no use either. The lucky clutch of the heart that came when we stood, about 6.30 of a late July evening, at the foot of the bridge across the Wye at Bredwardine, had little to do with 'grand folk', or an illusion of permanence. It had been felt in other places, other countries, a combination of light and shadow and texture. In this case, a shining horse grazing, some still sheep, an ancient pear-tree and grass as neat as a golf-course green up to the river's edge, ending abruptly in a little cliff of pink Herefordshire earth, the quietly moving water crossed by the eighteenth-century bridge of lichened brick.

We were about to embark on the next instalment of the 'Wye Valley Walk'. We had tacitly abandoned our idea of walking the river itself, as we had walked the Severn, along its banks. The Wye is different; too many loops, too many private estates. Last year we had resisted those little arrows on posts with 'WVW' above them: too prescriptive, too municipal for sinewy Severn veterans. Now we had learned to hanker for them, helplessly dependent; the difficulties were great if they were ignored.

But first we had somehow to deal with the ghost of the Reverend Francis Kilvert, diarist of these parts, which haunted us here even more persistently than last year at Hay, and Clyro (we were walking from the Wye source on Plinlimmon) when we stayed at the pub opposite his house, through the windows of which he had sadly watched the falling-down drunks who were his parishioners.

We had chosen Bredwardine because the bridge gave us a choice of banks. We intended to link up with last year by walking *back* to Hay, upriver, then moving from Bredwardine towards Hereford, downriver. We booked ourselves in for B & B at Bredwardine Hall and lo! Kilroy, or rather Kilvert, had been there too, a frequent visitor to the retired Vicar and his two unmarried daughters. Kilvert became Vicar there himself, for the last two years of his life, and is buried in the churchyard. Next to him, snuggled up so close that it is almost a communal grave, are the two unmarried sisters, older than he was, who died after him.

Behind the church was a hand-written sign on a gate – 'Bed and Breakfast' – and the gate led to a handsome white house with softly rounded battlements overlooking the river, and this was his Vicarage, where he died. Nothing for it but to move there the next night and sleep in what was surely Kilvert's room, watching the shivering of white poplar old enough for him to have watched, whose lower branches dangled lightly in the river. Even the old bridge, seen from his window, is Kilvertian.

He married in August 1879 and on his return from honeymoon his parishioners took the horses from his carriage on the bridge, garlanded him and his bride, and drew them both to the Vicarage. That night he felt unwell and within ten days he was dead, of a burst appendix. (A few months later was performed the first appendectomy.) He was 38. His diary for the Bredwardine period is disappointing. His wife removed all mention of herself, and we do not know what besides. She survived, unmarried, until 1911 and is buried in a corner of the graveyard, the places by his side having been taken long before by the two ladies of Bredwardine Hall.

It is a sad, strange story, and the telling of it has left little room for an account of the walk. In the morning, obedient to the 'WVW' signs, we climbed the steep Knapp, a symmetrical eminence above Bredwardine, a tawny triangle of a hill, in the July dryness, while below us the silver spools of the Wye unwound. There is something to be said for looking *down* on a river. On Merbach Hill we were among green bracken and foxgloves and, after an hour of solitude came upon an eager horse, unbridled, with the look of a thoroughbred. Shergar? We pondered as to what such a horse could be doing up there alone, and never found out. We walked on fields of camomile and clover, and along a disused railway line, so long disused it was darkened by trees and crossed by butterflies.

Then we were met by a gate so festooned with razor-wire it might have been guarding a cruise missile. Laurie suggested we plunge through an unpromising thicket of brambles at its side. Reluctant, I spotted through the glasses a WVW sign on a faraway gate. Equally reluctant (he was guardian of the map, and we were *right*) he followed me over the fence towards it and immediately saw, next to the barbed-wire entanglement, a nearer WVW sign. Democracy at work: he wanted one way, I wanted another; yielding, he found the right one. Timorously, I suggested we move quietly, the farmer so obviously detested Walkers. Stoutly, Laurie declared us to be on the Right Path, so to hell with him. We came to Hardwick Brook, a Greek, an Irish, sweetly running sunken little stream, above Hay, and anyone staying in Hay should climb up towards it; the track is marked on the Pathfinder map. (Just as anyone staying in Bredwardine should use the elegant and inexpensive Old Vicarage.)

Herefordshire is special, specially quiet and coloured, and seems full of English refugees. We were counselled to live there ourselves – 'It's like going back to the 1940s'. Doubtful whether I wanted this, I suggested that Hitler was no longer around. 'Oh yes,' said one, with a kind of surreal relevance, 'we were singing "Roll out the Barrel" in the village hall only the other week.'

Our way into Hay, coming down from the hills, was obstructed by a spanking new and deserted golf-course, much bewired. The Heroes of the WVW should look into this.

Next day we began towards Hereford from Bredwardine, 'The Monnington Walk'. We might have known that Kilvert was there before us:

> One great feature of the place is the famous 'Monnington Walk', a noble avenue of magnificent Scotch firs bordering a broad green ride, stretching from Brobury Scar (a red sandstone precipice beetling over the winds of Wye) ...

He was right about the wind; it scours between the trees till the earth below them is bare and white. We never saw the Scotch firs, but plenty of very old Spanish chestnuts, above The Scar, the tall red cliff carved by the river. Perhaps we shall see the firs next year (DV and WVW) when we move out of Kilvert's shadow. He was a good man, but it will be pleasant to be on our own again.

*August 1995*

# Stephens and Staring

With apologies to W.H. Davies – 'What is this life if full of care/We have no time to stand and stare' – there is something in us which says that instead of staring we should be changing the world, or changing work into money, or at least changing our shirts. Too much staring can produce a condition not far from sleep, and curiously related to melancholy.

Nevertheless, the heat of this August, a seemingly endless succession of Italianate days, has driven me to try and work outside under a tree (the roots of which, incidentally, have so undermined the building where the work would have been attempted *in*side, that the door now sticks against the floor, and has to be forced, which causes a soft susurrus of sandy material to fall from the new gaps between ceiling and walls; which is indeed a melancholy sound), and under this field-maple, writing materials on knee, there does seem a great deal to stare at.

A Brimstone butterfly, for instance, a handsome and sizeable creature, bigger than a Large White, which always seems to be alone. This is worrying, because how can it reproduce? Large Whites seem to buzz it, dance round it, doubtless resentful of its distinctiveness. I am at last forced to consult a butterfly book and learn that the female Brimstone is nearly white, so its pursuer is probably its mate and all is well. I also learn that all butterflies perhaps derive their name from this one, because it is early to appear, as well as late to linger, and is thought to be the colour of butter. Very light-coloured butter, in my view; a sort of pale primrose; a flower for which, I read, it is the chief pollinator.

There is also the extremely strange behaviour of a blackbird, which I have never heard described. It lurks in the dark shade of a bush, then it warily emerges, flops on its chest in the sun, spreads its wings on the ground, fans its tail upwards, opens its orange beak, cocks its head and stares steadily at me. The perfect circle of its iris, also orange, gives it a maniacal expression, and its open beak makes it look loopy. In fact it looks dead, and unimaginatively stuffed. When I move to the house to answer the telephone it hurriedly resumes its normal appearance and hops back into the shade.

On one such occasion I saw from a window that it was doing the same thing but with its back to me. Its cocked tail revealed an unfeath-

ered area with a little red scar in it. It was airing, or sunning, its funda-
ment. But if it is responding to the heat, why does it choose to come
into the sun to behave like this?

All this staring, this almost-entering into the life outside, has led
me back to James Stephens, a great starer, and listener, and one who
could effortlessly describe a conversation between an ass and a spider.
The ass had been brutally treated, which Stephens mentions without
comment:

> There was a spider sitting on a hot stone in the grass. He had a
> small body and wide legs, and he wasn't doing anything. [Clearly
> Stephens approves of that.]
>
> 'Does anybody ever kick you on the nose?' said the ass to him.
>
> 'Ay does there,' said the spider; 'you and your like that are always
> walking on me, or lying down on me, or running over me with the
> wheels of a cart.'
>
> 'Well, why don't you stay on the wall?' said the ass.
>
> 'Sure, my wife is there,' replied the spider.
>
> 'What's the harm in that?' said the ass.
>
> 'She'd eat me,' said the spider, 'and, anyhow, the competition
> on the wall is dreadful, and the flies are getting wiser and timider
> every season ...'

That is from *The Crock of Gold*, which also contains leprechauns,
Pan, Angus Óg, the Irish god of love, two hilarious Philosophers
married to the Grey Woman and the Thin Woman, and how can
Stephens deploy such a cast, as well as talking spiders, without for a
moment sounding fey? Partly it is his humour, as natural to him as
breathing, and partly his seriousness. His books are armatured by a
Blakean-Theosophical-Buddhist philosophy – witty and mystical
Irishmen will go almost anywhere to escape the embraces of Mother
Church (though Stephens was a Protestant) – which gives his stories
an under-surface strength and disinfects them of whimsy. His world
coheres, even if you think some of his generalisations barmy. He is
an enchanter, and little is known about him, even his birth date. He
was abandoned when he was six and was brought up in a Dublin
orphan school. His biographer says that he was 4 foot 10 high, or low,
but in a letter he claims 5 foot 3. Whichever it was, his height and his
manner seem to have made inevitable his later casting as a professional leprechaun, with which he cooperated, to earn his bread, and
because he was amenable. It its difficult to define his unique quality.
He tried to do it himself in a 1917 letter:

I think I portray *living*, or the sense of being alive... the beginning of chapters where one is only preparing for the story, the end of chapters where one is wiping up the mess which the action has made, into these I put all the energy I have got, much more than in the *important* places.

In other words, or so it seems to me, he most valued those places where he could describe the outcome of merely staring, with no irritable grasping after event, or action. He goes on:

Read, for example, the description of the awakening of the little encampment in *The Demi-Gods* ...

He considered *The Demi-Gods* his best book, which is encouraging, because so do I. It is shorter than the more famous *Crock of Gold* and better organised, with fewer and briefer philosophical asides. It takes equivalent risks. Three angels join a tramp and his daughter on their travels round Ireland What could be more whimsical-dangerous? Yet a critic has remarked, 'To say the book is subversive is to put it mildly.' The angels are as innocent of any sense of private property, or the rule of law, as is the tramp himself, and what he does to survive seems to them merely sensible.

He planned to write an Irish *Comédie Humaine* based on the old saga-cycles of Ireland. He only completed *Deirdre* and *In the Land of Youth*, both marvels of tone and psychological realism. But ill-health and melancholy intervened. He spent the second world war in Gloucestershire, publicly declaring himself an Englishman for the duration. He became a famous broadcaster. These talks read well, not too leprecorny, but you can see that he knew what the audience expected. On reflection I do not think it was the staring that made him melancholy. It was the best part of him.

A cloud of Cabbage Whites has just taken off, dancing, higgledy-piggledy, but always keeping together within that small space of air; then they disappear. Stephens would probably have had them conversing, and it would have sounded appropriate.

*September 1995*

# 'Is this shame eternal? I cried'

On the paperback of his *Apologia Pro Vita Sua* Cardinal Newman is called, as he usually is, 'a master of English prose' and it is open to question whether that would make anybody want to read Newman's graceful and candid self-examination. Maybe we reserve the phrase 'well-written' for books we have no intention of reading. We know when something is *badly* written because we have difficulty getting through it even when interested in the subject, but few readers, surely, in the midst of something they enjoy, pause to exclaim, 'Well written!' – though they might say, '*That's* good.'

As for bad writing, the worst I ever had to read was in the formal Evidence submitted to the Committee on the Teaching of English, most of it by professional English teachers, and in the end I understood what made it bad. Maybe they were inhibited by the formality of the occasion, but when you come across phrases like 'communication skills' you may have a rough idea what you could mean by it but you cannot be sure what the writer means unless he or she gives examples, and examples were as rare as golden orioles in Gloucestershire.

Remembering that rubbish (not all of it rubbish, but most) and shuddering a little, remembering also that George Moore in his self-examination, *Hail and Farewell*, covers pages proving to his own satisfaction that John Henry Newman couldn't write for toffee; remembering also that *Hail and Farewell*, though I disagree with nearly everything in it, is a book I would take to a desert island, it is so entertaining (and well-written), and wanting an excuse to advertise it, again; wondering whether the question of the 'well-written' was interesting enough to write about at all (well or ill) – while crossing an open space on the way to work – I realised that I was not only shuddering at the lifeless jargon I had read years ago, but also at the force, noise and temperature of the east wind.

At our 900-foot height above Gloucester an east wind, blowing hard, has no real impediment between Silesia and us. Perhaps further, but that is where the map on the wall ends. It blows along a green smooth channel at the top of Europe, up the Thames valley and reaches our front door with its Eastern European teeth unblunted. I saw the sky was bruise-black and like a bowl, with a primrose rim on the horizon, through which shafts came vertically down, not of rain, of struggling light. Even the sheep were huddled miserably at their hay, a close-packed row of dungy, mustard-coloured bottoms. One part of the field near a wall was almost entirely covered by their dung: they must have sheltered there during the night, processing the day's grass. There is a saying round here that sheep should never hear the church bells in the same field twice, and they are going to have difficulty finding a blade of clean grass among their droppings.

I was soon driven indoors, to be much distracted, as always, by dipping into the paperback *Hail and Farewell*. Meanwhile the yellow horizon-rim disappeared, all became black, the rain came, and now the windows have misted up and darkness has fallen. There is a model for this particularity in Moore's book. He frequently breaks off to describe the room he is writing in, what memories his (rather splendid) furnishings and pictures evoke, then he goes on. He does this so often that the earnest critic J. Middleton Murry, younger than Moore, and not often associated with humour, wrote a piece about him called 'Wrap me up in my Aubusson carpet'.

In *Hail and Farewell* Moore picks sentences from Newman's *Apologia* and defies his devout brother, The Colonel, to prove their 'prose mastery'. Gossipy, self-indulgent Moore is always useless on the subjects of love, sex and Christianity. In another book he treats of Irish legends and they lose their innocence, which is what presumably attracted him; he yearns after it, but his fondling only leaves smeared fingerprints. It is rather like that with his treatment of the *Apologia* in which Newman tries to make reasonable his forsaking of Anglicanism for Roman Catholicism, an act which must have contained as much emotion as it contained reason. He had not wanted to write the book at all, but was forced to, because of the public slurs of the xenophobic Protestant, author of *Westward Ho!*, Charles Kingsley:

… those proselytising priests, like Dr Newman, who have turned round upon their mother church (I had almost said their mother country) with contumely and slander.

Newman mildly asks where he has committed these slanders (wanting, of course, examples) and sighs at the end:

What is the use of going on with this Writer's criticisms upon me, when I am confined to the dull monotony of exposing him again and again, with a persistence, which many will think merciless, and few will have the interest to read.

Moore had the interest to read, perhaps annoyed that Newman

made his spiritual journey so enthralling, but his real motive was to destroy Newman in his Catholic brother's eyes. As with the Irish fairy tales he seemed impelled to test delicate things to destruction. 'The Colonel', white-faced, eventually quits the house and Moore is left to lament his own wicked, teasing nature. 'In life,' admitted Moore, 'I can play nothing but light comedy.' The reader senses tragedy, not comedy, in Moore's cruelty to his brother, and is thus flattered into imagining he knows Moore better than Moore knows himself, but that is one of Moore's many tricks. His subsequent attempts at becoming officially a Protestant are not light, but brilliantly high, comedy.

This comes about because the light-comedian Moore seems genuinely outraged when a reviewer in 1903 takes for granted his Irish-born Catholicism.

Words that upset my mental balance, forcing me into an uncontrollable rage. Is this shame eternal? I cried. Of what use is writing?

He announces his (non-existent, absurd in his hilarious account) conversion to Protestantism in a Dublin newspaper, thereby preparing the final, non-absurd rift with his loved younger brother.

Anyone who likes a good, fat book (774 pages, really three books, *Ave, Salve, Vale*) should try *Hail and Farewell*. Stories about life in Paris among the Impressionists, about the Irish Literary Renaissance – Yeats by the lake at Coole 'in his cloak, like a huge umbrella left behind by some picnic-party'. You can bob along in his creamy impressionism, laughing, wincing, until you arrive at the end and feel bereft of an infuriating, entrancing companion.

Everyone laughed at Moore, not only himself. The Fates are still laughing. *Hail and Farewell* was published in 1911, but I notice that the Colin Smythe paperback, 1985, is published in conjunction with 'Catholic University of America Press'. Is this shame eternal?

*February 1996*

# Ten Days in Winter

Flying to India for a ridiculously short visit is like going to a football match or an opera. Having done all three recently I feel justified in making these strange juxtapositions. There is the same sense of being flung into a self-contained and intensive world to which you do not belong.

At the football match it is the crowdedness that reminds you of India where, in MacNeice's words ('Didymus'), 'the world is on the boil'. The moment you arrive in India you know you have to expunge the words 'teeming', 'colourful'. But Stamford Bridge, Chelsea against West Ham, *teems*. Where did all these people come from? You saunter along the Fulham Road, vaguely aware that others on the pavement are moving in the same direction, but when you enter the ground – paying as much as for an opera ticket, Covent Garden take note – you are overcome by the inexplicable purposefulness of a mass of people criss-crossing each other, but with a cheerful and noisy intentness, which, given a happy mingle of animals, could be Indian.

Not even Indian colourfulness is lacking, though cunningly delayed. You squeeze through a dangerously spiky turnstile, enter dark caverns of concrete, clatter up stairs and passages for which the term 'brutalism' was invented, turn a corner, and there, below, is the defined open space, the beautiful emerald of the pitch in a banked setting that is quickly being decorated, in patient Moghul style, with an inset of 20,000 faces. Like Indian inlays also, the stands are patterned with angled aisles, gaps, that almost form the letters of an alphabet you do not know.

The players are already on the pitch, in tracksuits, doing Tantric exercises with the football – chinning it, back-of-the-necking it, kicking it with the side of the foot so that it curves through the air and lands miraculously on the outstretched instep of a colleague – tricks forgotten once the grunting collisions of the match begin by all but the dark-skinned, dreadlocked Ruud Gullit, who with feints and back-heels continues to enjoy himself. The West Ham supporters shout a version of the Red Flag (do they know it is that?), a thousand baritones in staccato unison, palms extended towards the Chelsea fans, like an opera chorus. Despite the power and precision of the singing, the words are hard to distinguish, probably just as well.

The previous night it had been the same at the opera, you couldn't distinguish the words there either, although it was the English National Opera, in English; and there was the same injection into an intent, criss-crossing crowd. What must the Coliseum have been like when it was a music-hall? In the dress-circle bar, where you had to queue, there were posters, pre-first world war, on which Sarah Bernhardt and the ballet shared the bill with Gillie Potter, 'The Squire of Hogsnorton' and 'the comedy juggler' W.C. Fields. Those audiences, more varied, must have been variously thirsty; did they also queue?

Then comes the Imperial splendour of the auditorium and a view of the private world of the pit orchestra, the red perm of a lady violinist, the chatting harpist, all of them tuning up, about to do difficult things beyond the reach of most of the audience. It was Bizet's *The Pearl Fishers*, set in India – well, in Ceylon – the set a raised platform covered with decorated cushions upon which the baritone slumbers, in boots, fanned by a servant. It must have been nearly like that in Fatehpur Sikri, where the Moghul emperor Akbar had a little summer platform, set amid cooling conduits of water, on which, in public, he took his rest. The opera stage was covered with coloured petals, Indian-style; at the match a section of the crowd must have carefully torn their tickets into tiny pieces: at the kick-off, in one concerted movement, they threw this confetti into the air and it descended on the pitch in a slow curve; not untidy, graceful. The footballers did difficult things – beyond the reach of most of the audience – and the soprano, Elizabeth Woollett, did complex coloratura things with her voice, beautifully, as did the player Ruud Gullitt, with his feet. Two intense worlds; a brief visit to each.

It was the confetti, in the end, that was most reminiscent of the short glimpse of India. Indians seem to go in for detail, decoration; a nearly infinite number of hands, and infinite patience. Everyone at the roadsides seemed to be making, mending, selling something, and it was usually small. Loping, crawling, standing among the squatting or bustling people were calm-eyed water buffalo, sacred cows, bristly pigs, monkeys, dogs, sometimes a camel, and the occasional plumed and caparisoned horse taking a cartful of people to a wedding. The tolerated animals looked bony, but healthy, as did most of the people, however poor; busy, free, uncowed. But what could we really know, just watching, as at a match or an opera?

It was cold at the match and it was cold at the Taj Mahal. The first time we saw it was in a white fog. Years ago a child put together a white cardboard model of the Taj which still stands in our attic, and the real thing looked familiarly like that. Very fine, but there was an uneasy feeling that some of the visitors standing rapt were actually worshipping it.

Across the Yamuna River is the 'baby Taj', an earlier mausoleum properly called Itimad-ud-Daula. A lovely mixture of geometry and decoration; the white marble of its surfaces is inlaid with flowers and patterns made from different coloured stones. One of these inlays is of brownish-red marble with fossil-like spirals and whorls which give it the look of a paisley pattern, or a detail from a painting by Richard Dadd. My companion kept saying, 'It's like a carpet' which it wasn't, but he was talking of the intricate designs covering the whole building. A professional historian, he was taking the wide view whereas I was looking at a detail perhaps an inch and a half across. I reflected that if our two temperaments could have been joined we would, I suppose, be God.

The Yamuna is wide with dry grey patches on which grey cattle eat hay that is brought to them. A woman stepping gracefully in a sari crossed the mud-flats with a silver bowl on her head. She was gathering cowpats. These are dried, stacked in a decorative pattern, and used as fuel. Everything is used.

We learned to fill our pockets with small notes to help allay some of the sights – 'Begging unfingered hands and mouthing eyes' (MacNeice again, same poem) – and there was a tiny girl carrying a baby I had seen before, so I was ready. I held out two rupees, about fourpence, and she plucked it from my hand with the rapt dignity of need. It was the quick jab of a thrush in a field, plucking out a worm.

*March 1996*

*Bywords*

# Flints in Gloucestershire

The spring equinox dawned promising; bright, clear, windless, a rim of white clouds on the horizon, but overhead a vault of faultless blue. It seemed a good idea to go on a tour of inspection, to see how far spring was advanced. It would not be far at this height, 900 feet; late March is an odd time, you sense things happening, but underground, underbark.

True, there was frog-spawn in the water-troughs, but in other years at this time these have been filled with tadpoles (though last year there were none). The frogs themselves seem to have gone (where? any tour of inspection fills itself with unanswered questions); in past weeks you couldn't go near the troughs without causing a boiling, bubbling sound, as the frogs, clasped together egg-fertilising, crash-dived to safety below the weeds. Now there is no movement at all, only rather chill-looking spawn with black dots inside it.

The grass has hardly grown, though become somewhat clumpy and irregular. However, it is filled this year with ground-hugging violets, very shy indeed. Each year is a 'good' one for some wild plant, and there have never been so many violets. These are the usual violet-coloured flowers, but further afield, observed on the tour and under bare hedges, there were carpets, or at least rugs, of *white* violets, taller and more daring, as though assured by the roofing shelter of the hedge.

Somebody said that 'description is revelation', and whether that is so or not, it seems likely that the various dismays and excitements, inside and outside us, the sense that everything most important in our lives finally eludes explanation, could in some way be tackled by looking as closely as we can at what is around us, this being the only 'revelation' we are likely to receive.

It can make you giddy. For example: last week the neighbour farmer ploughed up a pasture never disturbed in his lifetime. 'Min. of War and Ag', he reckoned, was the last to do so, by which he meant wartime Dig for Victory. After recent droughts the grass had become tired and he wanted to refresh it, wondered if he would find some old clay pipes, or flints. There is no flint in this part of Gloucestershire, so any that is found had been brought in, for tools or weapons.

The dizziness came because across this new-ploughed pasture there is an ancient track and this he had left untouched, a broad strip of green turf running straight through the gleaming waves of newly turned earth. Walking along this, looking for flints on either side, you did not need to be fanciful involuntarily to experience a sense of walking a green pier surrounded by a brown immobile sea. There were currents in the waves, because, ploughed lengthways, it was in some places ploughed across, so the earth-waves pushed against each other and you felt a sort of motionless heaving, even felt a kind of seasickness.

There were no flints. These stand out, especially after rain has washed the mud from them. One, found last year in another field, shone out so white and grey among the muddy yellow it might have been placed there, as a test, by some gamesome museum curator. It is maybe three inches long, pointed, an inch and a half across at the base. It could be a spearhead but such luck is unlikely. It is probably a 'scraper', carefully knapped at the edge used for removing fat from animal skins. It fits snugly between thumb and forefinger, but only in the left hand, so maybe its owner was left-handed.

They do gleam out, like white feathers, or bird droppings, so you often have the thrill of thinking you have spotted one, until you go near and look more closely. There were no flints and, after many such disappointments, there was time to wonder why so many dropped feathers – no, all of them – were white; though, of course, at ploughing-time the seagulls come.

The edge of the newly ploughed pasture descends into a thorn-bush-scattered and sedgy bank. In one of the small hawthorn bushes there seemed to be some agricultural plastic bag entangled – there have been high winds. It was a gull, dead, its breast almost unimaginably white, its wings grey, one stretched out, the other half folded against its side, as though caught in some acrobatic manoeuvre. There was no mark on it, no sign left by a predator. Do gulls have coronaries midair?

All this was seen during the day. In the evening, reading Peter Brown's *Saint Augustine*, I was startled to discover that Augustine, in his *Confessions*, blamed himself for enjoying observations like these, felt ashamed that he could be distracted by the sight of a hare, tempted to turn his horse and follow it. 'Indeed, unless You quickly showed me my infirmity and admonished me ... I would simply stand gaping at it. What is to be said of me? A lizard catching flies or a spider eating them as they fall into his net can hold me absorbed when I sit in my room.' Brown ends the quotation there. Surely a Christian should be praising God for his world? So it was a relief to find that Augustine goes on, 'It is true that the sight of them inspires me to praise You for the wonders of Your Creation ...', but he still blamed himself for being distracted by the created from the Creator. Which is altitudinous of him, though his thinking affected the course of Western Civilisation.

Our highest altitude has been glimpses of the miserably named Hale-Bopp comet, apparently intent on disappearing inside its own slipstream, before in fact disappearing into cloud difficult to discern as cloud because of the sad orange light cast up by the nearby town. No use complaining because what you do not want, others have decided they do want – the suburbanisation of England. The Vandals were at the gates of Hippo when the dying, mellowed Augustine said something even more encouraging about tours of inspection: the love of martyrs for the eternal was measurable, because 'they were capable of so much love for things that pass away …'.

Some of our decisions have been disastrous, we know. Next to the field of the dead gull are sheep. The grass is growing, but not quickly enough for them. As you approach they set up a throaty murmur, then they run towards you in full bleat, hoping you have brought them a supplement of hay, or those pellets that look like giant All-Bran. 'Protein', it said on the sack; few farmers knew that it contained minced sheep. They stare, with their long, horizontal pupils, almost butting you in their eagerness. It is luck they do not recognise the taste of flesh, they have not yet learned to bite.

*April 1997*


# Edward Thomas and Miguel de Unamuno


It is unhelpful to limit good poems too narrowly to their subject-matter, to what they are ostensibly 'about'. To talk of 'nature poetry', or worse, 'war poetry', is to slap a template of journalistic expectation on a poem that fits so badly the words underneath will be unable to breathe. (It also allows scope for comic prejudice. There is a story about Gavin Ewart and Ted Hughes judging a poetry competition. Hughes recommended a poem about a dead lamb. 'Oh,' said Ewart, 'I always throw the ones about nature away.')

Take John Clare, a 'nature poet' who wrote about hedges and birds and villagers with almost photographic exactness, but whose poems are really about himself, his past, his present, his sanity. They are a search for who that self is, and his fidelity to the facts is an attempt to anchor it, keep it sane, and the power in the poems lies not only in what they say but also in what they do not say. Once he famously cries this out loud. 'I am – yet what I am none cares or knows', and is led to the wonderful line, 'I am the self-consumer of my woes.'

Or take Edward Thomas, who lies under a double bind. First he was neglected because he was not a 'war poet'; although he took part in the war, he did not write directly about it, and this made him mysterious, even suspect. In fact, it is possible that if he had not managed to get himself killed in that war, he might have remained neglected altogether. He has been slowly resurrected, despite, like Clare, writing about hedges and birds and villagers, because his search for himself is more overt, and his apparent failure to find it is interesting, because it is something we can recognise and apply to our own experience. Nevertheless, he can be written off like Clare and diminished into a recorder of a rural England that was vanishing as he watched; a writer, in short, of poems about 'nature' that Ewart might throw away.

I have been rereading Thomas, and finding him more and more of a considerable figure, because I had agreed to give a talk on his poetry to the Edward Thomas Society. Just before that I had been rereading Miguel de Unamuno's *Tragic Sense of Life*, for no better reason than that I wanted to and found myself in Bilbao, where he was born. What seemed strange was how the thought of these two men, writing roughly at the same time, coincided at a surprising number of points. Or perhaps not so strange, that two such intrepid potholers, determined to descend into the darkest tunnels of their selves, should occasionally glimpse the flash of the other's torch, or throw up similarly shaped shadows.

It is a rare treat for me to read someone like Unamuno because he thinks in the way I do, only better; persistent, impassioned, unembarrassed. *The Tragic Sense of Life* is a prolonged battering on the door of reasonable common sense, determined to make it open and admit 'life', which for Unamuno is the opposite of reason, though both are necessary; or rather, their necessary opposition is what gives our life its tragic sense. Why he wants it to open, to allow in the unrational, is because he believes that our most urgent concern, the centre of our lives, is our passionate desire never to lose our individual consciousness, to believe, in short, that our souls are immortal. To arrive at this belief, he throws theology in the bin and replaces it with non-reasonable 'life'.

It is clear what he is driving at, and he drives with brusque conviction and does not cheat. The importance of his topic is obvious, but I am uneasy with what he takes for granted: that everybody wants eternal life. I find it difficult to believe in my own, but impossible to believe in the extinction of anyone dead whom I have loved. Cowardice, inability to face facts, doubtless; it is a position both rationally and religiously indefensible. In *Hail and Farewell*, George Moore goads his devoutly Roman Catholic brother, whom he derisively calls 'The Colonel', and at last gets him shamefacedly to admit that he believes in immortal life for others but not for himself. So perhaps my illogical position is not unique.

Edward Thomas's poems so often refer to a memory, of something glimpsed, not understood, nearly forgotten, that memory could be defined as his form of self-search So it is for Unamuno: 'Memory is the basis for individual personality, just as tradition is the basis of the collective personality of a people. We live in memory and by memory, and our spiritual life is at bottom the effort of our memory to persist, to transform itself into hope, the effort of our past to transform itself into our future.'

Thomas could be thought too self-referential; he not only sees the flycatcher, he ponders the effect of the flycatcher on him. Unamuno: 'If you look at the world closely and as inwardly as you are able to look – that is to say, if you look within yourself … you will arrive at the abyss of the tedium, not merely of life but of something more: at the tedium of existence, at the bottomless pit of the vanity of vanities. And there you will come to pity all things; you will arrive at universal love.' That tremendous paradox looks naked here, but he has led us by the hand towards it. So, to look outward according to Unamuno, is inevitably to look inward, as Thomas does, personalising what he sees. Unamuno: 'Love personalises all that it loves. Only by personalising can we fall in love with an idea.' Unamuno's personalising led him, unslavishly, to a personal God. Almost the last words Thomas wrote in his trench diary were, 'I never quite understood what was meant by God.' He was killed next day.

Unamuno's paradox – despair being the foundation of hope – his argued view 'that in the depth of human love there is a depth of eternal despair out of which spring hope and consolation' is expressed in what seems Thomas's last poem, written before he left England, but in the same trench diary. The first lines are –

The sorrow of great love is a great sorrow
And true love parting blackens a bright morrow:

Yet almost they equal joys, since their despair
Is but hope blinded by its tears, and clear
Above the storm the heavens wait to be seen.

'Despair is but hope blinded by its tears': in eight words, what Unamuno's Spanish eloquence and Basque doggedness climb towards in 300 pages. The two men may emerge from different cracks in the limestone hill, but into the same landscape.

*June 1997*

# Watching the Rain at Lord's

A warning: what follows is not about cricket but about attendance at a cricket-match, and for the sake of the transatlantic readership, also for the many in Britain for whom the word 'cricket' is a turn-off, a turn-page, there will be no obscure reference to the game itself, which in this case will be easy because during the five days of the match very little of the game was played.

It was a Test Match at Lord's (a 'Test' being a contest between two cricketing nations; Lord's cricket ground, in London, the headquarters of the game), England versus Australia, two countries which, for historical reasons, are particularly eager to beat each other. This Lord's Test match happens roughly every four years, and I suppose, off and on, I had been looking forward to it for about that length of time – together, of course, with hundreds of thousands, maybe millions of others.

This year, there are to be six Test Matches between England and Australia, each over five days, and that is worth considering for a moment, until the head spins. Each day consists of six hours' play (weather permitting, but more of that later), a total of 180 hours of combat, during each hour of which ninety balls must be bowled, every ball an attempt to knock over the batsman's stumps, or make him give a catch, or do something else which leads to his dismissal and his return to the pavilion. So that is 540 attempts a day, multiplied by five (days) equals 2,700 attempts a match, multiplied by six (matches) makes 15,000 attempts – or 'balls' or 'deliveries' – and at this point arithmetic has to be abandoned as one loses oneself in wonder. The sheer lunacy is its greatest attraction. And every ball is described on one of the main radio channels of the BBC. If it rains, the commentators chat about past cricket or describe the cakes they have been sent by grateful listeners.

Play begins at eleven o'clock, gates open at nine, and by half-past eight in the morning the queue waiting to get in is a mile long. For the first time (in my experience), while we are waiting, our bags are searched by polite youths. Looking for booze or bombs? I wondered aloud, causing laughter in the queue – everyone cheerful, excited; this, after all, was England against Australia, at Lord's – but no one seemed really to know the answer, and the youths just blushed. Certainly many of the bags were clinking with bottles; the rumour was that you were allowed a litre per person, but you could always say you were expecting friends. The search was just something to be endured and forgotten, like the grey clouds low overhead.

Once inside the ground, you saw its vast extent was covered with huge green sheets, from which overnight rain was being patiently swept with brooms. Sometimes these sheets were rolled back, when it looked as though rain might not be coming, and this was a complex process because air-pockets formed under them, they billowed up and a dozen men trampled them down, looking as though they were trudging, knee-deep, in green dunes. Then would come another flurry of rain, and the sheets would be rolled on again. We also had our first sight of a new figure who seemed the Bearer of the Hereditary Umbrella, John Jameson, a former England player, who, carrying no less than two mobile telephones, strode about, talking into them, sometimes his MCC umbrella furled (Marylebone Cricket Club; Lord's is not in Marylebone, it is in St John's Wood, but never mind), sometimes sagging half-open, and sometimes over his head, revealing the MCC colours, alternate panels of dried blood and scrambled egg.

It was a lively scene, sweepings, rollings, conferrings, but why did we all stay – the weather was terrible, it grew darker by the hour? Because, should there be play, and the covers at last rolled away, the damp air, the damp turf, would make the ball do unexpected things and this would be exciting. Mostly, perhaps, we stayed because we could not bear to tear ourselves away. The stands looked nearly deserted, but under the stands in bars like caverns noisy parties were under way. A voice came over the Tannoy urging us to behave (there had been rowdiness at the previous Test Match in a suburb of Birmingham), to remember the tradition of fair play. This annoyed us, because, as Heinrich Böll said about folklore, tradition is some-thing like innocence: 'when you know you have it, you no longer have it'. 'Is that chap a schoolmaster? Sounds like one,' came a voice. At one o'clock, there was another announcement, that no more alcohol would be sold. Whence this sudden puritanism? It didn't make the slightest difference, everyone had clearly brought their own. What was remarkable was universal cheerfulness, even when play was called off for the day (not that there had been any to call off).

Next day, the clouds were as low and grey, but the green sheets were off and the whole Australian party was lying on the turf slowly rotating, as though on spits. In another corner the England team played boyish games, running round coloured plastic nipples stuck in the ground, trying not to bump into each other; the Umbrella was raised, lowered, furled, two Mobiles uncomfortably juggled. At last, a day late, play began, very slowly; damp air and damp turf had played their part, and England were bowled out for their lowest total since 1988. Never mind, it would be as difficult for the Australians. It wasn't. Damp air and damp turf seemed not to help England's bowlers as much as it had Australia's. Then came more rain. An elderly jazz band played, well, under a dripping tree, the banjo player in a tweed motoring cap, *circa* 1910, with a bright pink tip to his nose.

Third day, the covers came off, in bright sun, and then were rolled back in near darkness. During what play there was, England managed to drop all the catches that came to them. At the fifth one missed, someone howled, 'I don't believe it!' and spoke for us all.

The fourth day began with a thunderstorm and a flood. I sheltered with a Maltese who had come from his island for this match only. There was also a man from Adelaide. Even the jazz band strode off, muttering. Sometimes the sun shone, and little engines with curved tin roofs the Reverend W. Awdry would have loved – Thomas the Sponge Engine – rode slowly up and down, round sponges fore and aft, retiring discreetly to beyond the boundary to discharge jets of yellow water, like the micturition of cows.

Still, there might be play, we scanned storms on either side of us, weather-wise as ancient mariners. At one o'clock a major cloudburst, the stand roof hissed and poured, the ground became a near lake and, broken, I fled to Paddington Station and home. By the time I reached it, maybe four hours later, there was, unbelievably, play and Australian wickets falling. Thomas the Sponge Engine had triumphed. Next day, the last, the sun shone, they played all day, I wasn't there and nobody won.

*July 1997*

# Angels and Montaigne

When you are told at an impressionable age (six) that everyone has a guardian angel, the idea is appealing. At least, it is to a certain kind of temperament; more and more it seems to me that whether you have a sense, or intimation, or even a wish, for the existence of any world other than this one, it is a matter not of reason or unreason but of temperament.

Should you take to such an idea, it pleasantly personalises the thinness of the membrane – or perhaps you could say the 'interface' – between this world and an intuited other. When, later in life, someone tries to shoot you, say, and misses, more or less, and is himself shot by somebody else, you have occasion to be grateful to your guardian angel while at the same time wondering where was his. It is the ability to live more or less comfortably with such unanswered questions that so infuriates and disgusts, sometimes justifiably, those of another temperament. When, as in my experience, the existence of the guardian angel was posited at the same time as the adage 'God helps those who help themselves', the ability to live with two contradictory ideas was inaugurated; indeed, at six, there seemed no contradiction at all, and perhaps there isn't one. When something goes wrong, it is easy to imagine the angel sorrowful, or irritated, or shrugging.

It seems we need angels, or some of us do. They are in Judaism, in Islam: at the end of Islamic prayers, I am told, there must be a glance to the left shoulder, and to the right, because on each shoulder an angel sits. In various forms they are also in Eastern religions. In Western art, their representation affords the opportunity for rainbow wings, for an escape from the limitations of gender. In the New York Metropolitan Museum, it seemed necessary to go back for a quick second look at certain angels, Dutch I think, sixteenth-century. The bottom of their robes floated back a little, still unsettled after the speed of their arrival. It was their expressions that were most particularly imagined. Not quite the mischievous detachment of Puck – 'Lord, what fools these mortals be' – but nevertheless a watchful uncertainty about these strange cattle they were dealing with, coupled with an implacable determination – the paintings were usually Annunciations – to deliver the message; a consciousness of the hugeness of the power they represented. Formidable creatures, not 'sweet' at all.

Human, however, in their depiction, because that is the best we can manage: they have eyes, noses, feet. The only odd thing about them is their wings. In other respects, they are 'ordinary', which is what makes them exciting. (Milton describes the digestive processes of angels.)

Montaigne praises Socrates, above all men, because of the ordinariness of his examples: 'His talk is always of carters, joiners, cobblers, and masons ... By these common and natural means, without exciting or pricking himself on, he expounded not only the most regular, but also the most exalted and vigorous beliefs, actions, and morals that ever there were. It is he who brought human wisdom down again from the skies where it was wasting its labour, and restored it to man ...' ('God helps those who help themselves.') Yet (or should it be 'and') Montaigne has an angel in the chapel on the lower floor of his tower: Michael, killing the dragon. He also importantly remarked, or so the guide-sheet claims, that, amid the appalling religious intolerance of his time, his sympathies were equally with Michael and the dragon.

Montaigne, after public life, retired to his library in the tower at the corner of his house. 'L'an du Christ 1571, âgé de trente-huit ans ... en pleines forces se retira ...' he says of himself. His editor Michel Butor cries out, 'Voilà une date qui doit appartenir à l'histoire du monde', and points out that he retired 'en plein milieu des troubles qui déchirent la France'.

Geoffrey Grigson, son of a vicar, did not allow himself easy commerce with angels. His poems, like a horse confronted with an unexpected obstacle, jib when they sense an approach to the transcendental. Grigson visited Montaigne's tower and called a late book of poems (1984) by that title. Typically, he is cautious:

Was it really here, in this tiled room
In this tower that Montaigne wrote?
I hope that it was so.

(There seems little doubt, but best to be careful.) Grigson sees Montaigne pushing back his chair across the tiles, standing and stretching, and going down the newel stair – at the bottom of which, Montaigne tells us, he had often forgotten what made him descend in the first place – and, a Grigson touch, has Montaigne seeing what Grigson saw and the present visitor sees, a douce landscape, with vines that cast 'black bars of shadow in row after row'. Back to the real, the visible, the more-than-sufficient everyday.

At Angers, however, is a banquet for the angel-fancier. 'The largest tapestry in the world – 103 metres long, 4.5 metres high, commissioned by Louis the First, finished about 1382, designed by Jean de Bruges, Court Painter.' It illustrates the Revelation of St John, the Apocalypse. Character-filled and busy angels are everywhere, almost as frequent as animals and flowers; not always benevolent angels, frequently they pour flasks of famine and plague and massacre on the earth, to purge its past impieties. St John himself is at the corner of each panel, in a sort of Gothic shelter, sometimes biting his fingers, covering his eyes from what he sees, sometimes merely gloom-filled, but also at times led by the hand, out of his look-out, by a firm and commanding angel, assuring him that all will be well. Horrors are not flinched away from, but there is a springtime feel about the whole work – made during the outrages of the Hundred Years War. Birds, flowers, animals; along the lower border, a homely rabbit keeps popping in and out of its burrow. It was made by people in touch both with reality and their imaginations. 'You clearly mistake,' said Blake, 'when you say that visions of fancy are not to be found in this world. To me this world is all one continued vision of Fancy or Imagination.' That the work is large is of no matter; what matters is that to look at it is to be enlarged. It is one of the wonders of the world.

*September 1997*


# Frank O'Connor and Donegal


There is something Heroic about Ireland; perhaps not if you were born and had to live there (though possibly, even so), but to a besotted and frequent visitor, everything, even its wearisome literary quarrels, seems pitched on a heroic scale.

'By 1947,' says Frank O'Connor's biographer, James Matthews, 'he had antagonised just about everyone in Ireland, not only the pietists and the patriots, but the mainstream literati as well, Flann O'Brien, Austin Clarke, Anthony Cronin ...' Even the Monaghan poet Patrick Kavanagh, whom O'Connor had spotted early and championed, to an almost universal sneering ('the lavatory poet'), even Kavanagh said that O'Connor 'had sold out to the Yanks' – because, his work banned in Ireland, O'Connor had been forced to the United States to earn his bread.

Even Seán O'Faoláin, with whom he had started out from Cork forty years before, two brilliant young men, intellectually self-made, sworn to awaken their country to its rich cultural history and the splendours of the world outside – even O'Faoláin was estranged by the end. And why? Because O'Connor argued, battled, as he said at the 1965 reinterment of Yeats at Drumcliff, 'for an Ireland where people would disagree without recrimination and excommunication … stop turning everything we love, from our language to our religion, into a test of orthodoxy', which is precisely what he and the others did, while wanting, in their different ways, exactly what he proposed. It was impossible for any of them to be 'pure' in the eyes of the others. There is something almost saga-like in such pigheaded bloody-mindedness.

Even the famous epitaph at Drumcliff, 'Cast a cold eye / On life, on death. / Horseman, pass by' was cause for dissent. O'Connor, and others, felt that it misrepresented the ebullient enthusiast they had known. They would have preferred a quotation from his late play *The Herne's Egg*: 'That I / all foliage gone / may shoot into my joy.'

Republican O'Connor stirred the pot further, with 'Instructions for *my* Gravestone':

Then take me to the Ulster Border,
And beg me a stone from the Orange Order.
A pillar of stone both tall and slender.
Frank O'Connor & 'No surrender!'

Ireland is also heroic, or at least grand-scale, in its new prosperity. On the coast of Donegal, in rocky fields that grew barely enough to sustain a donkey, there has sprung up a white crop of bungalows, jostling, craning for a sight of the sea (what rich cause for feuding there!). Older houses were set a little way from the sea, sideways on, usually placed within some sheltering rocks, and with a wind-tortured tree. These face the sea boldly, in parallel lines, and perhaps their new owners have not read O'Connor's translation from the old Irish:

Winter is a dreary season
Heavy waters in confusion
    Beat the wide world's strand …

That's outside, while inside:

Crude and dank and black and smoky;
Dogs about their bones are snarling,
On the fire the cauldron bubbles
    All the long dark day.

The inhabitants of Bunbeg seem not to mind this sudden change to their small town. (If you think of Ireland as a square, looking down at the map you see Bunbeg in the topmost left-hand corner.) They have a new church, a concrete wigwam, which has an original way of dealing with the 'heavy waters' that doubtless batter it. Down the angles, from the top to the ground, are broad conduits like children's slides. Inside, you discover these are made of some transparent material, and they light the church. It must be fun to be in there in a storm. Mass is in Irish, unselfconsciously, which, if you think about Irish history, is an act of successful heroism in itself.

We stayed with friends, then threw ourselves on the hospitality of Donegal, as it turned out, on the day that Donegal shut. (There is something heroically final, for the traveller, to find hanging on the door of a looked-forward-to hotel a notice saying, 'Closed till next year', especially when it has been hung that day.) In Dunfanaghy even the pubs were shut, except for one, the only customer a hunched man in a cap. However, you never know in Ireland, possibly a last rag of the Heroic still hangs round the shoulders of a Traveller. I put my predicament to the woman behind the bar: somewhere to stay, work, space to spread books. She looked thoughtful, as I hoped she would, made a telephone call and – to cut the story short – in an hour we had a house to ourselves in Dunfanaghy High Street into which, unasked, the landlady came when we were out exploring, and a turf fire was blazing by the time we damply returned.

Later, in the house of a Dublin friend, I picked up the biography of Frank O'Connor, *Voices*. He, with less luck, had also visited Dunfanaghy. In a way it is a heroic tale, of Irish chastity, which only a dolt could laugh at. In 1928 in Cork, O'Connor fell in love; he was twenty-five. The girl was intelligent and devout; he proposed marriage, she loved him too, but his inability to get near her physically drove him wild. After five years he managed to make her agree to come alone with him to Dunfanaghy, so that they could talk Irish in the Gaeltacht. She not only insisted on separate rooms, but on separate hotels. He found that these were miles apart (I think I know which they were): 'For three mornings he walked from his hotel to Nancy's, cursing the whole way; each evening he walked all the way back. Their meals were especially tense …' It is here the biography reader hesitates; surely there must have been more to her hesitations, perhaps more than he has a right to know. The next year, after six years of courtship, she wrote to tell him she had married somebody else, and O'Connor broke down.

The reader of a biography is in some way an emotional voyeur, too detached from the subject's pain; but biography has anecdotal pleasures. For instance, the story of Yeats, collaborating with O'Connor on an Irish translation, scolding him: 'You must always write poetry as if you were shouting to a man across the street you are afraid can't hear you, and trying to make him understand.' O'Connor's translations, from the seventh century to the nineteenth (*Kings, Lords and Commons*), became translucent.

The woods of Ireland were cut down after 1691 because they sheltered the remnants of the Irish army ('Kilcash'):

> What shall we do for timber?
>    The last of the woods is down.
> Kilcash and the house of its glory
>    And the bell of the house are gone.
> The spot where the lady waited
>    Who shamed all women for grace
> When Earls came sailing to greet her
>    And Mass was said in the place...

Of course the book was banned; there is mild obscenity in 'The Midnight Court' by Brian Merriman. There is even something maddeningly heroic in that doomed attempt to keep things 'pure'.

*December 1997*


# 'Father Ted'


It is a truism that Nature imitates Art. Returned from my first day of rehearsing a television farce in London, the small iron gate of the house where I would be staying seemed unwilling to open. I gave a small heave, to clear the latch of it, and the whole gate came off its moorings. The dog inside the house began to bark, my hostess for the next few days opened the front door a crack to see what was going on, and beheld her guest, feeling and looking foolish, holding her garden gate in his hands. It was soon restored, eventually even opening the right way, though that took a certain amount of anxious thought, and I went upstairs to wash and recover from my strange day. I switched on the landing light, an angled spotlight; there was a flash, a small explosion, the bulb sped from its socket and hit me on the head. None of this is an exaggeration, which would be pointless. The two things happened in the space of ten minutes, and were precisely the sort of misadventure we had been rehearsing all day.

The farce, or comedy programme, was an episode of *Father Ted*, in which various comic events befall an Irish priest on his mythical Craggy Island. I had been summoned three months before to read for a part in it, I don't know why. I used to be an actor, but had done nothing like it for twenty years – at least. Neither do I know why I obeyed the summons, except for a natural fondness for the receiving of cheques; and perhaps because the words 'variety is the spice of life' came into my head, which in fact I do not believe, having achieved a fondness for routine, even for monotony. At all events, I went up to London and read, for some pleasant, laughing people, mostly Irish, and was given the part of a priest who for fifty years had sheltered a German in a room filled with Nazi memorabilia; returned home and did my best to forget all about it until the time came.

Occasionally I remembered, and wondered, 'Can I do this?' All my life I have suffered from a mild form of dysphasia, if that is the term: the replacing of one word by another, especially names. A very long time ago indeed, in repertory, I was apt to call the Inspector in an Agatha Christie play by the name of the murderer (as yet unrevealed), thereby causing an interested susurrus in the audience. But then I was young, it was fun, and I sometimes suspected that it was an unconscious desire to liven things up; an Agatha Christie play can do with that. However, this semi-geriatric return was likely to be less friendly.

In short, arriving for rehearsal on the first morning (of the day the third Act of which was to reveal a man under Battersea street lights with a garden gate in his hands), I was nervous.

The rehearsal room was in an art-deco building oddly decorated with busts of Victorian worthies – Herschel, bearded Charles Dickens, chipped, noseless Matthew Arnold. Beneath their gaze, coloured tapes on the floor denoting different sets, actors sitting around chatting, doing the crossword, making themselves hot drinks from an urn of water that perpetually steamed. They were friendly, of course, that is part of an actor's life (derided: but it is easy to prefer 'luvvies' to 'haties'); all this was familiar. Then in through the door walked Vernon Dobtcheff, acted with many times in the distant past. He demanded to know what part I was playing, and I said I was the priest sheltering a German. 'Well, I'm the Jerry!' and we happily did our surreal – or perhaps sous-real – double act for the rest of the week; watched, contemptuously, by Thomas Carlyle.

No word was allowed to be changed; all had been thought out, planned. In one scene Father Ted, anxious to show he is not a racist, welcomes some approaching Chinese through his window. This had been inadequately cleaned (his housekeeper had fallen off the roof). A piece of dirt remained on the glass and coincided precisely with his upper lip, so that when he raised his arm in greeting, the Chinese saw Hitler giving his salute. This, when done on film, occupies a few seconds of screen-time, but to make dirt-blob and upper lip coincide on film would take much longer than that. (There was also a bicycling hamster, which caused delays.)

We must have gone through that half-hour piece thirty times. It is hard to think of any profession, apart from the Army, that bonds people so closely together when they are working. In the evening, to go out into the Bloomsbury dusk was like leaving a womb. It was also to emerge from a pleasant, classless, rogues-and-vagabonds cama-raderie. (Vernon Dobtcheff told the story of one actor meeting another actor who is carrying what looks like a box of expensive cigars. 'Ah, working?' 'No. Moving.')

We then went to the London Television Studios on the South Bank, to see the sets, to go through it again, and again. Between Waterloo Bridge and Blackfriars an astonishing series of develop-ments has gone up, all apparently built yesterday. The last time I looked, I think it was all old warehouses, which reminded me of what a country cousin I had become.

On the last day, after a supper of cold salmon and meringue tart, bowls of fruit, good cheese, for everyone on the set – on my script I counted the names of sixty-four technicians – they are no penny-pinchers, Hat Trick Productions, who were behind it all – we recorded in front of a live audience. During the inevitable delays, retakes and so on, a slick warm-up comedian of the kind I loathe kept the audience amused. Waiting in the semi-dark for my cue, I wondered for the first time just what I was doing there. He seemed to me charmless – and *Father Ted* survives on its charm. Then, hugs and kisses and well done darlings, a party, and a studio car to take each of us home. Next day, this cousin was back in the country, and some of the others on to yet another episode.

Here, the local farmer seems to have gone organic. Instead of nitrates, he now spreads manure, and long piles of it have for weeks lain on the skyline. In fact, from the bedroom window for a long time my horizon had been composed of dung, gently steaming, like the rehearsal-room urn. The stubble was a light fawn colour, today the clanking muckspreaders are shading it dark, almost chocolate. It seems a long way from *Father Ted*, which will be shown in early March, by which time the field will be greening. It, and my participation, will pass in a blur, will make me wonder what all the fuss was for, but I appreciated the care taken of us actors, and loved the almost infinite pains taken not to short-change, and to amuse, the people who will watch.

*February 1998*

# A Statue in Beaconsfield

The Trout at Godstow, near Oxford, now boasts a 'Morse Bar', because the famous television Inspector, connoisseur of Real Ale, was so often filmed drinking there. Across the bridge are the remains of Godstow Nunnery, picked clean since the Dissolution; all that now stands is the enclosure and the chapel of the Abbess. On the wall of that chapel is a plaque which hints at sexual goings-on between the nuns and 'the clerks' of Oxford, and this annoyed me. In the 300-odd years of its occupation, there were bound to be some untoward occasions, but surely it could be granted the dignity of having been, in intention, a religious foundation? After all, 'A serious house on serious earth it is'. Even the word 'nunnery' was bothersome; it is an old word, but the Oxford *SED* says that by 1593 it meant 'a place of ill repute'; so the post-Reformation propagandists, on that recent plaque, still have their say.

In the background there was the noise of traffic tearing along the nearby dual carriageway – metaphors become buried in language, but it was exactly the sound of material being ripped, and it tore at the nerves. We have certainly shattered the silence that must have surrounded the nuns in that beautiful place.

However, it was that plaque on the ruin that stuck in my craw. A guess is that about 70 per cent of any popular mention of God, Christianity, or religion, in the media of this country, is either negative or derisive. (It has been suggested that such grim secularism, far from being liberal, could become an obstacle to our acceptance of the Islamic population.)

What is certain is that whenever, in a TV detective story, we are taken inside a church, candles underlighting spooky statues, there is sure to be a corpse in the clerestory.

Those of us who think that all this points in the wrong direction – if it points anywhere at all – tend to keep our heads down. Nevertheless, occasionally we should speak up, it only to balance the scales.

Before Godstow, we had made a little pilgrimage to Beaconsfield, to try to find the statue of the Virgin Mary that G. K. Chesterton had given to his local church. He describes how he discovered it, in a London shop which sold such things. 'Here there was everything, from what some would call the conventional dolls of the Repository to what some would call the harsher caricatures of the Primitive. But somehow I felt fastidious, for the first time in my life.' What he saw left him, 'Not cold but vague.' He follows the proprietor upstairs to a lumber-room and at once sees what he is looking for, just unpacked, from Ireland.

> The colours were traditional; but the colours were not conventional; a wave of green sea had passed through the blue and a shadow of brown earth through the crimson as in the work of the ancient colourists. The conception was common and more than common, yet never merely uncommon. She was a peasant and she was a queen ... I have heard of one other man who felt as I do, and went miles out of his way to revisit the little church where the image stands.

We too had gone miles out of our way, and found it, in the Church of St Teresa, which is also called, possibly at Chesterton's insistence, the Church of SS John Fisher and Thomas More; he had wanted it dedicated to Our Lady and the English Martyrs, and his memorial fund paid for a chapel to those martyrs 'representing a cell in the Tower of London'. Chesterton, at least, was a determined counter-propagandist.

We visited his grave, a distance from the church, surmounted by an Eric Gill Crucifixion, dangerously weathered. His wife, Frances, is also in the grave, as well as – charming touch – his devoted secretary, Dorothy Collins, who brought some order into his famously absent-minded life.

Thence to Godstow, on our way to Oxford, because we had been invited to dine in College (pleasant, unaccustomed honour). After dinner I sat next to a philosopher friend to whom, years before, I had recommended Chesterton's *Short History of England*, so that he might see there existed an alternative view of English history, particularly of the Reformation. He had found nothing in it. 'I had hoped to learn something. It was just words, words!' Ah well, we decided, he is not Chestertonian; many aren't.

Before dinner, the Chaplain had remarked that 14 February was not just 'St Valentine's Day', it was the Feast of SS Cyril and Methodius, 'Apostles to the Slavs' (he was also Russian Tutor). After dinner I remarked to him that St Valentine's Day causes huge excitement round here, especially in the local pubs, because it swells their business, depleted because the new road bypasses them. 'Valentine's,' he said sombrely, 'they call it Valentine's.' To an Oxford-dweller, he lamented, 'They call it Frideswide's now, not St Frideswide's.' I remembered that chilling plaque at Godstow. To cheer us up, I quoted: 'Never mind, "the gates of Hell shall not prevail against it".' 'That I devoutly believe,' he said.

Before describing his discovery of the peaceful statue (which he does in a rare 1932 pamphlet, *Christendom in Dublin*), Chesterton had quoted a Donegal story of an apparition of the Virgin Mary, carrying her baby, and of what she was supposed to have said, which he loved the lilt of, and called 'natural literature'. Some may detect a touch of 'Kiltartan' Irish in it, but it worked for him and it works for me. He ends the pamphlet by quoting it again, as he regards that statue in the little church in Beaconsfield. No one could accuse Chesterton of keeping his head down.

> She looks across the church with an intense earnestness in which there is something of endless youth; and I have sometimes started, as if I had actually heard the words spoken across that emptiness: *I am the Mother of God, and this is Himself and He is the boy you will all be wanting at the last.*

*March 1998*

# W.H. Hudson and Buenos Aires

Travelling in England, W.H. Hudson – 'How does that fellow get his effects?' demanded Joseph Conrad; 'he writes as the grass grows' – met what used to be called 'a commercial', who described himself humbly as 'a traveller in little things'. Delighted, Hudson decided that he was such a traveller himself, and called the book he was writing by that title. Of course, to him what he described and 'travelled in' – insects, clouds, birds, ideas, thistledown, people met as he moved about watching these things, who are described with the same dispassionate objectivity he applied to the natural world – to Hudson these phenomena were not 'little' at all, but carried the observer and his reader into a world infinitely wide. Hudson was a fabulist, autobiographer, austere philosopher: *sui generis.*

Any visitor to Buenos Aires (this is being written in the lobby of a small Buenos Aires hotel, where you might indeed come across just such a 'commercial' whose job-description so pleased Hudson; he was born a few miles from here), any ignorant observer of an unknown city must humbly become a 'traveller in little things', a purveyor of first impressions.

It is a city that surprises by not surprising at all. You have to remind yourself that you are on the other side of the world, under the Southern Cross, Orion upside-down; the moon likewise, a cheerful golliwog, not a mournful face. You think, 'this is Barcelona, this is Milan', but it is without the competitive edginess of those cities. Yet Buenos Aires is not 'soft'; it seems gentle, in a way of its own, despite Argentina's political history. You glimpse miserable shanty towns below overpasses – there has been immigration from neighbouring countries. You hear loudspeaker demonstrations in the wide public squares, about pensions, about the Disappeared of the recent Dirty War. These are carefully named, some of them on a small monument, a fan with ribs of Argentina's hardest wood, *quebracho*, 'axe-breaker', the fan open towards the Palace of Justice. How important to us is the fact of naming, yet such a 'little thing'.

These indications of unrest take place in the tree-filled plazas: the many-trunked *ombú*; pot-bellied *paloborracho*, the 'drunkard tree' with its large pink flowers; *gomeros* of such a spread that, true to Dr Johnson's insistence on accuracy (he carried a measuring-stick to the Hebrides, a bludgeon against the exaggeration of travellers), it seemed worth pacing out, one branch to the other, and it came to thirty long strides, it was maybe 100 feet across. Among the pigeons under these trees are the red-tailed *horneros*, oven-birds, which build oven-like nests of mud with a curved entrance-slit at the side, like the opening of a huge seashell; exotics among the pigeons. An English resident of six months' standing confessed her surprise at discovering that what she most loved about Buenos Aires – a vast sprawl of a city – was its trees and its birds.

The first morning here, among the tree-interrupted roofscapes at the back of the hotel, there was a foreign-sounding three-syllabled bird-cry. It came from a bright yellow and black number, moustached, shaped and beaked like a large kingfisher; a kiskadee, known locally as a 'bienteveo', a more human onomatopoeic rendering of the sound it makes.

The traffic honks and fumes along narrow grid-pattern streets of high concrete blocks with balconies and window boxes that drip on the pedestrians beneath. Strings of yellow-roofed taxis cruise slowly like hopeful fish (should you enter one, you may be driven murderously). The windows of the many bars and cafés are filled with inviting sandwiches and *empanadas*, which are like little Cornish pasties that can be filled with anything and are the most delicious snacks in the world. The food everywhere is served with a democratic courtesy, even friendliness. Each grid-crossing is marked and named so that you cannot lose yourself, the buses are uncrowded and frequent; altogether the sense is of a clean, well-lighted place, even if the holes in the pavement are patched with wooden pallets.

A first impression of the Argentines themselves, mostly poets and painters and the like, is that they neither observe nor listen; are happy to discuss at large, say, the nature of Heraclitean fire, while, unnoticed, their trouser turn-ups smoulder. To a visitor from the Old World, this is both annoying and impressive; these are certainly not 'travellers in little things'. (However, oddly, they envy our sense of detail.) On the other hand, while, as with us, the fine arts move more and more towards the sensational, or the conceptual, among certain artists here the techniques of painting also have been retained and refined, so that the town contains original and contemporary pictures, with a New World twist, that it would be good to be able to afford.

W.H. Hudson (here G.E. Hudson: Guillermo Enrique), who intrigued Conrad by creating word-pictures without strain or flourish, was perhaps able to do so by taking his time, a leisureliness learned from his unschooled, untrammelled Argentine childhood. We were able to visit his birthplace, with the help of the British Embassy (for which gratitude, here recorded). It is about twenty-five miles from Buenos Aires; a small three-roomed cabin, Irish in its simplicity, in which there were in the end eight Hudsons (his parents were immigrants from North America). Their lives must have been spent almost wholly in the open air, in the middle of the flat pampa, with its huge sky, the world a green margin at the bottom of the picture, still filled with the shrieks, cries, tunes of amazing birds, as well as of other creatures. The young Hudson almost became a wild creature himself. He only left the Argentine when he was thirty-three, and never returned. Strange to think of him ending up in a dark house in Westbourne Grove, in time to befriend Edward Thomas.

Here he is, in his seventies, in the London of 1910, remembering the kiskadees of this childhood: 'In Buenos Aires the Bienteveo is found in every orchard and plantation; it is familiar with man and invariably greets his approach with loud notes – especially with a loud three-syllabled cry, in which people fancy there is a resemblance to the words *bien-te-veo* ("I see you well"); while its big head and beak, and strongly contrasted colours, especially the black and white head-stripes, seem to give it a wonderfully knowing look, as it turns its head from side to side to examine the intruder.' The fellow writes, not so much as the grass grows, but as though part-bird himself, observing, narrow-eyed, a neighbour species.

A visit to the country, the *campo*, proves Argentina to be filled with birds of such variety and glamour, unshy, and in such numbers, from flamingos and spoonbills to the extravagantly named Southern Crested Screamer, that they take away the breath. This piece, begun in Buenos Aires, is now being finished in Patagonia; but more of that, and of the birds, later perhaps.

*April 1998*

# Grass

The hoe scrapes earth as fine in grain as sand,
I like the swirl of it and the swing in the hand
Of the lithe hoe so clever in craft and grace,
And the friendliness, the clear freedom of the place

And the green hairs of the wheat on sandy brown.
The draw of eyes towards the coloured town,
The lark ascending slow to a roof of cloud
That cries for the voice of poetry to cry aloud.

That's Ivor Gurney, who is quoted because I have been using a scythe,
I 'like the swirl of it and the swing in the hand', and am encouraged
by Gurney to say so.

Strange, that we need such encouragement to speak out, some
confirmation from others. (This is, incidentally, what makes so much
of current academic literary criticism unreadable – 'As Foucault
reminds us …', 'If we apply the Lacanian formula …', which sounds
democratic, but do these critics have no unsupported preferences of
their own, 'free of useless fashions' (Gurney, again)? Gurney is bless-
edly unselfconscious in this way, and from him I gain permission to
be bucolic, without apology. I am further fortified by a letter from a
correspondent who lives in France and addresses me as 'Dear Young
Kavanagh', which suggests she must surely be of a certain age. Among
other matters she mentions that she too uses a scythe, or what sounds
like one: 'I have now got a new, miracle, blade for my "débrous-
sailleuse" with which I can surge through grass, hogweed, nettles and
blackthorn suckers, leaving a wake like the *Queen Mary* …' I can't quite
manage that – nor, alas, can the *Queen Mary*, which is probably rusting
somewhere – but I understand her satisfaction.

The advantage of a scythe is that it is silent. I have a little bit of
rough pasture to deal with, and a combination of warm May and wet
June wind have made parts of it a tangled mess. Now that the cow-
parsley is over and can be cut, the growth is beyond the scope of any
machine except the largest: so, the antediluvian scythe.

As all the world knows, a scythe has an attractively curved shaft
from which project two little handles at different angles. Sometimes
these slip and become awkward to hold. On one old scythe they
became hopelessly loose, and I went to the Garden Centre to ask

about a replacement. 'Try an agricultural museum,' said the man, turning away. However, West Midland Farmers had racks of these shafts (though I never saw a West Midland Farmer using one), and the site of that Garden Centre has been built over by Tesco.

Perhaps moving to the country years ago was a mistake. It seemed a cheap place to think, work and watch the seasons. What we couldn't have guessed was the pace of the psychological urbanisation going on behind our backs. Visitors from the town, friends, bright ones, seem increasingly unable to see what is in front of their eyes, their eye is 'out', as mine is if I go away for too long. It takes time to adjust, to slow up. (Maybe you can slow up too much, and they might say that was the mistake.)

An example of this ignorance, of *rus* as a foreign country: if you do not cut grass, it doesn't remain grass but becomes docks, nettles, thistles, briars, goosegrass; you would imagine every townee could know that, they only have to look at urban waste patches. But they don't know, not any longer. If you let grass sow itself naturally, and grow to seed, it is extraordinarily pretty and various. I counted five different types of grass-head just now, with tall buttercups among them, clover, and a small pink flower I don't know the name of. In late summer, the grass dries, yellows, and you cut it with a scythe and then with a mechanical mower (which is a noisy bore). If you don't do this, it returns to rankness; if you do, the thistles and so on disappear, and you have a meadow which, in our case, has paths cut through. And what do our visitors think? Just that we're too lazy to cut the grass …

Earlier this month, I was chatting outside with a guest and absently picked out some cow-parsley from the seeding grass. 'Don't you *like* cow-parsley?' she said. Elsewhere the place was awash with it, foaming with it, but in grass it takes over; has a carrot-like root, and at the base of the stem a ground-level fan of leaves which prevents the grass. Why should I blame her for not knowing something it took me seasons to learn? I cop it both ways; prefer such sentimental ignorance to the purist who, observing my late-season mow, shouted accusingly, 'But I thought *you never* cut the grass', as though I had ratted on my own eccentricity.

Perhaps this minor ignorance is because English country effects, on the whole, are themselves minor, and do not call attention to themselves. In March, there was a visit to an *estancia* a couple of hundred miles west of Buenos Aires. It was after rain, and in slight depressions in the otherwise flat pampa water had gathered, creating meres that reflected the vast sky and the curiously neat little puffs of white cloud. Feeding on these sheets of shallow water was such a vast variety of birds, in such abundance, that it made you gasp: what seemed every kind of wader, small to large, together with spoonbills, flamingoes, white egrets, glossy ibis. It was unforgettable, as was the little bird with a tail twice as long as itself, two curved feathers that crossed, like scissors, and the glow-worm that faded as the moon rose, as though it could not compete, or the gong-sound of the frogs at night, a Balinese gamelan.

English effects are not like that: shy subfusc hedge sparrows, warblers distinguishable from each other only by ornithologists, and then not always with certainty; little pink flowers in the grass the name of which you look up one year and have forgotten by the time they reappear. Gurney thought we concerned ourselves too much with even the mildly striking; too much written about the rose, for example, which as a consequence he called 'ink-proud' and referred us to the beauty of drowsy cabbages. His last line of the hoeing poem – 'That cries for the voice of poetry to cry aloud' – might seem far-fetched in such a context, but such moments can come when you use a silent implement to the sound of larks. And Gurney liked seeded grass, he noted that the floods of the River Severn 'ensured all June's / Dark fan-grasses of the pretty head'. We have no floods up here, but there are dark heads, fan-like, among the other grasses, in the patch now freed of cow-parsley, and pretty is the word.

*July 1998*

# A Night in Italy

It was in Le Crete (the Clays) not many days ago; Southern Tuscany, the less fashionable part – so much so that you can eat in restaurants surrounded by Italians, rather than by other foreigners in shorts. In superior Chianti the region was described as, at best, a place merely to drive through, and in winter the ploughed grey earth, whitey-grey, is stark, but also wonderfully sculptured. The empty hills undulate in graceful swoops and scoops; newly harvested, the dark gold of the stubble-stripes and the brilliant yellow of the lines of straw seem to lie on top of relaxed muscles, and can put you in mind of a vast recumbent tiger.

The hill-towns are good, too; anciently walled, quiet. This one was called Chiusure, and we were staying with friends near by. There had been births among the friends, and there was much grandmotherly cooing over the newly-arrived. I had already done my duty in this respect, and when a second adoration was mooted, late at night, I bade the glowing grandmothers a temporary farewell, stationed myself on a bench under one of the few street lights in the village, and settled down to read. I was wearing a hat, as a precaution against mosquitoes, and my trousers were tucked into my socks. The local ants are large, not quite as large as tigers but in their own way as ferocious.

I was conscious that I must have presented an odd sight. Italians are a sociable people, and I cannot remember seeing one read alone in public; certainly not in a nearly deserted village under a street lamp towards midnight.

The book was *The Path to Rome* by Hilaire Belloc, picked from the bookshelf of the friend's house. I had always shied away from Belloc; his heartiness, his brand of Catholicism, his bellicosity ('there is something so sundering about Hilary's quarrels,' sighed Chesterton) or, at least, the impression of these that I had picked up from him.

*The Path to Rome is* not really like that at all; it is freewheeling, digressive, vulnerable, filled with a carefree determination to write only about what interests him; if he comes to a place that bores him, he chooses to tell a story instead of describing it. Occasionally, a precise-minded 'LECTOR' interrupts and complains. 'AUCTOR' replies that at least the story has advanced his journey, and his account of it, thirty nondescript miles.

What is most surprising and endearing is his honesty, his confessions of fatigue, pain, self-doubt, loneliness. His desire for companionship is so overwhelming that it makes him lightheaded. The heat of Tuscany almost knocks him out, and he barely describes the place; he must have come through Le Crete after it was ploughed, 'as though the soil had been left imperfect and rough after some cataclysm'. He was not even competent, he had come at the wrong season and blames St Augustine for 'talking like an African of "the icy shores of Italy"'. However, he is tough, he reaches Rome, barely mentions it, and ends with some doggerel. What he does brilliantly suggest is the sheer youthful, virginal thrill of reaching his Holy City, the seedbed, in his view, of all that he loved and reverenced in his beloved Western civilisation.

As all the world doubtless knows (nevertheless, as the book, published in 1902, is now, alas, out of print, recapitulation might be useful), Belloc vowed to walk from the Moselle valley to Rome *in a direct line*, as far as that was possible, and he was strict about it. To do so he had to wade flooded rivers, sometimes on a guide's back; risk blizzards on Alpine passes (defeated there, his guide refused to go on, although Belloc offered him all the money he had; there is something manic in his determination). He was arrested and briefly imprisoned; seriously threatened with a knife at another place; but mostly it was trudge, trudge, up and down, his interior compass needle (he had no compass) set on Rome. He appears not to have even carried a change of clothes. The one detail he omits, very noticeable in view of those fearsome Tuscan ants and other, unseen, biting creatures that can raise a weal on you the size of half a golf ball, with a horrible, weeping centre, was the experience of any kind of insect. Yet he slept mainly rough, in 'sweet-smelling' hay surrounded by chomping oxen, under pine trees and in the weedy corners of fields. No bites? Perhaps he was immune.

It was a Christian pilgrimage, which is probably why he thought it best to go alone. Yet even his Catholicism is healthily tinged, even more than is usual, with the pagan. He vowed to go to Mass every morning (and failed), but his reasons are practical: such attendance clears the mind (true); ritual is good for us (also true); and people have been doing it 'for thousands upon thousands of years' – not going to Mass, surely: worshipping a deity, or the gods, certainly. All one to Belloc. He also vowed never to go on wheels, and at first, exhausted, he is careful only to hang on to the tailboard of a cart, keeping his feet on the ground. Soon, however, he is cheerfully jumping on board behind a dozing driver, and when he runs dangerously short of money, he blows his last francs on a train to Milan.

I can't pretend I had read that far under the Chiusure street light, from which a cobbled street ran down to a little bar where the elders of the village sat outside on straw-bottomed kitchen chairs, with children playing around them. After a while, I became aware of small faces peering at me from the warm shadows: 'Come si chiama?' came the shy whispers. 'Patrick,' I said, shortly, but the sharp Anglicised syllables alarmed them and they retreated a little. Relenting, I tried 'Patrizio', and they ran back to the light of the bar, crying, 'Ciao, Patrizio! Ciao, Patrizio!' Eventually the grandmothers returned from their celebration of the infant, and we moved towards the car and home. From shadowy doorways came the shy chanting, 'Ciao, Patrizio!' and I felt somehow Bellocian.

LECTOR: Why are we being told all this?

AUCTOR: Because it is what I best remember from eight days in

Italy: that, and the cream butterflies, with chocolate stripes, that furled their wings behind them, funnel-shaped, and presented the open end to the breeze, so that they blew about like exquisitely patterned leaves, and in no butterfly book can I find a picture of them.

*August 1998*

# Yeats and Holy Places

The first surprise in Ireland was Verdi's *La Traviata* in Longford. 'Will it be in some Georgian gem?' one visitor wondered, longingly. Not at all, it was in the local Gaelic football club, home of the 'Longford Slashers', and was moving and marvellous. The production was by an Irish company, Co-opera, and if I cannot keep the surprise out of my voice, it is because of the difficulty in imagining such a performance in an English football club.

We were on our way westwards, and stopped to look at Clonfert Cathedral in Galway: 'west of Banagher – the devil of a place to get to,' said Frank O'Connor, 'but well worth it when you do get there. It is one of those "cathedrals" established, not because they were suitable sites for a diocesan see, but because the spot had been sanctified by the cell of some hermit saint. It could be conveniently lost in any respectable English parish church.' So it could. Now, it belongs to the Church of Ireland, and its inside is not inspiring, seeming to be laid out for some Parish meeting or bunfight, but its twelfth-century doorway is a wonder. Recessed inside five successive layers of carving, crowned by a huge triangle containing sculpted heads of saints, the entrance itself is so small and modest it is like the nest-opening of an architecturally besotted oven-bird.

As O'Connor suggests, the church seems oddly sited for a cathedral. There is no formal approach to it, it is angled awkwardly in relation to the present quiet road. There are the ruins of a little building at the gate, maybe a gate-lodge, but all behind that is hidden under scrub, containing at least one abandoned car. Puzzled, wandering along the road, a new wall enclosed the scrub, with a gap left carefully in it. In the shadows on the other side of the wall there were some odd details of colour hanging from a branch of a not very old sycamore; these turned out to be sets of rosary beads, their different colours glaired with exudations from the scrub. It wasn't a special tree, but was this a special place 'sanctified by the cell of some hermit saint'? Or was it a secret protest at the Church of Ireland? My teasing companion suggested that they were votive offerings for the success of Galway in the forthcoming All Ireland Gaelic Football Final – every telegraph pole was wrapped in a Galway flag, and sometimes on garden walls there were teddybears dressed in the beautiful Galway colours of burgundy and white. It was a good thought, but the beads had been there too long; pinned to the tree was a little notice, under plastic, the words on it faded past reading. There was no one about, to ask, and the cottage opposite was a ruin. Nor would I have asked; Ireland is a talkative place but it keeps its secrets. I was happy just to stay surprised. (Galway won.)

By evening we were at Kinvara, on an inlet of Galway Bay, with its little houses round the harbour, painted in colours like varieties of ice-cream, and Dunguaire Castle, with its toes in the quiet-water, among oyster-catchers and curlews. The story is that Edward Martyn gave the castle to Oliver St John Gogarty for a bottle of champagne, but Gogarty never got around to reroofing it.

Our destination was the nearby Burren, in County Clare: those many square miles of limestone plateau, its parallel fissures a botanist's dream, sheltering growths from the Arctic to the Alpine, its grey hills stepped like ziggurats; its apparent barrenness littered with ruined monasteries, churches, stone tombs, fortresses of every time, and with holy wells: its grass, where there is any, famed for its lushness.

There, we turned up a little lane to the twelfth-century Cistercian Abbey of Corcomroe, dedicated to 'Holy Mary of the Fertile Rock', in a beautiful patch of green, its stones whitening, like bones. Irish Abbeys, after the Dissolution, were not cannibalised or turned into great houses; they remain presences, implacable, petrified memory of what an explosion the Dissolution was. We heard of older ruins nearby, ninth century, at Ought Mama, just above Corcomroe, within sight of it, at the very edge of the fertile, almost on the bare rock itself, 'one of the most perfect sites to be found anywhere in the country, its setting rivals Glendalough, architectually it rivals Clonmacnoise itself'. We climbed across fields, could see white ruins, in the shadow of the grey shale mountain, but were foiled by ancient walls of round stones, impassably fortified by hazel scrub. It was October, the skies were darkening. We would come back. We were now, as Heaney might say, 'a hurry'. The site was indeed dramatic, looking down on milky Corcomroe in its patch of green, as though, 300 years later, even the twelfth-century Cistercians had gone a little soft.

'"Corcomroe", Yeats set a play there!' they cried in Dublin. *The Dreaming of the Bones*, (1919), about Irish history and the need for one last act of forgiveness, to bring about a healing.

There they all are, the names in it:

This pathway
Runs to the ruined Abbey of Corcomroe;
The Abbey passed, we are soon among the stone
And shall be at the ridge before the cocks
Of Augnish or Bailevelehan
Or grey Aughtmana, shake their wings and cry.

It was Bailevelehan we had come from, and grey Aughtmana (Ought Mama) was where we had failed. We had unconsciously been on a literary pilgrimage. Of course, Yeats knew the Burren (we were surprised to have forgotten): he used to pass it with Lady Gregory on their way to Durrus where they first dreamed up the idea of the Abbey Theatre, in order to put on a play by Edward Martyn. That was in 1897.

A character in Yeats's (timeless) play is on the run from the 1916 Rising and hopes to be rescued by curragh from Finvara Point, near Bailevelehan. This is not far from 'The Flaggy Shore', the name of which rang a powerful bell in my head. Heaney mentions it in his poem 'Postscript', the last in his latest book, *The Spirit Level*, but surely he is referring back, to some earlier text; Ireland has more layers than most. Heaney is good on the subject of surprise (also, albeit cautiously, on the need for forgiveness):

And some time make the time to drive out west
Into County Clare along the flaggy shore …

where you will see the surface of a slate-grey lake, lit 'By the earthed lightning of a flock of swans'. That's the Burren all right, and Heaney's subject is the healing nature of surprise:

Useless to think you'll park and capture it
More thoroughly. You are neither here nor there,
A hurry through which known and strange things pass
As big soft buffetings come at the car sideways
And catch the heart off guard and blow it open.

*September 1998*

# Thomas Merton and Starlings

An advantage of midwinter is the lateness of dawn, which can be watched in the prone position from an eastward-facing bedroom. 'Smudgy dawn scarfed with military colours' can be murmured – one of Ivor Gurney's arresting first lines which make it difficult for the rest of the poem to keep up. There are days, of course, when darkness merely lightens, without conviction, but there was a coloured one recently, salmon and cucumber in slanting stripes; not so much a scarf as a Garrick Club tie. This put me in mind of Laurie Lee. Whenever he did wear a tie he favoured that one. I found this surprising in him, but refused to think it was touching; he was too individuated a personality to be patronised. Besides, with him, it was likely to be a complex tease.

Later in the day that had begun so neatly pink and green there was a flock of starlings in the cloudless sky, many hundreds of birds packed tightly together, moving as one bird, as they do. At a certain point the whole flock had an edge to it that was briefly round as a coin, which obviously involved a multitude of birds immaculately keeping station, to the inch; a wonder, that made a straggle of competing rooks look like a ragged army. Perhaps such sights mean more, are a greater solace, as one grows older and is tempted further towards what Thomas Merton, the American Trappist, called 'the forest'.

In a conference given to some contemplative nuns in the Far East, shortly before he died, Merton praised the Hindu system of dividing life into four phases: the celibate student, the householder, the forest hermit, the homeless wanderer. 'When the continuity of the family has been guaranteed through the birth of grandsons, the householder may leave his home for the forest, intensifying his spiritual practices until in very old age, in anticipation of the end of his earthly existence, he may become a homeless wanderer, completely detached from earthly ties' (Alexander Lipski, in *Thomas Merton and Asia*).

That last bit sounds risky, and would probably seem so to most Hindus, but it would have appeal for Merton, who was an all-or-nothing man. After a vigorously heterosexual Greenwich Village kind of life in New York, publishing poetry, drafting novels, he converted to Roman Catholicism and almost at once became a novice Trappist in Kentucky. There he remained for the rest of his life until his Abbot at last gave him permission to visit the Far East in order to study

Oriental religions. Merton, a clumsy man of headlong enthusiasms and great energy, was naturally accident-prone. His literary agent told him fondly that she couldn't help noticing, 'it's your visitors who get locked out of the church, and your server who forgets things, and your vestments that get caught in the folding chair'. In Bangkok he was electrocuted while plugging in, or unplugging, a fan in his hotel room. His understanding biographer, Monica Furlong, comments on 'the black humour' of this death, which she, and most of his friends, find strangely suitable: going out, as it were, with a bang.

He was certainly a headache to his Abbot. Although religiously keeping to his vow of obedience, he couldn't help but argue. (Like Laurie Lee, like most poets, he was a tease.) The odd thing was that most of his arguing concerned his desire to leave the community of the Cistercian Trappists, which, with its silence, its confinement and its meagre food, sounds harsh enough, for the isolated life of the Carthusians who, the reference books say, live largely alone: 'Abstinence is perpetual and sleep is broken for nearly three hours by the Night Office; the hairshirt is always worn.' Merton certainly was a whole-hogger. Yet, listening admiringly to him in his journal, *The Sign of Jonas*, fearful of his intensities (leavened with humour), the reader, wondering sometimes if Merton in his search for God is becoming overheated, is also uncomfortably reminded of certain remarks in the New Testament about 'the lukewarm'.

*The Sign of Jonas* (Jonah) is the promise of the Resurrection, and Merton confesses in the introduction to the book, 'I find myself travelling towards my destiny in the belly of a paradox.' A priest, vowed to live in a community, who wants to be a hermit. But first, the saving humour: after eight years in the monastery Merton is at last ordained priest, in 1949, a longed-for occasion. 'Overwhelmed by the vestments which I cannot describe as I am insufficiently familiar with the language of dressmakers … I wormed my way into these horrible decorations and proceeded to the altar palpitating with misery … I tried to begin Mass with my eyes shut, ignoring the gilt bookstand covered with little bits of red and green glass, and the chocolate frame of the altar cards … It suddenly occurred to me that I was really saying Mass in a bazaar in Cairo.' It would be difficult not to love such a man; unless you were his Abbot.

At long last, after twenty years, he was granted part of his desire: he was allowed to build himself a hermitage of breeze-blocks in the wooded grounds of the monastery; he has moved to 'the forest'. At first allowed there for only a day at a time, in the end he is permitted to live in it, though still Novice Master, still unwillingly involved in

Order politics, still in receipt of a worldwide correspondence. But he watches the deer, and the starlings – he was always good on them, and the way they moved together with one mind, but he is a solitary bird – and eloquent on the sound of rain (as, incidentally, was Gurney). Merton sits alone, 'cherished by this wonderful, unintelligible, perfectly innocent speech, the most comforting speech in the world, the talk that rain makes by itself over the ridges'.

At the end of his 1968 conference to the nuns, mentioned earlier, he suggests that the Catholic Church had made insufficient provisions for semi-monastic life for householders. His experience had taught him that 'some married people in their later years were ready for a monastic existence' (*Thomas Merton and Asia*).

A good idea. This might present some refuge from the uncertain joys of family Christmas, which now seems to extend further and further into the New Year. A curmudgeonly thought, no doubt, but Merton would agree that it would allow more time for the mature contemplation of bryony berries, from emerald to orange to pillar-box red, climbing up hedges like some glorious discarded necklace; and to watch the patterns that 'murmurations of starlings … over wolds unwittingly weave' – W.H. Auden, too, had watched starlings; and enjoyed teasing the alliterative ghost of another poet-priest – Fr Gerard Manley Hopkins.

*January 1999*

# Buddha in Kilmainham

Last summer, in Dublin, a pleasant little ceremony took place. The Irish President, Mary McAleese, visited the Buddhist Centre at Kilmainham, on the twenty-first anniversary of its foundation. She was greeted by a 'meditation practice' called 'The Shower of Blessings', sung in Tibetan. In other words, she was given the works. After taking off her shoes, she made the following graceful remarks:

> This is the first time that I, as Head of State, have addressed an audience barefoot. I am so pleased I am doing that in a holy

place, and for reasons that are important, important to you and important to me … My coming here to the Buddhist Centre today establishes a personal connection with Buddhism that parallels my own faith as a member of the Roman Catholic denomination …

She goes on to say that she has used Buddhist meditation and contemplative practices and that she owes much to the great Buddhist masters. Whether that is true seems hardly to matter. What is clear is that Mrs McAleese writes a good speech or has a well-chosen speech-writer. And what is immediately striking is the rooted, unpatronising confidence, of a member of one faith proclaiming that faith while addressing members of another. A confidence which could not, or would not, be shown by our own Head of State. For all sorts of historical reasons, for all sorts of embarrassment about 'racism' and the miserable muddle we are in about that, there would have to be some fudge about 'multiculture' and 'multi-faith' which would make all hearts sink.

Lest it seem that I am merely criticising England (Scotland and Wales are another matter, and Northern Ireland yet another), because of my name and (doubtless sentimental) attachment to Ireland, I ought to explain something about my own 'racial' background.

I was born and brought up in England. I have experienced mild forms of discrimination, both positive and negative. As for the positive, if that is the word, I found from early on that I was expected to be 'wild', 'amusing' and a good rugby player (which I was not, but tried to be). Negatively, I have been accused of support of IRA murders and, because of my 'race', considered clearly insufficiently intelligent to tie up my own shoelaces.

My maternal grandfather was an immigrant, from County Roscommon; my paternal great-grandfather was an emigrant, from County Carlow – a voluntary emigrant to Van Diemen's Land. About him I remain puzzled. Why a young man, in 1842, before the Famine, should want to take his wife and baby halfway across the world, to a penal colony, I cannot discover. It seems he was reasonable affluent; certainly his wife's family were, and well-connected in a native-Irish way. His wife's uncle was a priest who became Cardinal Cullen, a name which even today strikes in Irish breasts an ambiguous awe. 'That was one tough fella!' gasped the novelist Benedict Kiely when I mentioned the connection; it was as though he'd been punched in the solar plexus. I have always intended to find out more about Cullen but, with what I suppose might be called Irish indolence, I have not yet got round to it. As for the great-grandfather, when I asked in Carlow why he should have wanted to leave, the answer invariably was, 'Why not?' The unspoken assumption being that for a very long time Ireland was not a comfortable place for a reasonably ambitious young Irishman to be.

One personal anecdote, which presumably is to do with 'race'. Years ago, at Rome airport, I was approached by a stranger and asked, in careful English, whether I was Irish. Startled, hardly knowing how to reply, unwilling to disappoint, I countered by asking him why he asked. He said that he was a Soviet Jew, at last granted a visa to go to Canada, this was his first day out of his country, and I corresponded exactly to his mental picture of what an Irishman looked like. I was born in Worthing.

To return to President McAleese and the Buddhists. Kilmainham, where she was speaking, shoeless, contains a famous gaol, behind the doors of which the leaders of the 1916 Easter Rising were shot, and a terrible beauty was born. It is also the place where St Maignenn (thus '-mainham', 'Kil-' meaning church) founded his monastery 1,400 years ago; and it was the site of a holy well, destroyed in the 1900s. A Buddhist Lama recently did some water-divining, found the spring and, with his companions, restored the well. They also caused a cast to be made of the original monastery bell, which is in the National Museum, and keep the cast in their Centre.

Mrs McAleese mentions all this and calls it bridge-building. Naturally enough, in this company, she refers to the epoch when Irish monks travelled the world teaching and founding monasteries, building bridges 'to unknown worlds'. 'Nowadays,' she points out, 'there can be a tendency to promote sameness and at the same time, ironically, to exclude those who are different. It is important that we each maintain our identity and yet at the same time be prepared to open our minds to others.'

This comes well at a time when, in this island, we are asked to lash ourselves into frenzies of penitence for what has come to be called, in a dangerously blurred and blurring phrase, 'institutionalised racism'. Surely tribalism ('maintenance of identity') is the most natural thing in the world, and only repressed after severe psychological distortion, and most racism is tribalism. Of course, we must recognise other tribes, and commerce between all of these must be as just as possible; in this way we might discover that, in her words, 'to exploit diversity and difference enriches each of our lives, if only we will let it'.

The Cohens and the Kellys: that Russian Jew at the airport and the startled Irish Englishman. Neither group is likely to miss a decent opportunity for group-promotion, and Mrs McAleese uses this Buddhist occasion to launch a new book about an Irish saint, *Molaise, Abbot of Leighlin and Hermit of Holy Island*, by Dr Colum Kelly. This flagrant opportunism is made delightful, even witty, by the fact that St Molaise and St Maignenn (of Kilmainham) were friends, and Holy Island, off the coast of Scotland, is owned by the Buddhists …

The speech, the water-divining, the bell, the book-launch – it all seems so friendly, serious and, in a good way, funny. A plaque was unveiled beside the holy well, in Irish, Tibetan and English. 'A sort of fanfare was played on a pair of Tibetan *gyalings* and the Kilmainham bell was sounded.'

*April 1999*

# Pilgrimage

We at last reached 'the Holy Land' – it has to be called so in this instance because we were not really come to visit the State of Israel but were on a pilgrimage to New Testament sites, as we were all gently reminded by the three Benedictines, whose parish group we had been allowed to join. Indeed, what contributed most to the saving of the trip from becoming a blur of early rising, of mounting and dismounting from the coach, from turning into a confusion of sites and churches, was the presence of these cheerful Benedictines. One of them would gather us together at an appointed time, read a passage from the New Testament relevant to the place we were visiting, talk about it, talk about us, and then, almost before you noticed, because he continued in the same conversational tone, he was into the liturgy, as though it was a natural part of life. Clearly, it was so for him, and so it became, during those two weeks, for us. When they were over, we missed it: the familiar ritual words, the force created by that brief, communal concentration.

This could take place anywhere: in the hotel lounge, on two occasions in the hotel bomb shelter – opposite us, on the other side of the Lake of Galilee, were the disputed Golan Heights – but most often, in Galilee, it was in beautiful church gardens, with chattering birds and bougainvillaea, red, orange, purple. Perhaps the best of these gardens was on the Mount of Beatitudes, traditional site of the Sermon on the Mount. There the Franciscans had scythed the grass and allowed it to grow, with just the right touch of informality, so that it now contained cockle flowers and scabious and wild scarlet anemones like poppies, only more red.

This place was so special that on our 'day off' (from being coached about and led and talked to by our Israeli state guide, Joe, an erstwhile Londoner), three of us hired a taxi and went back to the garden on our own and sat there. Of course, we were not on our own, coachloads arrived by the minute, but because of the way the little hillside is laid out, with stepped, enclosed gardens, where groups gathered almost out of earshot of each other, people seemed to be absorbed into it, disappeared, and it was strangely peaceful, the wafting sound of distant singing making it seem even more so.

From there we walked down to the lake through a cut hayfield (rare in that rocky place) to the traditional site of the miracle of the loaves and fishes, Tabgha. (All of the sites are traditional, it doesn't do to be too literal-minded; and most of the churches are surprisingly new, successors to a series of churches built on the same sites, destroyed by floods, earthquakes and bloody invasions.) At Tabgha, not long ago, they found a fine fourth-century mosaic floor with lovingly, comically observed lake-birds, alert, necks askew, sleeping, or poised for take-off.

If a god wished to come to earth he could do worse than choose Galilee, undramatically handsome, compact – the places of Christ's ministry mostly within walking distance of each other – enough to eat (fish in the lake) and the lake itself useful for longer journeys. It is a long step from Nazareth to Bethlehem, however, and a rough one – a hilly coming they had of it. Now Bethlehem is almost a suburb of Jerusalem and there, as at Nazareth, is evidence of the colossal building-programme the Israelis seem to have embarked on. Perhaps they have no choice, because of immigration, but it looks as though their Promised Land will soon be one long series of high-rises, on every hillcrest, dominating, with old Arab villages huddled in their shadow.

Jerusalem, on the other hand, at least as seen from the Mount of Olives, is saved by the Jewish and Muslim dead. The sides of the little Kidron Valley – the small scale of these fabled places is constantly surprising – are lined with flat-topped cream-coloured graves, some very ancient. No flowers, no grass; from a distance the valley sides look as though they are covered by arid shale; no building allowed.

The Israeli poet Yehuda Amichai says: 'Jerusalem, the only city in the world / where the right to vote is granted even to the dead.' The dead-vote, here, allows Suleiman's ochre wall, neatly castellate like a child's toy fort, to rise suddenly out of the creamy, flat gravestones with a lovely clarity and emphasis; behind it the glowing gold dome of the Shrine of the Rock. Jerusalem (Amichai lives there),

> An operation that was left open.
> The surgeons went to take a nap
> in faraway skies, but her dead gradually
> formed a circle all round her
> like quiet petals.

The rock, under that dome, is the one upon which Abraham was about to sacrifice Isaac, and also the rock from which Muhammad began an ascent to heaven. That rock alone, the stories attached to it, make you tread warily in Jerusalem. (A bearded American outside the Jaffa Gate, twanging an odd-looking instrument, singing 'Majesty! Majesty!', and wearing a gold crown; black-hatted Hasidim with ringlets, striding past, their mouths moving in prayer.)

The ancient Armenian church, with Armenian massacres splashed in red on a map outside it, is suddenly filled with black-browed young men who take their places among the smoke-darkened icons and bellow lustily, antiphonally, and file out, pulling off their black robes as they go, throwing them over their shoulders.

Abu Ghosh – that was not in Jerusalem, but a Crusader church on the road to Emmaus – monks facing nuns, who wear white hooded mantles, singing Psalms in French, male voices and female voices alternating and resonating among the smudged frescos on the pillars. The church set in a garden like that of an Italian palazzo – eucalyptus, palms and, on a shaded path, a perfectly placed earthenware bowl of violas. Outside the wall, an Arab village with broken pavements, and a new muezzin tower that looks right down into the garden.

One treads carefully. We could see the olives of Gethsemane from our bedroom window. While we were there in the Garden, a minor doctrinal dispute broke out, Jewish, Christian; there, where Christ wept, looking across the valley to Jerusalem, because nobody had understood the message, 'Blessed are the peacemakers …' A friend remarked, 'Religion is impossible without humour; otherwise it just becomes eye-rolling fanaticism.' Our Benedictines were humorous; so, for that matter, was our Jewish guide.

Of the Beatitudes, Gandhi said, 'they contain a message that would save the world. What a pity that Christians have been listening to that message for two thousand years, but they [the Christians] are like stones lying in the water for centuries, never soaking up a single drop.' Well, yes, but maybe more brightly coloured for lying in the water. Take them out of it and the brightness fades.

*June 1999*

# An American Poet

The literary Festival at Cheltenham coincided this year with a spell of strangely perfect late-October weather: azure, sun-filled, windless, so the leaves were intact on the trees, autumn-coloured. This made the sixteen-mile round trip into the town, whatever the luminaries on display, seem like a sacrilege.

So we walked in the hills, Peter Kane Dufault and I, or he sat in the sun learning his poems, which he had come from the States to read or, rather, recite, at the Festival. He is hardly known in this country (though Ted Hughes was an admirer), but these recitations, in his relaxed Yankee baritone, are worth travelling to hear. Not for him the book clutched defensively between him and the audience, like a breastplate. He leans, elbow on the lectern, apparently plucking the words from the air, as though making the poem up, but the rhymes and rhythms, unobtrusive, the observations and philosophical musings, make it clear he is not doing that, these poems have been exhaustively worked over; he and his work are both slack and taut at the same time, like a tightrope. That is precisely what the audience feels it is watching and listening to, a tightrope walk from phrase to phrase, cadence to cadence, and there is a sense of danger, a fear that he may stumble and break the spell.

Although (or is it because?) he is the genuine article, he is not all that well known in the States either, but there are belated signs of notice being taken: regular appearances in *The New Yorker*, a hefty chunk of his work now in the *Norton Anthology*. He is not easy to quote in a piece as brief as this, because he often writes at length, teasing out his thought until it rounds itself off, or leaves it hanging at just the point where it should be left. School of Robert Frost, you could say, but he is his own man. Here, for flavour's sake, is a short example, 'The Way of Her'.

It was like clear water
or like clean air:
No particular taste to it,
no odor, no color, nowhere
anything put up in front or in back of it,
so you saw clean through
and never knew it was there.

Until it was taken away
and you knew at once you'd begun
dying for lack of it.

He is a man of distinctive appearance, with a neat, upward-jutting and white beard. When travelling with him in Virginia we stopped at one of those gleaming chrome palaces of the sundae, and the Southern belle behind the counter gasped, 'Yo-all are the most distinguished men ah evah did see!' We both preened a little, but it was soon clear that by 'men' she meant 'man', and that was Peter. I can't remember what he was wearing on his head that day, but he has an exotic taste in headgear, from a red bandanna to a green Glengarry (donned when he plays the bagpipes). For our walks he favoured a dun-coloured creation that would have caused a gleam of interest in a mycologist's eye. So dented and twisted and (artfully) convoluted of brim, it looked like the top-piece of a rare and jaunty fungus. He clearly loved that hat.

The pleasure of our walks was enhanced by Dufault's unfeigned delight in the Gloucestershire countryside, which was indeed laying itself on for him. He called it a series of gardens, rather than a landscape and one of the lanes he declared to be exactly the lane he had dreamed of walking along, in a grey flannel suit, after the war was over, when he was a young Air Force pilot in Southern Italy. Why grey flannel? 'Because it was better than goddam khaki!' We lunched at a pub and the steak pie was the best he had ever tasted and the cider was out of this world. Then we discovered he had lost his hat.

Picked up by our wives in the car we drove very slowly back along the way we had walked, each of us given a quarter to examine, right left, fore, aft. Peter decided that this was the best way to drive, concentrating, peering for unusual shapes. Perhaps, he suggested, there should be a profession, a leaver-of-hats-on walks, to create not so much a *bout de promenade* as a *bout d'exploration*. We found the hat, where he had taken it off to put the cord of his wife's binoculars round his neck. What hat, I suddenly wondered, had he dreamed of wearing, with that grey flannel suit?

*November 1999*

# Thinking About Time

An invitation to a Millennium party had 'Time present and time past are both perhaps present in time future' written across it, which T.S. Eliot possibly borrowed from St Augustine's *Confessions*. He was a deft finder. Several commentators have pointed out how the opening words of his 'Journey of the Magi' are lifted without change from a seventeenth-century sermon by Lancelot Andrewes – 'a cold coming they had of it ... just the worst time of the year ... the ways deep, the weather sharp... the very dead of winter'.

Augustine is more direct than Eliot (he has to be, he is talking to God), but is honest about the difficulty: 'What, then, is time? I know well enough what it is, provided nobody asks me; but if I am asked what it is and try to explain, I am baffled.' He wrestles with the problem for the whole of Book One, and sometimes it is possible to catch his argument, as you might think you have caught a butterfly between your cupped hands, but when you open them there is nothing there. Time 'can only be coming from the future, passing through the present, and going into the past. In other words, it is coming out of what does not yet exist, passing through what has no duration, and moving into what no longer exists.' Augustine bursts out (to the Lord), 'I am in a sorry state, for I do not even know what I do not know!' He tries the idea of duration in music, and Eliot does the same – 'Words move, music moves / Only in time ...'

Two Christians, trying to grasp (in two cupped hands) such elusive concepts as 'eternity', 'immortality', 'in the beginning'. Nevertheless, time exists, as Augustine has to admit; we measure it, divide it into minutes, hours, days – millennia. One sublunary way of dealing with it, or at least an attempt to alleviate the gloomy sense of it dribbling away, undifferentiated, is to keep a journal. In this respect, the reissue of William Allingham's *Diary 1847-1889* – the period which saw the publication of Darwin's *The Origin of Species*, that huge revision of our sense of time – is of particular interest; it shows that the great figures Allingham rubbed shoulders with – Tennyson, Carlyle, Emerson, Browning – cared little for the significance of Darwin's theories, but cared very much about Time, the immortality of the soul, and most of the things that are contained in the idea of God. They talked about them easily. The elderly Tennyson, in 1884: 'I have always felt that there must be Someone who knows – that is, God. But I am in hopes that I shall find something human in Him too.' Earlier, there is a memorable little scene as he and Allingham walk together on the Isle of Wight: 'T. "You're not orthodox, and I can't call myself orthodox. Two things however I have always been convinced of – God – and that death will not end my existence." W.A. "So I believe." T. (stopping and turning round) – "Do you hold these?" W.A. – "I do."' That stopping and turning are vivid.

Years before, in 1868, Darwin himself is expected to lunch. He doesn't show up. Perhaps he often failed in this way, because Allingham comments; 'Has himself been called "the Missing Link".' In his absence, Tennyson and Allingham walk again, talking of Christianity '"What I want," he said, "is an assurance of immortality." For my part, [adds Allingham] I believe in God; can say no more.'

Carlyle to Allingham, 1878: 'One thing Browning told me the other day was a saying of Huxley's, "In the beginning was hydrogen." Any man who spoke thus in my presence I would request to be silent. No more of that stuff, sir, to me!' Allingham loved Carlyle but suspected the Orator in his prose. 'When the Reader has recovered breath he may sometimes suspect that a claim has been made upon his attention and nervous system disproportionate to the real importance of the matter.'

In his long essay on Boswell's *Life of Johnson*, Carlyle certainly repeats himself, but comes up with a sublimely simple Johnsonism, and on the eternal preoccupation. A clergyman, 'with placid surprise, asks "Have we not evidence enough of the soul's immortality?" Johnson answers, "I wish for more."'

Emerson is liked by Allingham, but considered 'a maker of sentences', however lofty. Writing on 'Love', Emerson describes 'the actual world – the painful kingdom of time and place. There dwells care and canker and fear. With thought, with the ideal, is immortal hilarity, the rose of joy.' That surprising word – 'hilarity'; you know at once that it is right. Saints have it, you suspect Augustine of it; it is there, surely a stratum, beneath the brusque gloom of Tennyson, the public-bounce of Browning (not so sure about Carlyle).

'Hilarity' must contain a sense of the comic, of proportion and disproportion, and the good Doctor, Jonathan Miller, first made his name as a comedian. Now a sage, he has just delivered himself on a topic appropriate for the first week of the year 2000: 'Although I am not a Christian, the idea of a God that incarnated itself into its own creation, in order to suffer the experience of being its own creation, is a fantastically productive metaphor.' Fair enough, respectfully to remain on the levels of metaphor. Augustine himself says that he wants to write, 'so that a reader would find re-echoed in my words whatever truths he was able to apprehend. I would rather write in this way than impose a single true meaning so explicitly that it would exclude all others …'

*The Tablet*, this last week of 1999, prints graphs that show church attendance to be falling. Also fair enough; perhaps those who attend now do so because they want to, not for show – 'Our worship be inward only, with our hearts and not our hats, as some fondly imagine' (Lancelot Andrewes).

Allingham, recorder of the literary great, sometimes takes a small flight of his own. 'T. is unhappy from his uncertainty regarding the condition and destiny of man … to step outside the human limitation is not granted even to him … We must turn our eyes and thoughts to the noble aspect of things, and never let the scalpel of Science over-bear pen, pencil and plectrum.'

It suddenly occurs to me that I have always indicated my desire for a restaurant bill by miming a pen or pencil scribble. The March of Time ('the painful kingdom', the effects of 'the scalpel of Science') suggests that now it should be a computer-tapping motion – to mime the use of a plectrum would only confuse.

*January 2000*

# Quoting Augustine

In an odd way, if you have quoted an author in public (as I quoted St Augustine), you feel slightly alarmed, slightly guilty. Have you misrepresented your source, or misunderstood it? At least, so it is with me, and I am forced back to reread in and around whatever I filched for my own purposes, in order to reassure myself, or blush.

Chapter Eleven of his *Confessions* deals with the elusive nature of Time – it seemed appropriate to quote that in a piece destined to be published in the first days of the new millennium. Impelled, however, to go back and look again, to check whether I had made a hash of Augustine's careful cogitations, was to be reminded that in the previous chapter, Ten, he examines the equally tricky subject of Memory, which leads him to consider Happiness: is that in our memory? If so, in what way, why, and memory of what?

It is hardly a digression, at this point, to remember sitting years ago in a dark Dublin pub, with a group of ungloomy Irish friends who were meditating how long each of us had experienced happiness, in total, in our whole lives. The opening bid was half an hour; I think the record low was two or three minutes. The pub was dark because it was mid-afternoon and what used to be called 'the Holy Hour' when the bar was briefly shut and its lights switched off. This may have cast a shadow on the conversation – we were waiting for the lights to be switched on again, and the place be back in business – but I don't think it was that. I said nothing, because I could remember days, weeks, years … Indeed, I was happy now, with these intelligent friends, one of whom I had known and loved most of my adult life and whose consistent cheerfulness I particularly admired. Perhaps we were not using the word in the same sense, or their demands for happiness were exorbitant? Or maybe they were talking about joy? Even in that case, I thought to myself, I could up their durations considerably, but decided not to say so from fear of depressing them. And why, anyway, do we expect to be happy, whatever our definition?

It was after that, I think, I wrote a novel called *A Happy Man*, in which nearly everything awful befalls the central character who retains his capacity for observation and enjoyment (that is, happiness). I remember that in some quarters it was greeted with puzzlement.

We all know people who will never be quite 'happy' whatever happens, or so it seems; we mustn't judge, but they can indeed be irritating. Others can exude, and transmit, a happiness they appear to have little occasion for – some of the very poor, in India, for example. Whereas in London you can sometimes pass a startling number of unhappy faces, particularly among young women. That is only an impression – perhaps I particularly notice young women; maybe they are not as disappointed as they look. Other people are a mystery to us, as we are to ourselves (as St Augustine himself might say).

Perhaps best to drop the 'St', it puts a barrier between us and a man who is bent on opening himself up for us, though 'Augustine' sounds a little abrupt and overfamiliar. There is a famous story, again a Dublin one, of a Protestant teacher of theology who grew uncomfortable because one of his pupils spoke of 'Paul'. He mildly burst out, 'Will you please say St Paul or, if you think that appellation savours of superstition, you may say Mr Paul.'

Augustine picks away at the nature of memory. Some comes through the senses, but what about numbers, grammars, imageless, non-sensory things? Augustine's excellent biographer, Peter Brown, calls Chapter Ten 'amazing', which it is, it sounds so modern. He says it caused irritation, even disgust, among Augustine's Catholic contemporaries. Up to Chapter Nine it is an account of a journey towards a conversion; they thought it should have ended there; Augustine reborn. But, Brown says, 'he regarded a man's past as very much alive in his present', and for a further three chapters he continues to argue with himself.

He turns to the mystery of the desire for happiness. 'Where did men learn what it was, if they have learnt to love it, where did they see it? … Is it to be found in the memory in the same way as Carthage, which I have seen, is present in my memory? This cannot be the case, because happiness cannot be seen by the eye, since it is not a material object.' That last careful clause shows how determined Augustine was to make himself as clear as possible. Does he make himself clear?

Probably not, in the end, or insufficiently to convince all, because not everyone can follow him in his last jump, when he can go no further, and leaps from intellectual argument into faith. 'All desire to rejoice in the truth. I have known many men who wished to deceive, but none who wished to be deceived. Where did they learn the meaning of happiness unless it was where they learned the meaning of truth?' For Augustine the truth was synonymous with God with whom, by now, he is almost chatting But there is no QED, no slamming of the door in our faces, argument proved; the examination of memory is close and brilliant until it reaches the point where it can go no further, there is only unknowable Truth. Or that is how I understand him. The last sections of the chapter are confessions of his continuing weaknesses, of lust in dreams, greediness for food, religious distraction. They can seem overscrupulous, but that, presumably, is why he is a saint.

His self-observation is modern, but one would like to think that his Creator might forgive a moment of distraction caused by his own Creation. However, one must be cautious, and not 'chatter away as somebody in the know', as Augustine confesses that he did himself when he first read the Neoplatonists, and became puffed up with his new knowledge: 'Had I continued to be such an expert, I should have gone to my destruction.'

*February 2000*

# Neruda the Parakeet

The sun was going down into the sea when a dramatic bird glided over the waves below us; large, black-backed, with ragged wing-tips. 'What's that?' I exclaimed, imagining some kind of osprey. 'A duck,' said my companion, barely glancing, and after the bird had gone. He continued his wrestle with some abstract matter that concerned him. Perhaps the desire to name and identify the external is indeed a petty matter, and our avoidance of larger topics at home (this was Uruguay) is too glib an evasion. Or possibly the New World is too newly settled for nature to be regarded as anything other than a threat, or a bore.

In fact, there were not many birds along the endless white sands of Uruguay, near Punta del Este. Mainly gulls, of an English appearance. If, however, you penetrated through the dunes at the back of the empty beaches, you came across immaculate rich houses, with well-watered lawns, shorn smooth, and glossy black birds, being no sort of snobs, gratefully buried their curved beaks – they looked like ibis – into their barbered surfaces. Among them fluttered green parakeets, smaller than parrots, larger than budgerigars. These seemed to be nesting, or at any rate were flying about with dry, strawlike leaves in their beaks. These they entwined into a column, creating a vertical pillar of nests like a high-rise building, each bird in its nest-flat, peering out, one above the other. Odd, because now was the Uruguyan autumn, but questions about this unseasonal behaviour caused such blankness of response it seemed better to talk about Shakespeare (who could, I was not above reminding myself, tell a hawk from a handsaw). This communal nesting, such upwards-building, reminded me of something, but I couldn't for the moment remember what.

Uruguay is an extraordinarily pleasant place to look at, and (now) to visit, popular with its neighbours. Those discreet dune-hidden holiday houses belong, for the most part, to wealthy Argentines who come in the season (January) in elegant gangs. Even at that time most of the wonderful beaches must be empty, because Latin Americans tend to huddle together. The interior of the country is green and gently hilly, reminiscent of parts of Tasmania and parts of Ireland; the eucalyptus trees are probably Australian, and the green pastures are interrupted by smooth outcrops of rock, as in the West of Ireland.

For no particular reason I suddenly remembered what those nesting parakeets reminded me of: Pablo Neruda, and his house in Santiago, on the other side of South America. He seems, like those birds, to have been a compulsive builder, upwards. Admittedly, his house in Isla Negra is only two-storied, an old sea captain's house perched almost among the restless ice-blue waves of the Pacific, but his houses in Valparaiso and Santiago are really a series of flats, of nests, burrowed one above the other. In Santiago, each floor is connected by an external companionway, up and up, and all his houses contain public house-style bars, behind which only Neruda was allowed to preside. These are hung with enamelled notices, filched from elsewhere, 'Défense d'Uriner' and so on. In Valparaiso, there is a metal plaque advertising William Lawson's whisky, a favourite of mine, unobtainable in England. We had just bought a bottle of that, spotted in a locked cabinet in a little Isla Negra shop. It was astonishingly cheap. Later, in Buenos Aires, we discovered that Lawson's, rightly, was the most expensive blend of all. Was that lone bottle in Isla Negra the last of an order uncollected by Neruda, there since his death in 1973, still at the old price?

Santiago is set in a neat cup of mountains, brown and orange, their colours blurred because of the smog. Our friends told us that Neruda said that he had to get out of Chile every six months, in order to breathe. I wondered if it was the traffic fumes he wanted to escape, but no, they said, it was Chile itself that suffocated him. Perhaps it is a narrow country, in more than the obvious sense. The seaside towns at first suggest the picturesqueness of Italy, but then you see they are an uneasy compromise between the half-hearted New and the dilapidated Old. Elsewhere, the rich appear to have sequestered themselves in new fenced-off ghettos, with guards on the gates, dry scrub outside and, inside, glossy lawns, the grass bullied into weedless subservience, the sprinklers constantly turning. Pinochet must have felt at home in Wentworth. Ortega y Gasset, the Spanish philosopher, decided 'Chile didn't exist'. This may have been bad temper on his part. I could imagine myself settling happily, grahamgreeneishly, into one of those sagging seaside *residencias*, comfortably deploring the new and unrentable mustard-colour high-rises, relishing the older smaller buildings which to me are reminiscent of the Hollywood Wild West; raising my glass – possibly of William Lawson's whisky, if found at the Neruda price – as the Brown Pelicans flap slowly past, line astern. If relations between the classes seem strained in Chile, such a boozy expatriate might help to build a bridge between them, as Neruda tried to build a bridge (or companionway).

Back in Buenos Aires, bound for home, there was just time to notice the inexplicable you come across when you touch the surface of any unknown city; at the Recoleta, for example. This is the old white-painted colonial church which acts as a focus for that part of Buenos Aires, with its tended gardens outside, and its vast trees. On our very first evening in the town, barely unfolded from the cramps and deprivations of the twelve-hour flight, we had been approached by a well-dressed young man and asked coolly, specifically, for five dollars.

'Why?' I asked. 'Because I need it. I am a student.' Helplessly aware that on this night I had pockets full of the things, out of cowardice (I would have thought less well of myself if I had walked on), I reluctantly gave him his three quid plus. On our last night, we were there again and wandered into the church, its wide doors open. Inside it was unusually dark, the only illumination two candles on the distant silver altar. It took time to realise it was entirely filled, by young people sitting entirely still and in perfect silence. 'Noche de los Jovenes,' said the Orario. It was unforgettable.

Beggars remain a problem we all have to sort out in our minds; they will increase. Shawled women with babies, rumoured to be 'Romanians', 'Albanians'; blind men standing on street corners selling, of all things, magnifying-glasses. I asked a painter friend how he dealt with the beggars in his mind, as he strode purposefully past their outstretched, beseeching hands. 'Mafia!' he snorted; he has to use some category or he would have been broke, or downhearted, before he reached his studio every morning.

Chile, Uruguay, Argentina; this is 'European' South America. Do they feel cut off? Of course not, but dislike European neglect. A Chilean was reading the autobiography of A. Alvarez, he had known him at Princeton in the 1960s. 'We went on a fascinating expedition together in Mexico. He doesn't mention it! *Too Eurocentric.*'

*May 2000*

# Remembering Peter Levi

The chestnuts had not cast their flambeaux, indeed they were just creamily spiking up through leaves so fresh they were almost lettuce-green. Past these, with cow-parsley brushing the mudguards, we made our way to Oxford in mid-May to take part in a Memorial Service for Peter Levi. The town was filled with buses, and the crowded pedestrianised streets smelled of chip-fat, but I was probably in a gloom because it is not cheerful to go to a Memorial Service for a friend who was almost the same age as myself. Also, I never felt that Oxford sufficiently appreciated Peter. He was a Fellow of St Catherine's but not, I think, ever more than that. In the 1980s, he was Professor of Poetry, but that is an appointment made by election, not by the University itself.

Perhaps no institution can avoid a certain sourness, and Peter was such a colourful, carefree, even careless figure, and of such striking appearance, that he was bound to become a target man for the begrudgers; possibly he delighted in this. As a result, his books, especially his biographies of Edward Lear, Milton, Tennyson, Shakespeare and others, were often reviewed in terms of the mistakes they contained, which never seemed heinous, and there was no mention, or little, of their zest and the communicated enthusiasm. He wallowed in words and ideas like a dolphin, joyously splashing. David Pryce-Jones in his Address said that he once showed Peter a list of mistakes that someone had found in one of his, Pryce-Jones's, books, and Peter waved these aside: 'Mistakes are the plums in the pudding.' Levi also said that a scholar is someone who claims to know more about some tiny thing than the only other man to make the same claim. Not a wise thing to let fall in Oxford.

Not that I ever heard him complain about this neglect I resented on his behalf, or about anything else. Even his eventual near-blindness, caused by diabetes, was an occasion for interest: not merely a loss of sight but a different view. He had his fans in surprising places. I once mentioned his name in passing to an American painter in Italy – 'You mean you know the translator of Pausanias!' – as though I had dined with Apollo himself.

Greek Pausanias wrote his guide to Greece in the middle of the second century AD and in some ways has a character similar to that of Peter; painstaking but also risk-taking, gullible, in the sense that he wants to believe in wonders, but also observant and shrewd. In the introduction to his Penguin Classics translation, Peter remarks: 'In writing the footnotes I was preoccupied with brevity', which is a laugh; the footnotes, in smaller print than the text, take up about a third of every page, and are so entertaining they are at least part of the reason why the American nearly fell out of his chair. For example, Pausanias quotes the Pythian priestess using the word 'acorn-fed'. Note: 'One of Vergil's peasants is *uvidus de glande*; he has been giving his pigs acorns steeped in water, as recommended in Ministry of Agriculture pamphlets during the Second World War ...' and so on, for twelve more lines about Classical acorn-eating. Levi scoffs at Sir James (*Golden Bough*) Frazer's account of the length of certain walks: 'Olympia is a hilly walk away but much closer ... Samikon is an afternoon walk. Frazer has a bulky appearance even in his youthful photographs, and confesses to a dislike of heat and steepness.'

Almost thirty years later, Peter Levi writes: 'All in all, if I had to start my life over again, I would still start again at Pausanias; he is a satisfactory study for second-rate minds like mine, and one that does not come to an end.'

'Second-rate' – the word itself has a chilly academic ring. No mind so furnished, so curious, so exuberant, could be second-rate; though parts of it, doubtless, like the minds of the rest of us, could be third-class or even steerage. He had a memory like a cheerfully disordered library, in which only he knew his way about and understood the connections between the shelves. He could be an Ancient Mariner, detaining his companion with unfollowable leaps and diversions, never boring, and leavened with laughter. That remark about Pausanias comes in a late book, *A Bottle in the Shade*, which is much as its title implies: a journey back to his beloved Greece late-ish in life, to see an old poet friend, visit a grove or two, and check again on Pausanias.

The journey began with a fall, on his boat's arrival at Patras. 'In the press of people I had to negotiate a downward-moving staircase, something I can hardly do on dry land, and I tripped up.' Nothing worse than a broken watch-strap. I once saw him fall; he had had polio in his youth, and was a big man. His foot caught in the invisible projecting claw of a movable partition and he went down like a tree. It seemed the whole place shook, and people came running. He was on his feet before they arrived, continuing his conversation, even, like a batsman hit by a fast bowler, disdaining to rub the places where it must have hurt.

I have said he did not complain but perhaps he did, by inference, complain of old age. This was irritating because neither in fact nor in appearance was he old, nor was he old in mind. I once told him to cut this out, we were the same age. 'Oh no, you're much younger than I am. I have Alzheimer's of the soul.' 'Peter!' I was shocked, at the phrase and its evident inappropriateness to the man whose company I was so enjoying. He was delighted. 'What's the matter? I thought it was rather funny.'

Like all of us, he had regrets in retrospect about his whole approach to life:

> To count intelligence by funniness,
> sparkle in the eye, spring in the footstep,
> look for the lurching of the coming friend,
> or think all prizes were God-given
> and fell by nature to one's dearest friends,
> was a mistake of course, easy to make.

That is from his last book of poems, *Reed Music*, and from an elegy for Angus MacIntyre, an Oxford colleague killed in a car accident. Levi's poetry tended towards elegy. He had been a Jesuit priest before his happy marriage, and he also, in the same book, tended towards affirmation. From 'For Easter (1995)', some syllabics:

> What was my morning is my afternoon
> and sixty years or more drench my head in
> the ashes of my own and Adam's sin
> but I am washed as white and clean as bone
> and shall arise out of my death and shine
> and be revived and go where he has gone
> whose resurrection takes another turn
> with life and time and all things they feed on.

If I had to recommend one book by Peter Levi to give a new reader his special flavour, it would be *The Frontiers of Paradise: A study of monks and monasteries* (1987). It is written in bite-sized chunks which control his discursive style (and extensive mental library), it is on a subject he knew and cared about, on which he had meditated long, and is infused with a quality particularly his, surely one of the most encouraging – amused love.

*June 2000*

# Saul Bellow's Bucket

Somewhere in his essays, that observant writer Alan Bennett ruefully admits that he always finds himself writing 'to one side' of his inner-most preoccupations. Every writer does, even if the melancholy Louis MacNeice claims, of poets

> … Crude though we are, we get to times and places
> And, saving your presence or absence, will continue
> Throwing our dreams and guts in people's faces.

This is of course precisely what the classically minded MacNeice wouldn't dream of doing; he would know that his audience, if present, would soon go absent, tired of wiping itself down.

Any bucket containing bits of guts an author feels impelled to fling must be of a certain shape, its contents ordered and depersonalised, and as a consequence some desired immediacy will be lost, or merely feigned – 'the truest poetry is the most feigning'.

The master bucket-designer of our time, who manages to cram in all that concerns him most – which also concerns us – must be Saul Bellow. He can talk easily and entertainingly of matters so serious that elsewhere they are hardly mentioned at all, because of the sheer diffi-culty, even embarrassment, of referring to them.

His latest novel (he is in his mid-eighties and newly recovered from a near-fatal illness) is *Ravelstein*, and in it he once again rehearses his essential preoccupations, which are the essence of all our lives. As in *The Tempest*, there is a sense of summing-up, but unlike Prospero he leaves his book open, still floating, not drowned.

Ravelstein is a maverick political philosopher/educator of genius, with huge intellect and ravenous appetites, homosexual, HIV-positive, and dying; his friend Chick, the narrator, also Jewish, is a quietly observant writer, a lovingly sceptical admirer of Ravelstein. Bellow, as usual, skilfully but almost without concealment, sets up a dialogue between parts of himself into which just about anything can be introduced, an infinitely capacious bucket.

The condition of being a Jew is always very important to Bellow, but never in a way that makes a non-Jew feel excluded. It is hinted more than once that to be a Jew now is to know that the whole twentieth century tacitly agreed to your elimination. That view can be argued against, but that the idea can exist is obviously true, and has to enter our consciousness; like the bomb on Hiroshima, it alters our view of ourselves.

It is a book about America, which is our world, our time: fountains playing in university plazas, while nearby are districts where even the cops warn you not to stop at a red light, 'the sanctuary and the slum'. Ravelstein is both of this contemporary world and beyond it. 'You must not be swallowed by the history of your own time.' He quotes Schiller on the subject, 'Live with your century but do not be its creature.' (I found myself putting little marks in the margin, for future use, me quoting Bellow quoting Ravelstein quoting Schiller.)

Bellow can even get round to mentioning the soul, and in the opening pages; or rather, Ravelstein/Bellow can.

> In his classroom, always packed, he coughed, stammered, smoked, bawled, laughed, brought his students to their feet ... He didn't ask, 'Where will you spend eternity?' as religious the-end-is-near picketers did but rather, 'With what, in this modern democracy, will you meet the demands of your soul?'

What a question, and what a container into which it can fit naturally in the course of a narrative description, without pretentiousness or strain. Another mark in the margin: 'Nothing in the sexual line is prohibited anymore, but the challenge is to hold your own against the general sexual anarchy.' That's Chick/Bellow, not Ravelstein, who later asks Chick what he thinks death will be like. 'The pictures will stop,' says Chick ('I, who lived to see the phenomena, who believe that the heart of things is shown on the surface of those things').

Chick and the dying Abe Ravelstein discuss the afterlife, in which Abe does not believe and about which Chick is tentative. This drove me to rummage again for something in George Moore's *Hail and Farewell*, something that Moore's Catholic brother had said: that he could believe without difficulty all that his Church taught; Transubstantiatation, the Immaculate Conception ... 'He found it difficult, however, to believe in the immortality of his own soul.' My position exactly; impossible to think of the extinction of others (childish and cowardly evasion, no doubt) but equally impossible to imagine the continuance of oneself. Against such illogic there is no defence, but it was cheering to find that Moore's brother thought as I did. And how many others? These are interesting matters and there seems an embargo on discussing them. Not, however, in *Ravelstein*.

Ravelstein dies, Chick writes an account of him (this book) and finds that his friend in an odd way is *present*. This is a novel, Bellow's invention Chick is talking, but clearly Bellow is not writing 'to one side' of his preoccupations.

> Many people want to be rid of the dead ... I, on the contrary, have a way of hanging on to them. My persistent hunch – it should be clear by now – is that they are not gone for good. Ravelstein himself would have dismissed such notions as childish. Well, perhaps they are. But I am not arguing a case, I am simply reporting. I know one loses mental respectability by acknowledging such fantasies ... Nevertheless he had strange ways of turning up ... This should not take the form of a discussion of life after death. I am not inclined to argue. It's only that I can't sit on information simply because it's not intellectually respectable information.

There are brave ones who can insist on a final extinction, but it never quite rings true, there is bravado in it. 'If Ravelstein the atheist-materialist had implicitly told me that he would see me sooner or later, he must have meant that he did not accept the grave to be the end.' An old man keeping his courage up, or fleshing out his fictional character? Perhaps. It sounds more like an insistence. 'Nobody can and nobody does accept this. We just *talk* tough.'

*July 2000*

# English Manley Hopkins

Reading Geoffrey Grigson's *The English Year* this late summer, to see what writers have said about this time of year, Gerard Manley Hopkins leaps up, by making you see what he saw: 'Elms at the end of twilight are very interesting: against the sky they make crisp scattered pinches of soot.' Any anthology put together by Grigson is an eye-opener; he knew quality when he saw it, and was a sharp observer; the utter blackness of the word 'soot', would have caught his eye, and the justness, tactile as well as visual, of 'crisp'.

The *Journals* of Hopkins are composed of such precise observations: 'Take a *few* primroses in a glass and the instress of – brilliancy, sort of starriness – I have not the right word – so simple a flower is remarkable.' His use of 'instress', 'inscape', 'haeccitas', when he has not 'the right word', can be distracting: 'brilliancy, sort of starriness' will do. He concludes with a practical reason for this effect: 'It is, I think, due to the strong swell given by the deeper yellow middle.' (The chastity of the italicised 'Take a *few*' is attractive; no need to despoil the ground of too many, and with too many you might miss the individual glow.)

'Strong *swell?*' Hopkins's idiosyncratic use of language can annoy some. Indeed, is there a fashionable swell of opinion against him? In on of those Reappraisals that appear in Sunday newspapers, somebody chose Hopkins as an example of the hopelessly overrated, which is preposterous. In an enthusiastic discussion of recent essays by Bernard Bergonzi, *War Poets and Other Subjects*, a reviewer finds the last section, on Catholic writers, 'less engaging – not for theological reasons but essentially because the two essays on Hopkins deal with a poet whose linguistic tics I've always found insurmountably irritating'. As a confession, this will do, but not as a public dismissal, to describe this poet's wordplays, neologisms, syntactical leapfroggings, the energy and inventiveness of his assault on the inexpressible as 'tics' is – well – preposterous. They were what he had to give to English poetry, and why he wrote it.

His prose – given some 'inscapes' and 'scapings' here and there – is clear to the point of pedantry, because he wants to retain and remember. For example, a special greenness sensed in a park among 'tufts and patches of grasses': 'marked this down on a slip of paper at the time, because the eye for colour, rather the zest in the mind, seems to weaken with years …'. It was not 'tics' but simplicity and accuracy that he admired. 'I went to hear the Lord Chief Justice summing up in the Tichborne Case. I was pleased to find how simple and everyday, not undignified though, his manner was.'

He could also track down the workings in his own mind with such detailed particularity that, as with Coleridge, we identify the workings of our own. When he daydreams during an address by his Rector, while still hearing the Rector, he sees

> one of the Apostles – he was talking about the Apostles – as if pressed against by a piece of wood almost half a yard long. I could not understand what the piece of wood did encumbering the Apostle. Now this piece of wood I had often seen in an outhouse and had that day been wondering what it was: in reality it is used to hold a heap of cinders against the wall which keep from the frost a piece of earthenware pipe … It is just the things which produce dead impressions, which the mind, whether because you cannot make them out or they were perceived across other more engrossing thoughts, has made nothing of and brought into no scaping, that force themselves up in this way afterwards.

(It seems we cannot escape 'scapings'. He had to express them, rather than merely name them, by using verse.)

There is in Hopkins's last poems the richest expression of dryness in literature – 'send my roots rain'. Earlier, he could suffer in prose, and use the same image. In August 1873, risen at 4 a.m., sailing from the Isle of Man to Liverpool, he and his companions walked through heavy rain to their seminary, 'We hurried too fast, it knocked me up.' They arrived to further discomfort:

> almost no gas, for the retorts were being mended; therefore candles in bottles, things not ready, darkness and despair. In fact being unwell I was quite downcast: nature in all her parcels and faculties gaped and fell apart, *fatiscebat*, like a clod cleaving and holding only by strings of root. But this must often be.

Bergonzi makes much of the conventional, rooted, Englishness of the Jesuit Hopkins. Despite public suspicion of his Society, Hopkins found no contradiction between his radical Tory Imperialism and his internationalist Jesuit priesthood. It was different when he was sent to Ireland. There he found himself among Irish Jesuits and other clergy who felt quite otherwise about England and Empire; there indeed he began to feel his roots wither, 'one archbishop backs robbery, the other rebellion'. He wrote to Cardinal Newman about this, and Newman, who had his own sad experience of Ireland and Irishness, during his struggle to found a University there, replies with a gentle rebuke, agreeing with Hopkins about the difficulties, but adding, 'If I were an Irishman, I should be (in heart) a rebel.'

So 'English' was Hopkins, so passionate about clarity of thought and expression, that he flies to the defence of Dryden in a letter to Robert Bridges quoted by Bergonzi. 'My style tends always towards Dryden.' *Dryden?* 'What is there in Dryden? His style and his rhythms lay the strongest stress of all our literature on the naked thew and sinew of the English language ...'

His last years, in Ireland, make sad reading. He is buried in Glasnevin, the Dublin Nationalist cemetery, his name one among those of 200 Irish Jesuits interred below the same slab, most of whom would have cared more for the Irish than the English language.

That poem about dry roots which begins, 'Thou art indeed just Lord', quoting Jeremiah, wonderfully ends:

> ... birds build – but not I build; no, but strain,
> Time's eunuch, and not breed one work that wakes.
> Mine, O thou lord of life, send my roots rain.

There are 'tics' in that, sure enough – or you could say 'naked thew and sinew' – and how, even in the 'inscape' of barrenness, the work wakes.

*August 2000*

# Topical Johnson

There is not much new to be said about Samuel Johnson, but there remains a debt to him, gratitude for his existence, and the need to express this. He is the columnist's columnist. The temptation is to let him write this one, to allow him to help, as sometimes, by using hefty chunks of quotation, he allowed others to help him. Twice a week, Wednesdays and Saturdays, upwards of 3,000 words for *The Rambler*, he could be excused some padding. That was 1750 to 1752, and between 1758 and 1760 he was at it again, weekly this time, in *The Idler*. This was meant to be lighter in tone than *The Rambler*, but he was soon moralising in it; it was a moralising time, as though after the tumults and accommodations of the seventeenth century, the middling classes of the mid-eighteenth had time to look about them, and comment on their own fashions and follies. Johnson's was the firmest (as well as the kindest) voice.

Being wise, he remains effortlessly contemporary. If we think of our serious present-day preoccupations, Johnson was usually there before us. He was, for example, sympathetic to women and detested their undereducation. Writing in the persona of a woman ('Tranquilla', No 119), he says what many of us think about the present gender conflict: 'Sir, As, notwithstanding all that wit, or malice, or pride, or prudence will be able to suggest, men and women must at last pass their lives together, I have never therefore thought those writers friends to human happiness, who endeavour to excite in either sex a general contempt or suspicion of the other.'

There is unwisdom in listening to daily bulletins on the radio. Speculation about an announcement to come, then the announcement, and in the evening analysis that had already been contained in the morning's speculation. 'The tale of the morning paper is told again in the evening and the narratives of the evening are bought again in the morning. These repetitions, indeed, waste time, but they do not shorten it' (*The Idler*, No 7). We are given more information than we can take in: 'The most eager peruser of news is tired before he has completed his labours; and many a man, who enters the coffee-house in his nightgown and slippers, is called away to his shop, or his dinner, before he has well considered the state of Europe.'

We are told today of harsher penalties for certain fashionable offences. 'The lawgiver [114] ... enforces those laws with severity that are most in danger of violation ... This method has long been tried, but tried with so little success ... yet few seem willing to despair of its efficacy.' Johnson's was a time in which capital offences proliferated, and he invites his reader, in a terrible image, 'to reflect on the days when the prisons of this city are emptied into the grave'. He favours leniency, and, lest his reader suspect him of being radical, like a true columnist he gives a flick to the tail of his piece by ascribing this opinion 'to its author, Sir Thomas More'.

So, gender politics, panicky legislation – what about animal rights? Walter Jackson Bate, in his definitive *Samuel Johnson*, has a story of Johnson on a trip to Wales with Mrs Thrale:

At Gwaynynog, they were visiting Colonel John Myddleton, whom Johnson liked ('the only man who in Wales has talked to me of literature'). While he and Johnson were talking, said Myddleton, the gardener caught a hare among the potato plants and brought it to Myddleton, who ordered it to be taken to the cook and prepared for dinner. As soon as he heard this, Johnson begged to hold the frightened hare in his arms for a moment, 'which was no sooner done, than approaching the window then half-open, he restored the hare to her liberty, shouting after her to accelerate her speed'.

An example of eighteenth-century 'sensibility'? Hard to imagine the sturdy Johnson being so fashionable. It seems more like an act of instinctive protectiveness, a sort of fellow-feeling. It was certainly decisive, probably discourteous. It makes us like Johnson, and wonder what his host thought. Jackson Bate found the story in the Colonel's *Diaries*, and it is such discoveries that give depth of texture to a good biography – 'The biographical part of literature is what I love most,' said Johnson.

'I have often thought that there has rarely passed a life of which a judicious and faithful narrative would not be useful.' Useful, obviously to the moralist, but what is it that makes Johnson the moralist so entirely convincing? Surely it is his oddnesses, illnesses, poverties, despairs – and his humour; we feel he has 'been there' and has returned, perhaps briefly, shaking his head like a great dog, to clear his thoughts for our benefit, and for his own. 'In the ability to arouse – and sustain – an immediate and permanent trust,' says Jackson Bate, 'no other moralist in history excels or even begins to rival him. To begin with, few moralists have lived as he did – so close to the edge of human experience in so many different ways … he, least of all writers, is not overlooking, disregarding, or falsifying anything at all.'

Johnson knew his own life was not exemplary, at least in his own opinion. Had he the right to moralise? In our own day, the vice most self-righteously detested – perhaps the last one to be scorned – is hypocrisy; anyone not living up to their aspirations is torn from place with delighted cries. Johnson knew the delusive nature of this truth-lust: 'It is the condition of our present state to see more than we can attain: the exactest vigilance and caution can never maintain a single day of unmingled innocence.' In *Rambler* 14, he meets the idea head on: 'Nothing is more unjust, however common, than to charge with hypocrisy him that expresses zeal for those virtues which he neglects to practise …' He seldom mentions his religion, because he does not think himself worthy. He does not even wish his readers to meet him, anyway not in his guise of moralist, 'friend to human happiness'. He mistrusts his person, knows 'the treachery of the human heart' (his own), but trusts his considered experience so long as it is written down:

> A transition from an author's book to his conversation, is too often like an entrance into a large city, after a distant prospect. Remotely, we see nothing but spires of temples and turrets of palaces, and imagine it the residence of splendour, grandeur and magnificence; but, when we have passed the gates, we find it perplexed with narrow passages, disgraced with despicable cottages, embarrassed with obstructions, and clouded with smoke.

*September 2000*

# The Hawk and the Shadow

A small natural event, a mildly disturbing one, witnessed the previous evening and still somewhere at the back of my mind, probably made it unwise for me to listen to the Minister of the Environment on the radio next morning. He was defending changes in the regulations concerning the erection of advertising billboards in the country. He said there were now places protected from such intrusions which no longer qualify as 'country' at all. But, I thought crossly, if advertisers want more billboards, why should the Government ease their way? What's in it for the Government? Besides, his chief defence during his interview was that there would in fact be no changes at all. In which case, why change the regulations? The whole business sounded like a con-trick, especially when he ended by passionately telling us we had no need to fear, that he, as much as anyone, wanted 'the countryside to remain as beautiful and tranquil as we know it is'.

Perhaps it was that small happening the previous evening, an event that doubtless takes place all the time, but was never before seen by me, that made me react to the Minister's passionate affirmation of the beauty and tranquillity of 'the countryside'. Towns can be beautiful too, or should be, and that farmland is not 'tranquil' is a commonplace. These words are being written in a room that is between two fields: the one to the east is being chain-harrowed with attendant tractor-roars and clankings; the one to the west is being sprayed by what looks like an aeroplane trying to take off, the tractor its fuselage, the vast spray-bars behind it, on either side, its wings. What is de-tranquillising about the country is not its agricultural busyness but sudden natural events.

For some days now a fledgling blackbird, full-grown but still the light-brown fledgling colour, has been nonchalantly hopping and pecking about the place. What is surprising about this bird is the way it does not startle. You can almost walk up to it before it moves, and then it only does a couple of hops and stays watching you, its head to one side. Mindful of the household cat, I made a quick movement towards it to see if it could fly and it did, perfectly well. However, it seemed to prefer to keep me company and I grew fond of it, because most birds are maddeningly quick to vanish if you want to look at them, they even cease to sing if you stop to listen. They hide themselves further and further on the wrong side of the tree. This one stayed, and I was grateful.

Last evening there was a rustle and a flap low down in a young tree, and, just above the stone wall a hawk flew. There was something extraordinary about its appearance, it seemed to have a large dark undercarriage, then it appeared to be not a monoplane but a biplane and – it was only a short sight I had of it – I realised the hawk was carrying in its talons a bird almost the size of itself, which also had its wings outstretched. Then both disappeared behind the slope.

Whether the hawk had seized that fearless and companionable fledgling, I cannot be certain. It seems likely. How is one meant to react to such a sight? A mouse in its talons, yes, or a vole, but a full-grown fellow bird? What does one celebrate, the hawk's triumph, doing what it had to do? Or prose on about 'nature red in tooth and claw' which has always seemed to me both true (enough) and absurdly anthropomorphic? My own reaction, I think, was mild lament, that such fledgling curiosity and trust, or at least lack of caution, should have so swift a nemesis. Yet not so swift either, it had seemed to be still alive, wings out, in that strange biplane construction. Perhaps that fledgling was born to be hawk prey, as some creatures are, as, in a different fashion, are some people.

For behind all this lay the irritation of the human analogy, the thought of the Hawk which hovers over All – the aneurism, the fatal diagnosis, the car crash – which is too glib, even if it is true. At bottom, I felt that fledgling had deserved better luck, which is to say I hoped that for myself.

Irritation with analogy because I remembered my disgust with a line of poetry I read when I was fourteen or fifteen – 'Sitting in this garden you cannot escape symbols ...' That annoyed my egalitarian self because it presumed (a) the possession of a garden, which in this case I did not have, (b) leisure to sit in it, which in this case I would not have been allowed, and (c) because of my thoroughgoing dislike of the idea that one thing can *represent* another thing; I believed (and believe) that everything is only and wholly itself; it may give rise to other thoughts and connections, but it remains itself, and that is the point of it. Possibly this is a Catholic way of thinking, a literal-mindedness – the Presence is Real, not symbolic ...

Yet the hawk is real and is also the Hawk, the shadow or the Shadow we try not to think about too much. However, without the knowledge of it, in perfect tranquillity, how would we ever grow? Indeed, looking out of the window into the garden and wondering whether that patch of grass needs cutting, I decide not, except where it is in shadow, and there it clearly grows most lush.

I even found the book in which that line appears, an Everyman, *Poems of Our Time, 1900–1940*. It is the first line of 'A Phoenix Answers' by Anne Ridler, a good poet who will easily survive a schoolboy's dismissiveness. It is a difficult work, and perhaps I never got past the first line which has stuck for so long in my head, but I notice that she gave me a let-out clause:

> Sitting in this garden you cannot escape symbols,
> Take them how you will ...

*October 2000*


# Wallace Beauties and a Bell


The refurbishment of the Wallace Collection in London seems a complete success, because it is the same as it always was, only better. The walls have been hung with new crimson silk, the inner courtyard delicately glassed over and turned into an uncluttered restaurant, and the basements opened up.

I lived nearby with my parents when I was a boy, and, during holidays from a severely girl-free boarding school I used to wander past the suits of armour, the cases of majolica, the ingeniously hideous eighteenth-century furniture, in order to peek guiltily at the Bouchers (and dream). These can still startle with their pink voluptuousness. They were too much for Paris in 1753: 'One commentator complained that their excessive nudity was so shocking that one should not take one's wife or one's daughter to the Salon.' Which is odd: one would imagine one's wife or one's daughter were acquainted well enough with their own nudity, whereas, if anyone should have been kept away from 'The Rising' and 'The Setting' (of the sun), it was sons. They made me feel guilty because I felt I should have been appreciating Art, not breasts. How annoyed Boucher would have been at such a perverse resistance (however half-hearted) to his flagrantly obvious intent.

The Collection not only contains Bouchers and Fragonards, and Poussin's exquisitely static 'A Dance to the Music of Time', it also contains *things*, objects, and among these, only a few inches in size, is St Mura's Bell which strangely moved me when I first came across it not long ago, and only partly because I knew by then where it had come from.

In the north-east of Ireland, in County Donegal, there is a sort of peninsula, almost an island, Inishowen, margined by two sea-loughs, Swilly and Foyle – its tip the Malin Head mentioned in every shipping forecast. It is in the Republic but just above Londonderry and therefore very near indeed to the Province. There, in a sense, the 'two Irelands' have met for centuries, Gaelic Ireland and Scotticised Protestant Ireland. On the Lough Swilly side, at Fahan (pronounced 'Fawn') the two Irelands come together in a strangely neat and significant way, which also has a Wallace connection.

Around the middle of the nineteenth century – when the fourth Marquess of Hertford, who owned chunks of Northern Ireland, was greatly augmenting his Collection – William Alexander was Protestant Rector at Fahan. He wrote poems, and his daughter put together a memoir of him, in which she remarks: 'Beside the Rectory garden is the picturesque burying ground The graves are scattered round the chancel of the old church.' That picturesque burying ground and ruined church is all that remains of the seventh-century Abbey of St Mura, wielder, presumably, of that beautifully decorated bell. In the seventeenth century, 1,000 years after St Mura, the Franciscan historian John Colgan, writing in exile, was still thundering about the desecration of this Abbey, insisting that it had contained 'splendid relics of antiquity which were preserved until the arrival of the mad heretics who desecrated, demolished and plundered everything sacred... Until modern times there also existed various relics of St Muranus but these have been removed from their place.'

William Alexander went on to become Church of Ireland Primate of Armagh, his poetry behind him; his wife, however, Cecil Frances, was writing verses which contain lines which must be the best-known in the English language, hymns such as 'Once in royal David's city', 'All things bright and beautiful', and 'There is a green hill far away'. Hymns, incidentally, which we did not know or sing at our Catholic boarding school, presumably because they were 'Protestant'.

What I wondered, once I had made the connection between the Rectory and the Abbey, was how much the Alexanders knew about John Colgan and his indignation, and about 'the old church' they could see from their Rectory, and whether they were aware that the Irish people they lived among certainly knew the history of the place, and were still having themselves buried in its precincts. I might be doing her an injustice, but the remarks of the Alexander daughter suggest that perhaps they did not know much; and so, it is a telling example of the historico-religious discontinuity in Irish history. The Alexanders were not 'mad heretics'; they were devout intelligent people, who doubtless considered themselves Irish.

Mrs Alexander also wrote *Poems on Subjects in the Old Testament* which Tennyson admired. Mark Twain was fond of quoting one about the death of Moses:

> By Nebo's lonely mountain
>   On this side Jordan's wave
> In a vale in the land of Moab
>   There lies a lonely grave.
> And no man knows that sepulchre
>   And no man saw it e'er,
> For the Angels of God upturned the sod
>   And laid the dead man there.

Alexander and Twain once met, at Oxford, when they were being given Honorary Degrees. 'They exchanged a few words and passed like ships in the night, and never knew of the strange bond between them.'

Anyway, there in the Wallace Collection in what was the Smoking Room decorated with Minton 'Turkish' tiles on the walls, there lies in a cabinet, among unrelated things, St Mura's little bell from Fahan. 'The decoration was applied in stages, the earliest is an Irish style of

Viking ornament, the filigree, rock crystal and amber were added in the 13th–16th centuries.' It was long-loved, therefore, before it arrived to lie among the armour, the painted plates and below the Bouchers. 'For hundreds of years the bell was valued for its power to alleviate suffering', says the Catalogue, adding breezily – and Protestantly – 'however, its last keeper was destitute and had to sell it.' Come to think of it (or I like to think it), since those early lurkings, bell and Boucher have both played a role in my life, to and fro – not necessarily a contradiction.

*October 2000*

# Percy French and Nosmo King

There is some more to be said about changes and continuances in Ireland, as they strike a frequent visitor. In the peat bogs of Galway, the gentle mountains in the background, men use long-handled, long-tined forks to throw out turves into a tractor-trailer. There are more men than could ride on a tractor, so their cars, good ones, are parked nearby on dry, stony patches. Separate piles of cut turves lie by the roadside year-long, drying. They never seem to be stolen and, presumably, belong to the men who cut them. I never saw anyone cutting, or collecting, before; it must have been the season, mid-September. They are cut at angles, ziz-zag, six inches one line above, six inches at another angle on the line below, and so on down until the brown cliff of the turf-cutting has a herringbone pattern. In the centre of Ireland, Westmeath, they just scrape off the peat wholesale, using huge Japanese machines, creating a dark desert.

In that same county, at little Fore Abbey, with its whitey-grey abbey ruins, its water meadows lush even by Irish standards, so that against the grey and the green the flanks of contented cows shine like newly opened conkers, the woman behind the bar came from nearby Mullingar. We remarked on the amount of new building in that town. 'Oh,' she said, equably, 'there's people there now I wouldn't know *who* they were!' She liked our (genuine) admiration of a veteran iron stove in the corner, patched, wired together; she looked at it with affection and told us it gave out a great heat in the winter. There are doubtless neophiliacs in Ireland, and there will be pressure to keep up with the O'Joneses, but from a thousand little incidents that you notice when you travel, it does seem as though the comfortable, the familiar, the human-sized, has more chance to survive, even in a newly prosperous Ireland, than in most countries; something to do with the scale of the place maybe.

In Ballyjamesduff, Co Cavan, the last nun, at a great age, has left the huge convent. It is now the Cavan County Museum. Driving away from there on a Sunday morning we came across a traffic jam in almost every small town; people coming out of Mass and climbing into their cars; change and continuance.

The great William Percy French wrote a ballad, 'Come back, Paddy Riley, to Ballyjamesduff', even going so far as to liken that modest little Cavan township to 'paradise', so it is only natural the hotel there should call itself proudly 'The Percy French'. There is another one in Strokestown, Roscommon: 'We all want to lay a claim to him,' said a local. Perhaps he was seduced by the melodious name and never visited the place. Possibly he did, because he was that county's Inspector of Drains:

> The fair maids of Cavan (this William maintains),
> Tho' I think one should take it with salt, a few grains,
> Have left in a body their woe-begone swains
>     For William, the local Inspector of Drains.

French deserted his profession, engineering, to write 'Abdallah Bubul Ameer', 'Phil the Fluter's Ball' (my father's party piece) and 'Where the Mountains of Mourne sweep down to the sea'. He performed them in public, and he sounds delightful. Floruit 1880–90, I should guess, but back in England I could find very little about the man for whom two Irish towns contend. In a London bookshop, I looked him up in the Drabble *Oxford Companion to English Literature*, but, as was to be expected in that Roundhead and Cambridge-domi-nated compilation, not a word. As I had the book in my hand, I wondered if I was in it and discovered that I went to 'Merton College, Cambridge'. What is the matter with OUP these days … ?

My ex-medical-student father, helplessly seduced from his studies by his passion for music hall, and into writing comedy for radio, would have loved the ex-engineer Percy French. He (my father) had friends with names like 'Nosmo King' (after a sign he saw in a railway carriage); I have his card pinned to my wall: 'Nosmo King, BBC Entertainer', and it is a sovereign specific against pomposity, social pretension, over-seriousness. 'Dear Old Nosmo', my father would murmur, smiling fondly.

Percy French songs, says *The Oxford Companion to Irish Literature*, 'have an alluring appeal and charm because of their affectionate use of Hiberno-English and a satiric edge'. Nevertheless, did not French patronise the Irish with his comic stereotypes? I nervously asked in Dublin. 'Undoubtedly,' said a friend, 'but he had impeccable Nationalist credentials.' (In Ireland the unwitting visitor is never more than a footstep away from tripping over politics.)

An example: after crossing the border into the Six Counties, we stopped to telephone because we were running late. I took the opportunity to step into a bar and foolishly offered Irish money for my drink, forgetting where I was. This threw the hospitable lady into a flutter. 'No problem,' said a man with whom I had fallen into conversation, 'give me the pleasure', and he paid for my drink in sterling. 'That was very kind of you, Bob?' I heard the fluttered one whisper behind me, wonderingly, as though he had never bought anyone a drink before, whereas I left delighted at yet another example of Irish hospitality. 'Puzzled at the sight of Irish money?' snorted our host, later. 'That place is an IRA stronghold!'

John Taylor is Member for one of the most beautiful constituencies in the Kingdom, Strangford, the 'strang fijord' of the Vikings, bird-haunted (the Brent geese had just arrived); you cross it by ferry between two townships that look like idealised eighteenth-century filmsets. Taylor talked unhelpfully against the Irish Agreement, speaking, not of Loyalists or Unionists or Protestants, but of 'the *British* majority community'; and Mr Patten would want to reform the RUC, wouldn't he, 'him with his roots in the west of Ireland' (news to me). And this was said in Ireland, as though all things Irish, as opposed to 'British', were threatening and malign. Meanwhile in England, a headline screamed, 'No decommissioning without a united Ireland, say IRA.' So little change, too much continuance.

'Ach, I dunno', to quote Percy French. Enough of these impotent indignations against extremes of both sides in that longing-to-be-peaceful place. Time to invoke the surreal spirit of Nosmo, or sing a ditty by Percy, in 'Hiberno-English'.

*October 2000*

# Dietrich Bonhoeffer

This has been a strangely anxious, jumpy time, mid-November: not only for me, I think, but for most of us. Perhaps we catch it from each other, what T.F. Powys called 'moods of God', and it reminds us how mutually vulnerable we are. Floods, gales, railway accidents, faulty railtracks – the repair of which causes delays, confusions, blocked roads – the list could be longer; at the moment, the world's most significant power seems unable to elect itself a President. Yesterday, up here in Gloucestershire, safe from floods but not from high winds, a helicopter nosed noisily up and down the combes all day, as though looking for a burglar or a body. Perhaps this was anxiety-inducing for two reasons: the impossibility of discovering why it was doing that – who to ask? and to ask about so many mysteries? – and the extraordinary, pervasive racket of helicopters that makes you want to duck and hide, afflicted by some atavistic mouse-memory, fearing the shadow of the hawk.

In fact this is being written, or partly drafted, beside the swollen river at Henley ('in' Thames) where tall men in wet green waders stride purposefully about, as though returned from battle. Council rescuers? Rubber fetishists? What is certain is that being unusually and uniformly attired gives us a confidence that is obviously enjoyed, which makes it odd that nowadays we appear to abhor uniforms. These splendidly accoutred heroes – sometimes their waders downgyved to the knee, as a cowboy might unbuckle his gunbelt – stride past the gathered swans and coots which seem to prefer flooded pavements to the main fast-running river. You can look down on the backs of fully-grown cygnets, which are still coloured, powdered chocolate on the white foam of a cappuccino coffee.

Under my arm, as I watch them, is the bulky biography, *Dietrich Bonhoeffer*, by his friend and fellow pastor Eberhard Bethge. The Folio Society has reissued Bonhoeffer's *Letters and Papers from Prison*, which, enlarged, came out in 1970. As I have read this book and round it and have thought and talked of nothing else for weeks, I might as well talk about Bonhoeffer here. With hesitation (anxiety, again), because since earlier publication, theological ideas Bonhoeffer adumbrates in his letters have been analysed, defended, argued against, semantically pushed and pulled at with such vigour, that I wouldn't dare to say a word. All I know is that the letters themselves, and the ideas they contain, are more fascinating to me than I can easily describe, and for various reasons.

Take the first letter, to his parents, two weeks after Bonhoeffer was 'unexpectedly' arrested, 14 April 1943. He remembers his father's seventy-fifth-birthday celebration two weeks before. 'It was a splendid day. I can still hear the chorale that we sang in the morning and evening, with all the voices and instruments: "Praise to the Lord, the Almighty, the King of Creation"...' A suggestion of cultivated Berlin life, amid Allied bombing, that we might not have expected. Then we learn from Bethge (not from Bonhoeffer, whose letters were read by his interrogators, and not from the Folio edition) that, during the seemingly serene birthday party, they were all waiting anxiously for the telephone to ring and announce that the bomb plot against Hitler had succeeded.

We realise that, in every letter, Bonhoeffer, alone in his cell, is forced to play a double, triple, deadly game: to baffle his accusers, to give neither himself nor others away, to reassure his friends and family that he is all right, of his interest and concern for them, and also, by means of subtle ambiguities of phrase, to warn his fellow conspirators to stick to the same story, a story which, though not in itself untrue, was necessarily 'economical with the truth'.

Even the word 'conspirator' in English, as in German, has an unpleasant ring – Gunpowder, Treason and Plot. Bonhoeffer was loyal to Germany, to Christianity, not to the hell Hitler had made. What is astonishing is the extent of the conspiracy, not only pastors and intellectuals, but Admirals, Generals, people in positions of the highest authority. Churchill was told of this alternative Germany ready to take over, and dismissed it – 'a conspiracy of militarists, simply a case of the higher personalities in the German Reich murdering one another'. They were certainly toffs. Difficult to say even now that Churchill was wrong, the situation was so complex, the period so confused, but it does look as though an opportunity was lost, to try to limit the further destruction of Europe.

After a few months of his imprisonment, Bonhoeffer won over a warder and was able to smuggle his theological speculations to Bethge who was at the Italian Front; his ideas of 'religionless Christianity', of 'mankind come of age' which therefore could do without the idea of God – 'Before God and with God we live without God'. Above all, his sense that the Church had inevitably evolved into a form of spiritual privilege, because anyone who believes in God increasingly finds his friends unable to imagine how his mind works; they barely know the meaning of his terms, 'redemption' and so on. He therefore feels himself to be in possession of some private gift, a 'grace' denied to others, which is an intolerable position to be in, and un-Christian. Bonhoeffer not only faced up to Hitler, he faced up to the greatest question of all.

Incriminating diaries were at last found (of Admiral Canaris); now came the Gestapo, interrogation in cellars, Buchenwald. There, these 'special' prisoners met up again until the atmosphere was almost party-like in that terrible place. 'More aristocrats,' growled one guard. Hitler ordered the deaths of all of them. But Allied artillery could be heard (1945); chaos might save them yet. No, bureaucracy triumphed, they were hanged, within days of the end of the war and of Hitler.

A life of subterfuge, of which we know nothing in these islands, becomes a habit. Called out by his guards for what he suspected was the last time, Bonhoeffer took his copy of Plutarch and wrote his name in the front, in the back, and *in the middle*. It might reach his parents one day, and alert them of his fate. It did, years later.

Every eyewitness of this time remarked on Bonhoeffer's lack of anxiety (to go back to the beginning of this piece). Earlier he had written, 'I sometimes wonder myself at how "composed" (or do I mean blunted?) I am.'

Purely by chance, finishing this, I notice that it is the eleventh hour of the eleventh day of the eleventh month; an appropriate time to remember Dietrich Bonhoeffer.

*November 2000*

# Surprised by Aberystwyth

I have been looking through the four volumes of George Orwell's journalism, partly in the hope of discovering how he gets his effects, and mainly to see if he touches on a subject of interest to me, namely the strange fascination of British seaside towns in winter, especially when these are past their best, as they usually are.

He may write of this somewhere, but I have had no luck. Even the wonderful Index has been unable to help – 'miscellaneous observations: on blaming skunks for stinking; on authors and pregnant women; on throwing dead donkeys ...' This is a pity, because it might have been a subject that interested him, and he would have been able to analyse why this was so. As it is, I am left on my own (distracted for the moment by looking up the page reference for 'throwing dead donkeys'). You don't have to agree with all Orwell says in order to recognise that, as essayist, reviewer, columnist, he was a master. Dip in anywhere, however gingerly, and you find yourself swimmin'-along with George.

So, Whitley Bay, South Shields in the north, Deal, St Margaret's Bay in the south, what is the secret of their wintry, semi-deserted appeal? I once saw the sun come up on Whitley Bay, among the peeling Bingo Halls and disappointed-looking boarding houses, and dawn seemed an even greater wonder than it always is. I tried to write a poem about it, because it deserved one, or at least a song; but 'To see the sun come up on Whitley Bay' doesn't work, somehow. Why not, precisely? Deal, of course, is obviously pretty, with its shingle beach and little boats drawn up on it, its painted seafront houses and shops; the exquisite fishmonger's, on the sea, its inside painted blue and white and three fish, just three, lovingly placed in parallel on the grey slate slab. Nevertheless, even Deal, in its winter and tripper-free aloneness, withdrawnness, seems greater than the sum of its parts.

To be fair to the compass, there is Aldeburgh in the east, and my latest addition to the list is Aberystwyth in the west. We were there last week to look up something in the National Library of Wales, which is set high above the compact little town, looking down on its curving black-sanded bay, given definition by small green hills on either side.

The wonder of it is that Aberystwyth should be there at all. Its beach is not a harbour, there were lead mines, a few, and an occa-sional shoal of herring; Edward I built a castle there to guard the coast and keep the Welsh in order, and that's about all. However, being Welsh and proud of it, the place has a literate town guide (a thing maddeningly rare in England), and the quotation marks round the title of it give the reason for its sudden development from nowhere very much into '*A Fashionable Watering Place*'.

In the mid-1780s, it became seriously fashionable, it is not clear why. It is a handsome nook in the coast, even a cosy one, but it must have taken some reaching, even from Bath. What did they do, the 'quality', when they got there? Dress up, it seems:

In going to church we were preceded by a handsome young man walking mincingly along, in the very height of fashion ... The collar of his coat was low but surmounted by an enormous cravat, and this again was overtopped by a wide and stiff shirt collar cut into the form of the outward edge of a scimitar, indeed it almost seemed able to perform the duty of one, and stood up so high that we were in some pain lest it should cut off his ears … The points of his shirt collar projected two inches beyond his face, and, when viewed en profile, completely concealed it from his nose downwards. The sleeves of his coat were very short, but then, his shirt wrists, stiff as his collar, were continued two and a half inches over his hands. His pantaloons were white and of enormous bulk.

The Welsh, lead miners, fishermen, retaliated with 'Welsh Trowsers', blue, with a red stripe, but it doesn't sound an adequate response.

However, these people, dukes and their duchesses, lords and 'mere baronets' had to be accommodated, because they were valuable: 'as early as 1817 the visitors spent over £30,000 in the town', which is why, although some eighteenth-century houses remain, Aberystwyth became, and stays, a planned *Victorian* town of all Victorian styles, early and late, a period jewel.

However, in such a place it is the sea that draws you, the nearly people-less promenade, the boatless sea hissing and crashing on the black sand; Marine Terrace, begun in 1800 for all those visitors, finished in the same style in 1931. But it ends in disaster, its stub-end frayed, sea-struck, or at least sand- and stonestruck: Alexandra Hall, once a hostel for women students of the University, now window-less, boarded up, the safety fences round it rattling in the wind. The sea is not mocked.

Walk back along the sea, as dusk gathers, and there are soon again lighted houses along the promenade, 'Vacancy' signs and, incredibly in the near dark, one or two surfers packing up for the day. There is a sudden 'swoosh', and successive clouds of starlings, each cloud changing direction simultaneously as though directed by one starling-mind, as they come in to roost under the stubby pier; perhaps the spray does something to their fleas.

Near the pier, facing the sea, is the most extraordinary fantasy of a building, indescribable by me: Victorian Gothic – a grey Abbotsford or Amsterdam-mercantile; originally designed as an enormous hotel, it became the first Welsh University College in 1872, 'with 26 male students', and how they must have rattled about inside that vastness. It is still part of the University, but the main buildings of that are now high above the town.

As is the National Library of Wales, much expanded since 1912.

It would have to be: 'over two million books, thirty thousand manuscripts, three million deeds, documents, paintings, maps'. A welcoming, well-run place with a lofty view over the neat town below. We admire the view, sheltered by the front of the library, then turn a corner and are hit by an Orcadian, Skara Brae blast of wind you can lean your whole weight into. It is good to be reminded of the elements, the wind, the sea, and think of the swoosh of starlings taking confident possession of that storm-truncated pier.

That may be part of the attraction of out-of-season 'watering places'. Their impermanence, the evidence of change. The pillared 'Academy' – clearly a Calvinist-Methodist Meeting House, its whole architectural focus on the high wooden lectern under an arch decorated with the Ten Commandments in Welsh, turns out, almost unchanged, to be a pub. The Ceredigion Museum was a theatre, Gracie Fields sang there, they have kept the proscenium stage and red-plush seats in the circle and the gods; a good museum, and not the only one in which the most interesting, as well as the prettiest, exhibit is the museum itself. Perhaps it is a matter of temperament, but apart from the nearly perfect anthology of Victorian styles, what I most remember is the arrival, at dusk, of those confident starlings.

*December 2000*

# Tolstoy, *Anna Karenina*

'I've just been thinking about the critics,' announces Tolstoy. 'The business of criticism is to interpret the works of great writers, above all to single out from the great quantity of rubbish written by all of us – to single out what is best. And instead of this, what do they do? Force out of themselves, or more usually fish out from the works of a bad but popular writer some little platitude, and start to string their thoughts on this platitude, mangling and distorting the writers in the process. And the result is that in their hands great writers become small, profound ones shallow and wise ones stupid.' Thus Tolstoy in his diary of 1891, and it makes anyone tremble who intends to fish out some platitude about *Anna Karenina*, as I do, because I have just finished rereading the book and am unable to get it out of my head.

The diaries contain good things, as well as an astonishing and autocratic crankiness. It cannot be, surely, that so great a writer is without humour. It flickers in his imaginative work, but there is little sign of it in his account of his private life. In essence (platitude coming up), the diaries are an account of a man trying to be *good*, to live according to the teaching of the Gospels – from which he has filleted all miraculous elements, the Resurrection, the divinity of Christ – but one who is attempting to live, literally, according to the precepts of the Sermon on the Mount. This causes the maximum conflict with his wife, who is trying to bring up their children and pay the bills. He despises her himself and all who are not like him – which is everybody.

A.N. Wilson, in his 1988 biography of Tolstoy, pinpoints a story which encapsulates, in miniature, this lifelong or marriage-long struggle. The young literary journalist Desmond MacCarthy is invited to stay at Yasnaya Polyana. Tolstoy appears from the fields – 'the cap, the long white beard, the belted peasant shirt and felt shoes' – he is easy and natural and takes his guest to his pleasingly austere room. 'Oh, and there is just one small thing. If MacCarthy does not very much object, Tolstoy liked his guests to empty their own chamber pots. He felt it was demeaning to ask the servants to perform this task.' MacCarthy of course agrees, and Tolstoy shuffles off. Soon there comes the sound of brisker footsteps along the narrow corridor – Countess Tolstoy. Had he all he required? 'And, oh, did he tell you about the chamber pot? I must ask you most *strictly*, Mr MacCarthy, not to empty your own chamber pot.'

'I would like to serve God by actually spreading his truth abroad, not in word but in deed and the example of sacrifice, but nothing comes of it. He will not let me. Instead of that I live attached to my wife's skirts, subservient to her, and I and all my children lead a squalid and ignoble life which I falsely justify on the grounds that I can't destroy love' (1890). (And he wrote his diary for his wife to read. She retaliated by writing her own account. Wilson calls it 'the battle of the diaries'.)

There are good remarks scattered through the diaries which make this grim tragicomedy worth reading: 'A gentleman is the left-overs of a Christian. Wash the dishes where a Christian has been and you're left with a gentleman' (1889). The crankiness was occasionally extreme and, in the later diaries, repetitive and boring, but excusable in Tolstoy's place and time; he could barely leave his gate without encountering some example of State-induced misery. This he tried to alleviate, with soup kitchens, schools, relinquishing his own estates and copyrights as far as his quarrelsome family would allow. Crankiness can be influential; Tolstoy loathed authority because he saw that it was founded on violence; violence he also abhorred, so he developed the idea of passive resistance, which was taken up by Gandhi.

Meanwhile, what about *Anna Karenina*, Tolstoy as artist, not diarist? It is significant that from 1865 to 1878 he hardly kept a diary at all. He was writing *War and Peace* and *Anna Karenina*, books which could be called by his translator, R.F. Christian, 'surrogate diaries'. That these novels transmit a springing sense of life observed is surely because he was putting his daily experience into them, and had no need for diaries. For example, take Vronsky, on his way to see Anna (even the position of his legs in the carriage is described): '"Good, very good", he said to himself. Often before he had felt delight in the consciousness of his physical superiority, but never had he so loved himself till now.' This is not censorious, it is an observation of the author's self-content. Some have found Vronsky null, a sex object merely (the variety of readers' reactions to Tolstoy's characters is an indication of how alive they are), but Vronsky is surprisingly self-aware. He has to guide a foreign prince round the pleasure spots of St Petersburg; this is Vronsky's world. However, seen through the eyes of this dolt, he becomes disgusted with it: 'The Prince was a gentleman, and Vronsky could not deny the fact. Vronsky conducted himself in exactly the same way and was proud of it. "Stupid ox! Is it possible that I am like him?"'

It is the surprises that make you look up from the book and say 'Shakespeare!' (platitude). Like Shakespeare, Tolstoy gives you what you need and then a little more, which you might not have thought of but which you recognise at once to be true, and he does it with pictures. Levin is at last totally happy: 'he shut up his papers in a new portfolio, bought by his wife, he washed his hands in an elegant new wash basin, also bought by her, and, smiling at his thoughts, raised his head with a feeling that resembled remorse'. Wow! I thought, remorse inside happiness, that's brilliant, and laid down the book to think about this, which is why it took such a long time to reread *Anna Karenina*. Also, it had to be put down frequently because the misunderstandings between the lovers were so inevitable and accurately described that they became almost unendurably painful. And yet, about the time I was at last finishing it, a newspaper article appeared, by a similar rereader, who had found the book 'an immediate opening of a door to a brighter, more invigorating and cheering world'. Again the diversity of reaction: that two could be so different and equally justifiable, is proof of the life in the novel.

One last glimpse of the old, diary-writing sage, 1895. He is walking with his youngest daughter, Alexandra, and her friend. The two girls are excited by the thought of progress, about electricity, about 'flying in the air'. 'No,' Tolstoy tells them, 'the only progress is in brotherhood, unity, love and the establishment of the kingdom of God on earth.' He is right, of course, and is also lucky that the little girls didn't push him in the pond. Nevertheless, there is something fine and infectious about such relentless whole-hoggery. It was Alexandra who accompanied him to his deathbed on the station at Astapovo, who died eighty years later and – reports A.N. Wilson – 'was to keep a candle burning at her father's shrine until the end'.

*January 2001*

# Tolstoy and his Diaries

It is the height of unfairness to hold against anyone the things they say against themselves, especially someone as honest as Tolstoy; nevertheless, even the fair-minded and admiring editor and translator of his *Diaries* permits himself a mild exasperation: 'Perhaps significantly, the last word he wrote was "me".'

That is the point: central to the diaries, from the 1880s onward, is Tolstoy's struggle to eliminate from himself what he called his 'I': he describes his peace and happiness when he felt he had succeeded, his almost daily self-disgust when he realised he had not. His disgust, also, with almost everybody else, especially his family, because they seemed in his eyes not to comprehend the importance of this struggle, or be willing to undertake it themselves. He was surely an uncomfortable presence at the family dinner table: '… quarrels over money … But it can't be got otherwise than by sinning, because acquiring it is a sin. Nobody listened to me, and everyone was cross with me for talking such nonsense or uttering truisms. At which point the Sissermans arrived, and everyone was cross' (1890). Tolstoy even gave his fiancée, Sofya, his bachelor diaries to read and, says Christian, 'the shock which she' – a sheltered girl of eighteen – 'experienced on learning about his sexual promiscuity was one from which perhaps she never fully recovered'. Clean-sheet and know-me-as-I-am time: too much to ask.

It probably should not be surprising – nevertheless it does surprise – how directly Tolstoy's daily behaviour and daily reflections are mirrored in the fiction. Tolstoy's showing of his early diaries is an example; he makes his Levin do the same and Levin's Kitty is equally appalled. (Tolstoy's Sofya would have to transcribe the passage; she is being lectured.) Likewise, in his diary Tolstoy meditates grimly on man's lust for power; so, *Resurrection* begins with a joyous urban spring, unnoticed, according to Tolstoy, because 'what men considered sacred and important were their own devices for wielding power over their fellow men'. Tolstoy has been reading, with approval, the economic theories of Spencer and George. He wants to give away his property and is opposed by his wife. Within the first few pages of *Resurrection*, we find: 'Spencer's lucid and unanswerable argument against private ownership of land, arguments later brilliantly confirmed by Henry George.' He is continuing his quarrel with his wife in public; she would certainly have to transcribe this passage because Tolstoy's handwriting, says Christian, 'defies description'. 'My diaries are me,' said Tolstoy. So are his novels, in this particular sense.

After *Anna Karenina* and before *Resurrection*, there was a ten-year period when Tolstoy devoted himself to the reform of Russia, writing articles and pamphlets with titles such as *Time To Come to Our Senses* and *What Men Live By*. Because of the ideas these contained, an increasing trickle of disciples began to make its way to his door, called by his wife, dismissively, 'the dark people'. Tolstoy was also dismayed: 'to think you can change your life by changing its outward conditions is just like thinking as I did when a boy, that by sitting on a stick and taking hold of it at both ends, I could lift myself up.' That is an 1891 entry; six years later, he is more specific: 'There is no Tolstoyanism or teaching of mine and never has been. There is only one eternal, universal, worldwide teaching of the truth as expressed particularly clearly for me and for us all in the Gospels.' Like all writers, he could not understand why people wanted to meet him. In 1889, he growls: 'Sat down to dinner; the Americans arrived. Two pastors, one literary man. If only they would spend a dollar buying my books *What To Do* and *Life*, and a couple of days reading them, they could get to know me, i.e. what is within me, much better.' Sometimes he sounds desperate: 'It is one of the most difficult situations: a youth who has formed an exaggerated and false idea of me ... struggles to make his way to me and expects complete salvation; and suddenly there is nothing at all.'

Nevertheless he had founded a religion of a sort, secularised Christianity. By 1901, his attacks on the Orthodox Church had become so virulent that he was officially excommunicated. Perhaps it is a matter of temperament, but his parody of a religious service in *Resurrection* (admittedly it is taking place in prison and some of the 'congregation' are in chains) suggests that he had no conception of the human need for some transcending ritual. Just as his relentless search for clarity, his hatred of blur, led him to dismiss Shakespeare, so were, to him, church services meaningless mumbo-jumbo, and that was that.

He had not meant to found a religion, but it is interesting that, as a young officer in the Crimea in 1855, he was struck 'with a stupendous idea, to the realisation of which I feel capable of devoting my life. This idea is the founding of a new religion, not promising bliss but giving bliss on earth.' (At the same time he is gambling away his large house at Yasnaya Polyana; just as, fifty years later, pursued by members of his 'new religion', he is trying to give what remains away.)

All his life the one belief (unprovable, unclear) to which he clung, and seemed never to question, was in the immortality of the soul. Did this continue to the end? Possibly. 'When I am dying I would like to be asked whether I continue to understand life as I used to understand it, as a growing nearer to God, as an expansion of love. If I'm unable to speak, I'll close my eyes if the answer is yes and raise them upwards if it is no' (1901). Slyboots. You're going to close your eyes anyway, and to roll them upwards might take too much muscular effort.

1902: 'An astonishing thing. I know myself how bad and stupid I am and yet people consider me a man of genius. So what must other people be like?'

*February 2001*

# Foot and Mouth

In the local pub I was passed a 'Liberty & Livelihood' car sticker and a form that asked my reasons for not joining the pro-hunting march planned for the middle of this month. At first I thought this was a touch strong-arm – passions run high here in Gloucestershire – but then I understood it was only a headcount of those who would have gone if they could. The man who passed these things took it for granted that I would be on the right side, which is to say on his, so it was really a sort of compliment. Not to disillusion him, I scribbled a silly excuse – 'a broken leg' (without saying whose) – and left the form on the bar.

Within a few days, and oddly, because it had never happened before in many years, I found myself in the middle of the Hunt on the sunken road behind that same pub. The hounds were streaming all over the place, the scent presumably lost. Then something must have happened: a young man in a tight jacket, on foot, started urgently pulling himself up the steep bank, holding on to tree roots: a man in a pink coat, suddenly entirely concentrated, jerked himself forward in his saddle and put his horse at the bank, which wasn't far from the vertical, something I had not seen done outside a Western. It was thrilling, as well as brutal. On the road, grinning at me conspiratorially, were two young men in a mud-boltered moon-buggy, covered in mud themselves, brown, in brown woollen hats. They looked like murderers in an old play, and it was right that they should: clipped behind their buggy were two shovels. Their job was to dig out the fox if it went to ground.

Next day came the first reports of Foot and Mouth disease. There would be no more hunting, no march, no more most things for a while. The whole place fell silent, and it is still eerie. The unmoving quietness seems to contain a kind of grief, also a guilt. Footpaths out of bounds, golden bandages of disinfected straw at every field-gate, even across the lanes themselves, as they used to put down straw outside houses where there had been a death.

And it is like that. The word 'greed' has been used, in a hushed voice, by unlikely people: the greed of commerce, of farmers, of us. What was confidence is now suspected of having been hubris. Too much 'intensive farming', too many dull-eyed cows turned into barely ambulant udders, terrible journeys of live animals, too crowded, too far. If you complained of this, the nastier kind of farmer snarled: 'So you don't want cheap food?' and we said, Yes, but at what price? Why Either/Or; couldn't there be a compromise? We were considered sentimentalists, spoilers of a good thing, our questions were not answered and we stopped asking. We marvelled instead at the toppling shelves, the superabundance in supermarkets. We should have been warned when told that some of these chains had banned any picture of an animal, or part of an animal, from their stores and their literature; as little connection as possible was to be made between the neat carton and a beast.

My late father-in-law, Wogan Milford, farmed round here for forty years and became disenchanted with the whole business, though not for business reasons. 'Sheep eat the grass,' he said one day, meditatively, 'they piss and shit which makes the grass grow more, they eat it and then we eat them. Disgusting, really.' The directness of his speech was not that of a farmer but of a plain-speaking grandee, and a Communist. His first speech in the House of Lords was to demand the House's abolition. He believed in many things, in social justice for example, for which he fought, but his genius was practical: he did not believe in the way I believe, and this difference of temperaments intrigued me. I was so struck by a conversation we had on what was to be his last day here that I put it into a poem, called 'Politics', exactly as it happened, which is always, to me, more exciting than anything which is made up.

We were looking across at the hills where he had farmed, and which he had painted in semi-abstract oils often and well. A slight snow was falling, and I was admiring the light, not speaking. Suddenly, he said, as though I had indeed spoken, 'I want to see what's *underneath* those hills. I don't want light.' It was like a definition of his painting and of a difference between temperaments, an Either/Or perhaps, although it is always unclear to me why different temperaments should not learn from each other, as I believe we did, or I did.

This was many years ago, and I mention it here because of a letter by von Hügel, which exactly concerns itself with basic temperamental differences and uses my unspoken word 'light' in an interesting way. Hügel, patronisingly dismissed by his contemporary W. B. Yeats – 'So get you gone, von Hügel, though with blessings on your head' – was a humanist Christian writer on religious matters, the opposite of an Either/Or man, a soother of controversies, and therefore too middle-of-the-road to excite whole-hoggers. Here is the quotation:

Is the difference not this, that minds belong, roughly speaking, to two classes, which may be called the mystical and positive, and the scholastic and theoretical? The first of these would see all truth as a centre of intense light losing itself gradually in utter darkness; this centre would gradually extend, but the borders would remain fringe, they could never become clear-cut lines. Such a mind when weary of border-work would sink back upon its centre, its home of peace and light, and thence it would gain fresh conviction and courage to again face the twilight and the dark. Force it to commit itself absolutely to any border distinction, or force it to shift its home or restrain its roamings, and you have done your best to endanger its faith and to ruin its happiness ...

Wogan never 'forced' anyone, but his temperament wanted to know how things *worked*: geology, capitalism. Surely the 'intense point of light' temperament could usefully borrow that questing practicality, the two blended together, a dream of a compromise. The 'scholastic and theoretical' has had its own way too much. The other sort of temperament could never feed meat to herbivores, nor follow any so-called 'bottom line' relentlessly until it failed to notice it turning into a fuse that leads to an explosion.

Wogan was, of course, a 'progressive' farmer, a rational one (though not a cruel man), who in the 1950s kept battery hens in a shed. Now that is cruel (forget fox-hunting for a moment), the blistered breasts rubbed sore and featherless because of the closeness of confinement, the vocal desperation, the exaggerated stench. He wanted people to have cheaper eggs. Not at that price, we thought, and said so. For whatever reason, next time we visited his farm, the battery hens were gone. The mood here at the moment, during this silent nervy time, is that much of that sort of thing will have to go.

*March 2001*

# Philip Toynbee and von Hügel

If Baron von Hügel, the religious philosopher, round about 1900, divided our minds, 'roughly speaking, into two classes … the mystical and positive, and the scholastic and theoretical', Philip Toynbee was doing the same thing eighty years later: saint versus rationalist. 'There is a great gulf fixed between the two,' he says, 'and how well I understand those who prefer the good, sensible, unpretentious rationalist to the extravagant, often wild, often sickly, often "impossible" figure of the holy man. Yet it is St Francis who constantly excites my imagination, not John Stuart Mill; and I would rather read a life of General Booth than one of Voltaire.'

It was not always like that for Toynbee. In his introduction to *Part of a Journey* (1981), an autobiographical journal covering 1977-79, he cheerfully admits that, until his fifties, he 'was passionately and derisively hostile to Christianity, with a particularly sharp resentment against the Roman Church'. Not that his book is about a 'conversion'; it is what he calls it, a journey, published a few months before he died and followed by the posthumous *End of a Journey* (1988). Both books are addictive if you enjoy asides like, 'Always lurking in the mind is the mocking suspicion that this whole religious to-do is simply an old man's hobby.' After two paces forward (or upward?): 'The banana skin! I got roaringly, boringly drunk…' In that mood, he contemplates the weekly book-essay he has just contributed to the *Observer*: 'Rereading yesterday's review has been quite a ludicrous experience. The book was a life of Elizabeth Bowen, and the reviewer's tone of quiet authority and dignified self-confidence suggest a very different provenance from the bedroom of a man sick with a hangover and groaning with remorse.'

He says that he had 'a full array of childhood mistreatments for the benefit of any psychiatrist who might lay his hands on me'. Not, he implies, that he would permit such a laying-on of non-sacerdotal hands. He shoves on, day after day, astonished now to find himself nipping in to the local convent chapel to say a prayer, even attending Mass there, but attending also various love-ins and ad hoc ceremonies of a vaguely Eastern nature that take place among the commune to which he has surrendered his own house for five near-disastrous, educative years. There are no half-measures about Toynbee. He understands that it is the direction rather than the arrival that matters, but he does hanker to get there: he wants *clarity*.

Toynbee – a novelist, a poet, as well as an influential literary journalist – clearly belongs to the 'mystical, positive' of Hügel's two categories, about which temperament there is surely something medieval, which does not mean outmoded. No poet could be more mystical, or concrete ('positive'?) than Dante, who created physical pictures of Hell, Purgatory and Heaven, and made them almost tangible. A hundred years later, Botticelli illustrated Dante's poem with small drawings on sheepskin, remarkable for their realism, their clear, unambiguous outlines, exactly corresponding to the clarity of Dante. The sinners certainly suffer, gnawing each other or upside down in pitch, surveyed calmly by Virgil (who, after all, is himself a shade) and with varying degrees of alarm, disgust, pity and anger by Dante, who is only down there on a visit. The triumph is the *Paradiso* drawings, largely consisting of Beatrice and Dante alone, surrounded by a planetary circle or by souls in the form of flames: Dante flinching, hiding his eyes, Beatrice cajoling, encouraging, gently chiding until he gradually learns to trust to look up – and down. She wants him to see how far they have come. The last page, the arrival, is a white blank; inexpressible. The relationship of the two figures (he smaller than she), their varying facial expressions, all achieved on a tiny scale, their slight adjustments so that they could almost be illustrations in one of those little books you flick the pages of and the figures seem to move, these illustrations of humanity reaching its highest level remain intimately human. In other words, the defined and clear-cut can be warm, inclusive.

These ideas and emotions can be suggested in poetry and art, but whether they can be codified in prose is another matter. Hügel (1852-1925), son of an Austrian diplomat and of a Scots mother, resident in England since he was fifteen, struggles to explain and justify the teasing-out of the eschatology of the fifteenth-century St Catherine of Genoa (contemporary with Botticelli) – her ideas of Heaven, Purgatory and Hell. He struggles, because in his determination not to offend the Vatican and risk being cast out and his 'Modernist' liberalism be silenced, he piles clause after qualifying clause in her/his tentative description of what happens to sinners (not so horrible as in Dante – 'since everything, surely, points to a lowered consciousness in the souls in question'), so that he begins to read like an unpictorial Henry James. Toynbee says he has written in the *Observer* that the American Cistercian Thomas Merton was 'the greatest religious writer in the English language since von Hügel (and I might have added that what von Hügel wrote was scarcely English!)'. His impatience with von Hügel is understandable; and why, anyway, write in detail about what happens to us after death, when none of us knows? Probably because the 'scholastic and theoretical' part of our temperaments craves at least a working hypothesis of clarity; blur leads to further blur, as is certainly the case with religious ceremonies if those go slack, or trendy. There is a mysterious poem by the American Richard Wilbur called 'The Rule', which disturbs because we know the last line is true:

> The oil for extreme unction must be blessed
> On Maundy Thursday, so the rule has ruled,
> And by the bishop of the diocese.
> Does that revolt you? If so, you are free
> To squat beneath the deadly manchineel,
> That tree of caustic drops and fierce aspersion,
> And fancy that you have escaped from mercy.
> Things must be done in one way or another.

One of the attractive things about Toynbee is that he was not afraid to be grim in his pursuit of clarity, a Dantean and Hügelian one, and along the same lines as Wilbur. His normal temperament was humorous, though without being evasive. He was every kind of holy fool, but his questioning was sturdy:

> Beyond Good and Evil. You might as well say Beyond Truth and Falsehood: which no doubt has been said by some of the great mystics of the 'negative way'. But I come back to the fact that 'the Battle of Hastings was fought in 1066' is quite a different kind of statement from 'the Battle of Hastings was fought in 1067'. Satan the Father of Lies, etc.

*April 2001*

# April the Twenty-third

'Forty-two years ago (to me if to no one else / The number is of some interest) ...' That is Louis MacNeice, remembering himself as a four-teen-year-old scuttling from one window to the other of a corridor-less train in order to see 'the holes punched in the sky', the stars – 'partly because of their Latin names'. His modest parenthesis is perhaps fatally encouraging, because to me, if to no one else except others who were there, the date is of 'some interest'. The day on which I am writing this, 23 April, St George's Day, Shakespeare's birthday, and exactly fifty years ago, 2nd Lieut P.J. Kavanagh managed to get himself shot beside the Imjin River in Korea. The manner of it was for him – others were not so lucky – in the highest degree fortunate: it meant, thus far, fifty more years of life.

Not for all of us who were there: the American poet Peter Kane Dufault, ex-bomber pilot, hearing the tale, remarked drily, 'Survivors always have the best stories.' Yes, that's why real old soldiers seldom talk about such matters; they have heard the chat of too many friends stopped for good. However, indulgence; it was fifty years ago today, and the manner of it was strange.

Our little patrol seemed to have bumped into a whole Chinese army. (It had.) I was ordered to take all of us who could still walk back across the river and home, if I could. I stepped out from the copse where we had taken shelter and, unsurprisingly, found myself alone. Except for a Chinese soldier who had detached himself from his comrades and seemed determined to shoot me with his automatic gun, lying down to do so. I lay down too, regretting the brightness of my cap badge (it was a moonlit night). Most of his bullets went into the ground, splashing me with earth. Eventually one hit me in the shoulder, I cried out, then came a bang in my ear so loud that I thought my last moment had come, but it turned out that a brave man – whose name I never learned – had come from the trees, lain down beside me and shot the unfortunate and intrepid Chinese soldier. The others now came out of the copse, we walked to the river, to the pontoon bridge, the Chinese standing up to look at us. We crossed the bridge, and only when we were round the corner out of sight did they remember to shoot at us. There was nothing brave or soldierly on my part about this. As for brave, we were moving away from danger, which was sensible; I also had a superstition that if we broke into a run we were done for, that it was our orderly progress which puzzled the Chinese. As for soldierly, it was only afterwards that I realised the order had been to cross the river by fording it, swimming it; we were meant to take to the hills. As these hills were soon to be filled with Chinese soldiers running up and down them, firing and blowing bugles, this would have been a bad idea. Not that I even thought of it; to my civilian mind it seemed natural to cross a river by a bridge if there happened to be one, and go back along the road. All of our party arrived at our lines safely, and I was bundled into an ambulance, driven south to safety. Meanwhile, the Gloucesters were being almost wiped out, our battalion, the Royal Ulster Rifles, suffered dreadful casualties, so did the Royal Northumberland Fusiliers; some I knew became prisoners of the Chinese for years.

Later, an American surgeon told me that the bullet which had passed through my shoulder was 'a million to one shot', smashing nothing. Sometimes I am agape at the luck of it, and uneasy; have I justified my second chance? The Lord he knows; all I know is that I have enjoyed it, and am grateful.

It is strange what survives and what does not, objects as well as people; both can disappear, others stay with us as though glued. After I came out of hospital in Japan, we used to go, my friend and I (still a friend), to the American Officers' Club near our barracks. They were generous and hospitable, and it was there that an American wife gave my friend a book, which he, knowing my interest in poetry, passed on to me. Miraculously, I have it still: Louis Untermeyer's *Modern American Poetry/ Modern British Poetry*, first published 1919, this edition 1942, vast, but on thin paper, manageable. How in the world has that survived the movements of fifty years when so much else has not? I was looking at it the other day – nothing to do with anniversaries or Korea or Japan. I wanted to read Roy Campbell's 'Tristan da Cunha'. I must have had a complete Campbell once, but that has gone as Untermeyer has not, with his chunks of just about everybody, each with a biography and an appraisal.

From this side of the Atlantic, a reader can be forgiven for not having heard of some of the Americans – James Weldon Johnson, T.A. Daly, Paul Laurence Dunbar, but it may be ignorance, and Untermeyer's aim was to be inclusive. How could he be sure who would survive? One poet unknown to me even mentions him; Robert Hillyer, in his 'Letter to Robert Frost':

> Taste changes. Candid Louis Untermeyer
> Consigns his past editions to the fire;

His new anthology, refined and thrifty,
Builds up some poets and dismisses fifty.
And every poet spared, as is but human,
Remarks upon his critical acumen ...

Untermeyer's anthology, this nearly sole survivor from the first books I owned, could hardly be called 'thrifty'. If there were fifty left out for every one included, that number of versifiers would indeed be a depressing thought. Among the British names such as Gerald Gould, Theodore Maynard, Frank Kendon, even to a poetry addict, ring only sad and distant bells.

Louis MacNeice scrapes into this latest edition, rightly so. He wrote an 'Elegy for minor poets', 'who were too happy or sad, too soon or late / I would praise them in company with the Great':

Their ghosts are gagged, their books are library flotsam,
Some of their names – not all – we learned at school
But, life being short, we rarely read their poems
Mere source-books now to point or except a rule,
While those opinions that rank them high are based
On a wish to be different or on lack of taste.

Untermeyer gives us a chance to judge for ourselves and includes great wodges of people now unjustly near-forgotten as poets – Edwin Arlington Robinson, Edgar Lee Masters, Sylvia Townsend Warner. Did MacNeice think of himself as among 'the Greats'? Surely not, and he fudges his 'Elegy' by suggesting that the poets he means were not only minor but bad. Anyway, there is something disturbing about the word 'minor'. We cannot all be Miltons (or want to be); there are different instruments in the orchestra. MacNeice himself was 'minor' in this sense, but I can't believe it is my 'wish to be different or a lack of taste' that suggests his work will not become library flotsam but will survive. I read him at school and have been reading him ever since, despite the attempt of the brave Chinese soldier, dead instead of me, to put an end to all that (may he rest in peace).

*May 2001*

# Fragrant Fénelon

Fénelon, the late seventeenth-century French divine, always seems to get a press that makes him sound particularly attractive. Even the *Encyclopaedia Britannica* entry (1929), although written by somebody clearly unsympathetic to a man of his particular cloth, is reduced to praising him, admitting that around his political novel *Télémaque* 'there hangs a moral fragrance'. However, 'neither in his actions nor in his writings is there the least trace of that liberty of conscience ascribed to him by eighteenth-century philosophers.'

It would be surprising if there were, in a devout Catholic priest, and at that time. The Edict of Nantes, which promised toleration to the Huguenots, had just been revoked, Louis XIV was a bigot for orthodoxy, and the young Fénelon was put in charge of a mission to 'convert' the Protestants in the province of Poitou. From the first he set himself against violence: 'That,' he said, 'is not the true spirit of the Gospel... Compulsion never persuades, it only makes hypocrites. When kings interfere in matters of religion they don't protect it, they enslave it.' Brave words from a man appointed by *le Roi Soleil*. One of Fénelon's biographers, Charles Butler (1806) – whose book, it must be admitted, is near-hagiography – says of Fénelon: 'When he was presented to Louis XIV, the only request he made to the monarch was, that the troops, and every species of military parade, might be removed to a great distance from the province.' It says much for the famous persuasiveness of Fénelon, and also for Louis XIV, that the request was granted.

All this makes one sit up; here is a man in advance of his time, a man of good sense, and how different history would have been.

His educational methods are of interest because the King now put him in charge of his grandsons, the oldest of whom, the Duke of Burgundy, was, according to Saint-Simon, a six-year-old monster, 'born terrible, and during his first years, continued an object of terror'. Saint-Simon goes on at length about this wretched child: 'Often ferocious, naturally born to cruelty, barbarous in his raillery'; however, 'even in his passions talent beamed from him ... The prodigy is, that from the abyss I have described, there arrives a prince, affable, gentle, moderate, attentive to his duties, and sensible of their great extent.' It sounds a little like Shakespeare's Prince Hal, and how did Fénelon bring this change about?

His example might be useful, because there is much talk nowadays of how to help 'the socially excluded'. This royal child apparently felt himself excluded from normal social behaviour, therefore Fénelon (who did not want the job) was faced with the same sort of problem.

There is a dramatic scene in Butler's biography, between the Prince and Fénelon. How it can be known so precisely what passed between them is unclear, but life in Versailles was lived in public and Butler says that his account is taken from de Bausset, who 'seems to have access to all the papers of the family of Fénelon'. Anyway, it is a good story. 'On some occasion, Fénelon had expressed himself to the Duke, in a tone of great authority: the Duke was indignant; "Not so, Sir," he said to Fénelon, "I know who I am; and I know who you are."'His tutor, according to Butler, made no reply, gave his pupil 'a serious and sorrowful look', and withdrew.

> The following morning he entered the Duke's bed-chamber while he was asleep; ordered the curtains of his bed to be opened, and the Duke to be awakened; then, assuming a cool indifferent look, 'Sir,' he said, 'you yesterday told me you know who you were, and who I was. My duty obliges me to inform you, that you know neither. You imagine you are greater than I am; this, some valet has told you; but you oblige me to tell you that I am greater than you. Birth, here, is out of the question. You would pronounce a man mad, who should give himself a preference over his neighbour, because the dews of heaven had fertilised his field and not fallen on his neighbour's ... I have taught you everything you know; and what you know is nothing in comparison of what remains for me to teach you.'

There is more of the same; he tells the boy he never wanted to be his tutor, and would now take him before the King, and resign. This terrified the Duke, but their relations were only resumed after a long period of the Duke's good behaviour.

Fénelon was greatly helped by all the others round the Prince behaving as he did. When the Duke fell into a tantrum, everyone fell silent and looked at him as though he was mad. 'His books, everything used in the way of his instruction were removed from him, as useless to a person in his deplorable state.'

When Burgundy had calmed down, how did Fénelon instruct him? By taking a leaf out of the New Testament and using parables or, more precisely, fables, about shepherds enchanted by the sight of a happy young man – 'May the flowers grow under his feet!' About Melanthos: 'Last night, he went to rest, the delight of the human race; this morning, one's ashamed of him, one must hide him.' Delightful extended stories, some encouraging, some mirrors held up to the boy until, Butler says, he could not avoid look into them 'without sinking into the earth'. Fénelon had him until he was fifteen, and they became friends for the rest of the Prince's life. Fénelon was removed from his position (which was unpaid, and he would accept no favours from the King for himself or for his family) because he became suspected of Quietism, which the King regarded as a heresy, which it can be, but it is an almost infinitely subtle matter of emphasis. Fénelon defended himself publicly, the matter went to the Pope, who hesitated. Anglican Butler amuses himself about this endless delay, as he does earlier, about the inquiry into Jansenism. He wonders 'how an ill-written book, of an obscure Flemish prelate, containing five propositions on an unintelligible subject, was the origin of a dispute which continued for two centuries and convulsed both the Church and the state of France'. Quietism caused the same kind of confusion, and Fénelon retired to his bishopric at Cambrai where, says the *Britannica*, 'even Saint-Simon agreed his episcopal duties were perfectly performed'.

His *Letters to Men* and *Letters to Women* are both elegant and helpful, humble and clear. Although, of course, God-centred, they are filled with a modern consciousness of our talent for self-deception. Modern, also, in facing up, specifically, to the problem of depression. He sometimes almost congratulates the sufferer: 'Depend upon it, that comfortable vigour which makes everything easy, and congratulates itself on not knowing what hesitation and depression mean, is very treacherous … It feeds self-confidence and exaltation of heart … fostering an inward self-satisfaction and self-applause which is a most subtle poison.' *On Irresolution:* 'there is no argument so sensible as an honest confession of our own want of sense.' There *is* 'a moral fragrance' about Fénelon.

*May 2001*

# Thistles and *lignum vitae*

By the time this appears, the General Election will be over, it will nearly be midsummer, and I intend to celebrate things connected with the season. Enough has been said about the election, and what was remarkable was the abstract, non-specific nature of the talk. The season, by contrast, is always full of details. These may seem repetitive: same leaves, flowers arriving more or less on cue, but they never do so in quite the same way.

This year, for example, the bloom on hawthorn trees, the may, is creamy, maybe because of the wet winter. A few years ago, it was as thick and resplendent as it is now. There is a steep and boggy place nearby, undisturbed possibly for ever because of its inhospitable terrain, in which at this season, Whitsun, the hawthorn trees – and they have grown into trees, not bushes – were so densely flowered, so white-cushiony, some with delicate tinges of pink, so Samuel Palmerish, that they made you gasp. Impossible to know if they are like that this year because foot and mouth confines us to the lane above that field, and the footpaths are still closed. (A confinement not much referred to in the election, or so I had the impression.)

However, there is one field I can go into because I have responsibility for it. In late April and early May, it looked neat, satisfactorily green and smooth. Then grew untidy irregular clumps of a slightly different green, allowed by the sheep to grow longer than the grass: nettles, thistles, had arrived. 'Against the rubber tongue of cows and the hoeing hands of men / Thistles spike the summer air'; Ted Hughes announces such an arrival. Young green nettles are easy to deal with, they seem to collapse, sighing, at the sight of a scythe. True, they come back, but fewer, and weakened. Thistles are different. Cut, they flourish, as though grateful for the pruning. It is important that they do not seed:

> Mown down, it is a feud. Their sons appear,
> Stiff with weapons, fighting back over the same ground.

So it was, feeling chivalric, that I sallied forth with my own weapon, to do battle, a transistor radio in my pocket. (It is not a very entertaining feud, you have to provide your own entertainment.) It was good to be out of doors because there was a blessed light and a blue sky but also a cold breeze from the north, so that if you wanted to be out in that light you had to have a reason to keep moving, such as thistle-destruction.

It was no coincidence that the decision to tackle them was made on the Saturday of the second Test Match against Pakistan. The ball-by-ball cricket commentary is maddening to those not interested. If you listen to it through their ears, it is easy to understand why: a meaningless, juvenile chatter on a subject of no importance. I love it. So, behold him, single in the field, yon solitary midland loon, scything young thistles as close to the ground as he could, listening to the cricket commentary, but his conscience at ease because he thought he was also doing good to the field. Enjoying, also, the whitening litter of thistle-stalks, and the way the sheep with their lambs came tentatively to nibble the lush grass hitherto hidden under the spikes.

What was most striking about the commentary, after weeks of vague, unspecific political discussion, is its concrete, almost crazy, particularity. At last, here is detail; not just the pitch, the wind-direction, the bowler's grip, the position of the batsman's feet, but detail within detail – the white strip on the peak of Pakistani helmets; frayed? intentional? the commentators discussed that – until you begin to feel what is probably true, that nothing in the world matters, is of real interest, except precision, detail, in the face of the wholly unpredictable.

There is no end to it and it can lead anywhere. The previous day, for instance, the wind had been so strong the bails on the stumps kept blowing off. So, heavier bails were sent for. Or were they? (Further discussion.) By Saturday the emails were buzzing like wasps into the commentary box. Heavier bails? How heavy? Unfair because they might not be dislodged and a batsman would escape judgement? In what way heavy? It was long pondered whether they were ordinary bails with lead-shot inserted, or were made of a different wood. Of *lignum vitae* it was decided. 'Lignum *what?*' (There is an annoying, laddish convention among some of the commentators that they only know about cricket, that to reveal knowledge of anything else is to show off. No wonder some people are driven to distraction. Also, I learned later, friends who had switched on to learn the score were infuriated to hear nothing but a discussion about bails. You have to stay tuned and swim the whole distance.)

The scorer, Bill Frindall, Mr Stats in person, and allowed to be knowledgeable, came up with the information that *lignum vitae* is the only wood so dense it will not float. Wrong, came a telephone call, there are others. I missed what they were because I was whetting the scythe. That wood, emailed somebody else, was the foundation of the

Empire, it gave England command of the seas, because the cogs of the first instrument for measuring longitude were carved from it – and so on. The thistles were now lying down in greying rows, having, temporarily, given up the ghost.

But why 'wood of life'? A question fortunately not raised by anyone but me. I looked it up later, led by thistles and a cricket match to learn that '*guaiacum sanctum* or *lignum vitae* exudes a resin which, when boiled with salt, is useful both in acute and chronic sore throats, in chronic constipation and chronic gout and other forms of chronic arthritis'. The ingenuity (and attention to detail) of mankind never ceases to amaze. To make cogs out of the hardest wood available, which also lubricated themselves with these oils, is clever. To discover that pellets made from these oils can relieve some of man's greatest discomforts, the wood of life indeed, the 'holy' *guaiacum*, is staggering. Perhaps, because of its great hardness, it was invested with magical powers and investigations were made to see if it was magic in other ways. It was, and is, because apparently it is still used in pharmacology.

Meanwhile, a cricket match was continuing, which had its lulls but grew in excitement, and the thistles looked woebegone. More was to come from the commentators' box. Christopher Martin-Jenkins described a certain shot as being like a man scything thistles, meaning that a right-hander had hit the ball across his body to the left, or, in cricketing terms, to leg, as I was when scything. Wrong, came an email, that is not how to scythe. I pricked up my ears. What you must do is scythe to the off, to the right. A question of positioning your feet (and of attention to detail). I tried it this way, awkward at first, and the thistles were cropped close to the ground, beyond hope of resurrection – possibly.

*June 2001*

# Gurney and Sassoon

It is now midsummer, it is cold, and we are complaining, comparing this summer with other platonic summers we seem to remember. Not in 1792: 'Thunder and hail. A sad midsummer day' (Gilbert White). Nor 1779: 'Very cold indeed again today, so cold that Mrs Custance came walking in her spencer with a bosom-friend.' (James Wood-forde). Both quotations come from *The English Year*, edited by Geoffrey Grigson, and to the last one he adds a note: 'Mrs Custance, as a lady of fashion, would have worn her gown low cut; in the bosomy manner so often drawn by Rowlandson; in cold weather she would have needed the fashionable item of clothing known as the "bosom-friend".' He also tells us that Woodforde was a 'guzzling cleric as egocentric as Gilbert White was the reverse'. Unmistakable Grigson.

Nevertheless, it is cold, and we are disappointed: but hogweed has succeeded cow-parsley, there are pink wild roses in the hedges, and ash-tree boughs, now fully clothed, jiggle quickly back and forth, movement and countermovement, in the chill breeze. We think we are content and feel gratitude (that high virtue), although we hear unwillingly of fields poisoned which contained skylark fledglings, of cherry trees cut down in full flower to make way for a carpark (why cut in full flower?), and if a microphone were stuck under our noses we would be asked if we were 'angry and bitter' – always that curious formulation – and we might meekly agree because that is expected of us.

The question is as strange as the obedient response, because there isn't a spiritual/mystical tradition – or a medical one for that matter – which doesn't agree that anger and bitterness are bad for us. Indignation may be useful, if it leads to action. As for impotent 'anger and bitterness' – the field already poisoned, the cherry trees shredded and carted away – we know as soon as we feel them how bad for us they are. Maybe that is what Yeats meant when he said, referring to the poets of the Great War, that passive suffering is not a theme for poetry.

So, we think we feel content and gratitude and (speaking for myself) have reason to, because this is a fortunate time, for us. (To admit that is to risk 'You should be so lucky!' but let's say it for once, we know it is fragile.) Yet why, into the head of the thinker of this thought, sitting after breakfast in a sort of ash-tree bower looking across at farmland, does there enter a line of Ivor Gurney's remembered, or slightly misremembered, from one of his war poems – 'a farmer's treasure soon a wilderness'? Gurney means as a result of war, of an anger and bitterness possibly not felt by the destroyers but willed on them from afar. I looked up the poem, 'Riez Bailleul', and there is a 'perhaps' in the line; I had been trying to force it into a too regular rhythm – 'a farmer's treasure perhaps soon a wilderness'. That 'perhaps' is significant, suggestive of the *possible* destruction of contentment; of any 'treasure', fragility, uncertainty of continuance, is what we feel. Perhaps that is what we are meant to feel, I might say if this were a sermon.

Gurney was ambiguous about indignation: 'Fierce indignation is best understood by those / Who have time or no fear, or a hope in its real good' ('Sonnet – September 1922'). The other day I had to reread Siegfried Sassoon's famous 'The General', and it worried me. It was the only poem my second father-in-law could recite from, and frequently did.

> 'Good morning; good morning!' the General said
> When we met him last week on our way to the line.
> Now the soldiers he smiled at are most of them dead,
> And we're cursing his staff for incompetent swine.
> 'He's a cheery old card,' grunted Harry to Jack
> As they slogged up to Arras with rifle and pack.
> But he did for them both by his plan of attack.

It is indignation, it is justified, it very possibly did something to affect our attitude to war. It is epigrammatical and punchy – perhaps it is verse and not poetry, but let's not go into that – nevertheless, it seems to me, there is something wrong. It contains too much anger and bitterness, those terrible twins. We share his sympathy for Harry and Jack, but we feel more vividly his anger and contempt for the General and wonder if he, the writer, Captain Sassoon, would have made a better one. The 'plan of attack' was not disastrous on purpose, and it would be an unusual attack that did not 'do' for someone, which is why most of us are grateful not to be generals. There is another equally famous poem by Sassoon which is even worse in this respect, 'Base Details' – 'If I were fierce and bald and short of breath! ...' which tells us too clearly that Sassoon knew himself to be, so far, none of these things. Both poems, much anthologised, surely arouse the wrong sort of 'Ain't it awful!' indignation in the reader.

Ivor Gurney's 'Riez Bailleul' is not so famous, or not yet. It is not even his best poem. It does, however, contain a tenderness, a yearning, a memory of good, an absence of blame. In fact it could be said to be *above* blame, which is nearly always pointless anyway. It was written, or seems to have been written, after the War, and after his confinement in an asylum, 'to hide this pain and work myself free / From present things'. It is therefore courageous, because active not passive; heartbroken nevertheless. He wrote some of his best work after his confinement. He who still calls himself, elsewhere and towards the end of his writing life, 'the child of joy' knew too much about the fragility of joy, of any treasure.

The poem, and not at all incidentally, is a triumphant demonstration of the usefulness of rhyme for some poets. Gurney's determination to reach an end-of-line rhyme word, regardless of the length of line this sometimes required, because of his need to give the fluctuations of his thought some evident sonnet shape, creates not so much an irregularity, but a new and convincing music of his own.

> Behind the line there mending reserve posts, looking
> On the cabbage fields with other men carefully tending cooking;
> Hearing the boiling; and being sick of body and heart,
> Too sick for anything but hoping that all might depart –
> We back in England again, and white roads to walk on,
> Eastward to hill-steeps, or see meadows good to go talk on.
> Grey Flanders sky over all and a heaviness felt
> On the sense that no working or dreaming could any way melt…
> This is not happy thought, but a glimpse most strangely
> Forced from the past, to hide this pain and work myself free
> From present things. The parapet, the grey look-out, the making
> Of a peasantry, by dread war, harried and set on shaking;
> A hundred things of age, and of carefulness,
> Spoiling; a farmer's treasure perhaps soon a wilderness.

*July 2001*

# The Old Curiosity Shop – September 11

If Oscar Wilde did indeed say, of the death of Nell in *The Old Curiosity Shop*, 'a man would have to have a heart of stone not to laugh', etc, it must be his silliest attempt to shock. It is impossible to imagine any reader laughing. Yawning perhaps, if self-protectively sceptical, or clapping hands over ears to drown the noise of Dickens pulling out every stop on the console; but laughing, no. Dickens is so manifestly sincere, and within the heightened context of this extraordinary phantasmagorical book, of a wild imagination loosing itself to run entirely free, the final pathos rings true. It could be resisted, but why?

Perhaps I should give Wilde the benefit of the doubt (not having his *Collected Works* to hand). Interestingly, another wit to whom clevernesses not his own are sometimes attributed, G.K Chesterton, himself has some interesting things to say about Wilde, as well as about Dickens.

Chesterton admires Wilde the artist, but not Wilde the show-off, or, as he puts it, 'the charlatan'. He distinguishes 'the real epigram which he wrote to please his own wild intellect, and the sham epigram which he wrote to thrill the tamest part of our tame civilisation'. From *A Woman of No Importance* he quotes, 'Nothing survives being thought of', and says, 'That is nonsense, but nonsense of the nobler sort. "What is an immoral woman? The kind of woman a man never gets tired of." That is not nonsense, but rather rubbish.' He goes on, using his blue pencil, having fun, and he defines an uneasiness Wilde can create, even in an admirer. '"Life is much too important to be taken seriously"; that is the true humourist. "A well-tied tie is the first serious step in life"; that is the charlatan.' The essay on Wilde was printed in the *Daily News*, 1909 (collected, in 1953, in A *Handful of Authors.)* Dickens was co-founder and first editor of the *Daily News*, and Chesterton wrote a book about him.

Though an admirer of Dickens (in my private pantheon he is next to Shakespeare), I have no claims to being a Dickensian. So little am I qualified that, when I picked up *The Old Curiosity Shop* to reread it, I discovered I had never read it before, and it bowled me over. Chesterton even denies there is such a thing as a Dickens novel: 'They are simply lengths cut from the flowing and mixed substance called Dickens – a substance of which any given length will be certain to contain a proportion of brilliant and of bad stuff.' I'm not sure about that. Having just put down *The Old Curiosity Shop*, so complete is my state of bowled-overness that I can remember no bad stuff in it at all, certainly nothing I wanted to skip. Besides, Chesterton seems to contradict himself; if he says, surely rightly, that the novels are lengths cut off the substance that is Dickens, how can he say, disappointingly to one thunderstruck by it, that *The Old Curiosity Shop* is not as good as *David Copperfield*? Though he adds, savingly, 'but Swiveller is quite as good as Micawber'.

Ah, Dick Swiveller, layabout, tippler, spouter of ornate sub-literate poesies; perhaps it is his love of language that makes him lovable. The mysterious 'single gentleman' takes lodgings above the terrible office where Swiveller pretends to work. He goes to bed immediately, mid-aftenoon, and is not heard to stir for twenty-six hours. They think he may be dead; eventually they wake him, and he emerges furious. The startled Dick burbles, '"the short and long of it is, that we cannot allow single gentlemen to come into this establishment and sleep like double gentlemen without paying extra for it." "Indeed!" cried the lodger. "Yes, Sir, indeed," resumed Dick, yielding to his destiny and saying whatever came uppermost; "an equal quantity of slumber was never got out of one bed and bedstead, and if you're going to sleep in that way, you must pay for a double-bedded room."' Chesterton calls this 'perhaps the very best scene in the book'. Perhaps it is; there are others as good, and different (like the death of Nell). What Chesterton has no time to remark on, rushing as he is through the whole of Dickens's work, is the effect of this ridiculousness on the single gentleman, who beams, and invites Dick into his room for what Dick calls 'a modest quencher'. We thereby learn that the single gentleman is a connoisseur of the absurd, and so we like him, as we like Dick.

As Chesterton points out, there is absolutely no reason why the book should have the title it carries: 'Only two of the characters have anything to do with such a shop, and they leave it forever in the first few pages. It is as if Thackeray had called the whole novel of *Vanity Fair* 'Miss Pinkerton's Academy'. He goes on: 'Around '"Little Nell" of course, a controversy raged and rages; some implored Dickens not to kill her at the end of the story: some regret that he did not kill her at the beginning ... The beauty and divinity in a child lie in his not being worried, not being conscientious, not being like Little Nell.' True, but he might have added that what Dickens was risking is of the utmost artistic danger: he is attempting to describe genuine, unmixed *goodness*. He believed in it. Just as he believed in unmixed evil (Quilp). That this goodness is made to inhabit the body of a prepubescent girl is probably interesting but is not the point. It is possibly a pity, just as it is a pity that Quilp, the embodiment of vengeful evil, should have the body of a malignantly ugly dwarf. His readers were perhaps simple people, in some ways. In some ways perhaps, Dickens was a simple man. He was certainly in a hurry, he wanted to get on with the huge myth he was creating; realism, likelihood, thrown to the winds. It would be tempting to call this book his *Tempest*, except that it is mid canon; he does not drown his book, but his future ones are less unbridled.

Nell and her grandfather wander out of London on foot, Dickens conveniently forgetting how young she is – it is that sort of book – and encounter Punch-and-Judy men in, of course, a graveyard; Punch is propped on a gravestone. They travel with a waxworks, then with drunken bargees; weirdest touch of all, they enter the Industrial Revolution at its most horrible, and sleep on ashes, sheltered by a man who spends his life alone staring into an industrial furnace. In a book such as this, you really cannot complain at the unlikelihood of Little Nell. She finishes up in, of all places, the ruins of a monastery, surrounded by 'monkish stalls'. It is a vast and terrible vision of evil and injustice, shot through with bright gleams of good. A world of such imaginative scope and inclusiveness, it is large enough to contain the cataclysmic news, this moment arrived, of aeroplanes purposely crashing into New York. The vengeful Quilp would be gleefully rolling about. Quilps exist, and Dickens knew it.

*September 2001*

# Prophecies and Terror

Some books, picked up more or less at random, can lead in surprising directions. *Prophets of Palestine: The local background to the Old Testament Prophets* (1962) was a title mildly intriguing. Could anyone know enough about those mysterious men to be able to give them a 'local background'? A random dip suggested that Eric F.F. Bishop could, with justification, talk of Isaiah going for a walk in Jerusalem with his son, because Isaiah says so, ordered by Jehovah. 'Go out with your son Shear-Jashub, and meet Ahaz at the end of the conduit of the upper pool on the road to the Fuller's Field …' (Isaiah 7:3). 'It was doubtless a familiar walk with the prophet,' says Bishop, 'all unknowing of the joy to be occasioned to archaeologists in the nineteenth century AD in discovering the veracity of his remarks' (the 'upper pool' uncovered). 'Isaiah sauntered about the district… with his eyes open: "The daughter of Zion is left like a shanty in a vineyard, like a shed in a cucumber field" (1:8).' Still to be seen, says Bishop, happily, 'even as the motor car is driven along the highway. They are places to stay in during the harvest, deserted and neglected when the harvest is done.'

Bishop's aim was to give locality to the universal, and thereby make it more universal, rather than less, which is not nearly the paradox it sounds. The Irish poet Patrick Kavanagh in his little poem 'Epic' released a whole generation of poets when, fed up with the pettiness of a farmers' quarrel 'over half a rood of rock … Till Homer's ghost came whispering to my mind / He said: I made the *Iliad* from such / A local row. Gods make their own importance.'

Bishop's book was borne home, where it lay for a while on a table. Once picked up again, there was even surprise among the acknowledgements: thanks are given 'to the Reverend Sir Reginald Champion (an erstwhile District Commissioner for Galilee) for labours in proofreading'. In Galilee, where we were three years ago, the thought of a British District Commissioner would have seemed almost as distant in time as Isaiah. Mr Bishop, in short, was one of a band of people, between the wars, with a passion for Palestine in general, and Jerusalem in particular, whose mission it was, not to show that the three religions of the region were the same, but how much they had in common: after all, the Jewish scriptures are not only quoted in the New Testament but in the Qur'an (as he spells it).

Bishop is an Arabist, more than twenty years in Palestine, who knows whereof he speaks, and disconcerting some of it is: 'Dūlāb' (Persian 'water-wheel') means 'cupboard' in Gaza, but in Jerusalem 'bicycle'; in the colloquial version of Mark, 'shakhtūrà' means 'boat', but in Jerusalem it means 'stomach'.

The confusion, if that is what it is, extends to personages. The Crusaders conflated the great Elijah with their patron St George, 'but Elijah is also *al khidr* (The Green Man) in Islamic hagiology. This man belongs to everybody.' His point is that Palestine, the Holy Land, belongs to everybody, imaginatively. Whereas we, the West, have distanced the Holy Land from ourselves by making it quaint, foreign, and thereby run the risk of underestimating the transcendent quality of all three religions. 'In the Lukan version the Incarnation receives no enhancement when a congregation is told that Jesus was born in a "dirty" or "filthy" stable. Does not exegesis of this nature tend to suppress the Palestinian background of the Bible?' There is no need for a crib to be 'filthy'; one of his friends used to put his own child to sleep in a donkey's crib.

His insistence on the 'international' (the supranational) nature of Palestine exists on the secular level as well. Judah Magnes, first President of the then proudly new Hebrew University in Jerusalem, used to take his guests on the roof to look at the Mount of Olives, a watershed, 'the flora on the eastern slope predominantly *Asiatica* and towards the Holy City *Africana*'. And on the eastern slope lived the prophet Jeremiah, 'an afternoon's walk from Jerusalem'. 'Gethsemane', on the Mount, means 'winepress'. Always the familiar, the homely, in sites where things have happened, believe them or not, which have shaped our world.

Today, events in these places, and their repercussions, seem about to tear our world to bits. It has been bubbling and frothing in that place for millennia – when it was not being flattened. In 1919, Arthur Balfour wrote a Memorandum stating that the Four Powers were committed to Zionism, adding, with what Karen Armstrong calls 'astonishing insouciance', 'the Powers had made no statement that is not admittedly wrong, and no declaration of policy which, at least in the letter, they have not always intended to violate.' In other words, there *was* no solution to the Jew/Arab problem. After 1919, various things happen, until 'both Jew and Arab believe Britain is favouring the other side'. It is all set out in Armstrong's *History of Jerusalem* (1997). The Zionists 'showed a canny instinct. Whenever they were offered something by the Great Powers they accepted it ... the Arabs continually said no when offered anything at all.' Did not that happen again almost the other day? – bringing about a new Israeli Prime Minister, bloodshed, September 11, anthrax and (today) threats of smallpox, bottles of the virus in impoverished Siberia.

Bishop tells of an Australian General in 1946 who, seeing an inscription in Jerusalem, 'Peace upon Israel', suggested that it should be 'Peace upon the world'. 'The answer was,' says Bishop, 'that the two were intimately related; the latter could not come to pass without the former. As in Ezekiel, Jerusalem remained the centre of the world – not just geographically.' (Gods make their own importance.)

Bishop talks of Gog, in Ezekiel, the spirit of destruction. Jehovah is disgusted with man, with us. He whispers in Gog's ear to go and destroy 'those living secure, these stockbreeders and traders living at the Navel of the World' (Ezekiel 38:12). He will then destroy Gog, to such an extent it will take seven months to bury all the dead: the exiles will return from Babylon: a fresh start. Before that, the birds of the air 'will drink the blood of the princes of the world'. The field-fares and redwings have just arrived here, excited, from Greenland and elsewhere; they eat the berries in the hedges. This is a jumpy time, and one watches their voracious flutterings with a thoughtful eye.

*November 2001*

# Augustine and the Demonic

Writers, when writing fiction, sometimes find that what is happening around them, even the most trivial, is more alive, because more imme-diate, than what they are inventing. (By the time their characters are, say, caught in a blizzard, it is midsummer, and the curtains have to be drawn so they can try to remember the texture of snow.) In fact this is true of all writing, and an example happened recently which I was too inhibited to confess.

I had been re-reading Peter Brown's very good biography of St Augustine; his description of Augustine's preoccupation with demons, and his determination to expunge worship of them. Says Brown: 'in late Roman popular belief, the methods of demons were extremely crude: they would simply take on human shape to start a plague or a riot. With Augustine, by contrast, the nexus between men and demons was purely psychological. Like was drawn to like. Men got the demons they deserved…'

Now, by a perversion of religion (all such perversions Augustine was labouring to refute) a perfect bomb has been discovered, in the form of a large aeroplane flown by a man who believes his martyrdom worthy. I therefore decided to write about demons, or at least mention them in the context of St Augustine, because perversions of religion can become demonic, which is Augustine's point, or part of it.

I went to my room to do this, sat down at my old-fashioned type-writer, tapped away and was surprised to find that the page remained blank. Tapped again: still nothing. Peering into the machine I was dismayed to see the whole ribbon had been unspooled, part of it lying in folds, some of the rest entwined, even knotted, around the mechanism. Goblin's work: but I wondered very briefly what *human* malice could be involved. Nonsense, this was clearly the work of a mouse.

However, as I grimly tidied up the mess, I had to acknowledge two facts: I had been using that room and that typewriter for twenty-five years, and nothing like it had happened before; also, I had never before decided to mention demons.

How had the mouse got into the room, never mind into the covered typewriter? It would have to be a field mouse, the room is next to a field. Pretty creatures with long tails, delicate features and erect semi-transparent ears that glow pink when the light is behind them. Augustine would surely have liked such creatures, because what makes him so encouraging a companion is his entire certainty of the goodness of the created world.

Nevertheless the mouse had to go. There used to be things called Humane Mousetraps which caught mice without hurting them. I used one ages ago when a fieldmouse in summer walked through the open door, inspected me, and scuttled under a cupboard. It took the bait eventually, I let it out into the field and it bounded away in huge leaps like a miniature deer. That trap is lost, and I think they have been withdrawn, for humane reasons: people forgot to check them and the captive slowly starved.

So I shut the cat in the room and went away, requiring him to earn his keep. As far as I could judge he settled himself in my chair and went to sleep. Perhaps he did more. The new typewriter ribbon is still in place, though the machine is now absurdly wrapped in a blanket.

Augustine might have forgiven this digression, he was fond of them himself, and certainly would not have objected to the introduction of the cat, as much a part of Creation as the mouse. He quotes Genesis: '"And God saw everything he had made, and, behold, it was very good." Was it not meant to be understood that there was no other cause of the world's creation than that good creatures should be made by a good God?' Does such a quotation make Augustine sound cosy? He is never that, but his endless speculation is always warm. Warm, perhaps, until it leads him to a theory of the 'elect', but of this I can't talk because I haven't read it yet.

Nor do I apologise for this apparent evasion because Augustine often ducks away himself. He wonders if the three great questions about Creation – Who made it? By what means? Why? – are an early hint of the Trinity; but he pulls himself up, almost with a snort: 'This,

I say, is questionable, and one can't be expected to explain everything in one volume.' That is in Book Ten of *City of God*. In Book Twelve he returns to what is almost his obsession, the nature of time. He worries about the exact moment of the creation of angels. 'Let there be light' is his suggestion, and after many unboring pages on the subject it seems that at last he shrugs: 'I return therefore, to that which our Creator has seen fit that we know; and those things which he has allowed abler men to know in this life, or has reserved to be known in the next by the perfected saints, I acknowledge to be beyond my capacity.' He reckons God has given us hints enough in his Scriptures: 'For if an infant receive nourishment suited to its strength, it becomes capable; but if its strength and capacity be over-taxed, it dwines away instead of growing.' ('Dwine' is Scots for 'dwindle'. My Victorian translation was published in Edinburgh.)

I had thought this edition complete, but it ends at Book Thirteen and there are nine more books to go. He trails Book Fourteen, which is to be about Adam and Eve, at what point they lost their sexual innocence – the question of time once again. If this sounds too much like counting the angels on a pin, it has to be said that religion requires as much precision as possible, or it dissolves into the subjective, or, misinterpreted, hardens into ferocity. What Augustine is trying to do, therefore, is of the greatest importance. I look forward to the next nine books because he is good company. He asks serious questions and answers them with humility. 'Never was thought so abstract expressed in terms so popular,' says his translator, Marcus Dods. 'He handles metaphysical problems with the unembarrassed ease of Plato.' I don't pretend I always understand him, and sometimes I skip (especially when he gets on to the theory of numbers) but, it may sound glib but feels accurate, he gives me a sense of being released from the Humanist Mousetrap, and though I don't go bounding away, a miniature deer, like that field mouse long ago, I am happy trotting in his wake, panting.

*January 2002*

# Augustine and Billy Collins

There are times when almost everything we read or hear has a bearing on our immediate preoccupation. This week, for me, it has been a piece in the *Tablet*, a poem in the latest *Paris Review*, and St Augustine's *City of God*.

In the Christmas edition of the *Tablet* there is an article by William Dalrymple which deserves wide circulation at this time. As a young man, when he climbed the steps of the great mosque at Fatehpur Sikri, built by the sixteenth-century Mugal Emperor Akbar, Dalrymple was startled to be told by his guide book that the strip of Persian calligraphy framing its arch read:

> Jesus, son of Mary (on whom be peace) said: 'The World is a bridge, pass over it but build no houses on it. He who hopes for a day, may hope for eternity, but the world endures but an hour. Spend it in prayer, for the rest is unseen.'

Obviously puzzled to find an explicitly Christian reference at the entrance to one of the greatest pieces of Islamic architecture (what Jesus is quoted as saying is unfamiliar, but the sort of thing he could have said), Dalrymple has discovered since, during his travels in the East, that it is 'one of the several hundred sayings and stories of Jesus that fill Arabic and Islamic literature'. That Islam, like Arianism, has profound respect for Jesus as a divinely inspired prophet, while denying his divinity, we might already know; but that St John of Damascus (d. 749), brought up in the Islamic court of Damascus, first chronicler of Islam, did not regard Islam as a new religion at all, but a divergence from a Christian root, is, as Dalrymple says, 'intriguing'. At a time when small parts of Islam (secretly spread, alarmingly all over the world), are vowed to destroy the 'infidel' West, and the Western world is naturally and grimly determined to hunt down those hostile to it, his account of our apparent kinship needs to be highlighted.

We in the West are told we face a series of possible calamities. Well calamities do occur. After more than 1,100 years of steady and triumphant progress, in AD 410 Rome was taken and sacked. St Jerome set up a howl: 'A terrible rumour reaches me from the West, telling of Rome besieged, bought for gold, besieged again, life and property perishing together. My voice falters, sobs stifle the words I dictate; for she is a captive, that city which enthralled the world.' Many at the time thought that this was indeed the end of the world. St Augustine's reaction was less hysterical. Three years after the sack of Rome, he sat down to write *City of God*, and it took him thirteen years. He was fifty-nine when he began it, and seventy-two by the time it was completed.

It is, at first sight, a strange work. The initial ten books, at least, seek to point out the absurdity of the worship of demons. The editor and part-translator (1878), the Revd Marcus Dods, is frank about this strangeness: 'It is true we are sometimes wearied by the too elaborate refutation of opinions which to a modern mind seem self-evident absurdities … Some who have read the opening chapters of the *City of God* may have considered it would be a waste of time to proceed; but no one, we are persuaded, ever regretted reading it all.' He is right there; it grows on you, because Augustine is clear, sincere and intelligent.

The history of the book is fascinating: at first it seems to have had very little influence, but, says Dods, 'between 1467 and the end of the fifteeenth century, no fewer than twenty editions were called for; that is to say, a fresh edition every eighteen months'. Erasmus was a great admirer. However,

> Of English translations there has been an unaccountable poverty. Only one exists (published 1610) and this so exceptionally bad, so inaccurate, and so frequently unintelligible, that it is not impossible it may have done something towards giving the English public a distaste for the book itself.

If his is indeed the first translation since 1610, we owe Dods a debt, because it is elegant and easy to read. There is also something about the public courtesy of Victorian scholars that is attractive. One last bit of Dods, concluding his introduction: 'That the present translation might also be improved, we know; that many men were fitter for the task, on the score of scholarship, we are very sensible; but that anyone would have executed it with intenser affection and veneration for the author, we are not prepared to admit.' That last is clearly heartfelt, and, when you read the translation, you know it to be true.

One reason Augustine felt impelled to write his great work was that the rejection of polytheism by Christianity had been blamed for the fall of Rome, deprived of its deities and their intercessionary demons, which inhabited the air between men and gods. Perhaps Augustine himself believed in demons; Peter Brown in his biography of Augustine asserts that he did. He certainly did not believe in worshipping or propitiating them, and was concerned to replace them with angels (who were also not to be worshipped, but were not demonic). His book grows wider and deeper as it progresses, as it was bound to over thirteen years; Plato and the Neoplatonists are gone into carefully and respectfully, and Augustine's original conviction grows even stronger and firmer, that 'there is the City of God, and the city of the world'. Rome had fallen, his diocese and his African town Hippo were besieged, but, as Dalrymple read above the arch of the mosque, 'The World is a Bridge, pass over it but build no houses on it …'. Augustine's practical confidence in God's love and in another world did much to restore a balance in this one.

And the *Paris Review*? The American poet Billy Collins, just appointed Poet Laureate by the Library of Congress, is interviewed in it, and sounds humorous and agreeable. That only one poem of his is printed in the *Review is* a pity, but Augustine would have been interested. Too long to quote in full, eight four-line stanzas, it is set in Paris and concerns a sudden sense that the café is a play within a play, even within a third play and a fourth; to the writer sipping a Pernod, there seems 'a realm beyond cafés and rhododendrons … nothing but space':

> and maybe a few mythological creatures
> flying around in all this timelessness
> showing off their harsh, ferocious powers,
> dark wings spread, and their sharp teeth flashing.

Maybe, 1,600 years after Augustine, we still believe in demons, these days.

*January 2002*

# Lambs and Celandines

This time last year there were golden bandages across the lanes; hay, soaked in disinfectant. There was also a great silence; no ploughing, because seagulls might arrive and bring the disease with them, no movement of beasts, not even from one field to another; there was even a kind of silence in the pubs, low-toned mutterings from unlikely people about their own selfishness and greed, about supermarket pressures on farmers, all of which would have to change once the disease was over. Every week, the Foot and Mouth warning notices crept further up our hill, closer. There was a sort of horror in the air. As it happened, the disease never reached us, and whether anything subsequently has changed is difficult to know, local farmers not being unduly communicative. Also, whenever that terrible time is mentioned in newspapers, it is usually a political bickering about who took, or did not take, the right decisions. One undoubted side effect of the plague was the shadow it threw over last year's spring. If there were lambs in the field, we only peered out anxiously each morning, in case men from the Ministry had come and taken them away. This makes the clarity, beauty and speed of this year's spring even more dramatic.

Lively Peter Reading, a moralising Thersites, might not agree that this should be mentioned. He has made himself a brilliant poet of 'grot', and even invokes the stuff – 'Muse! sing the grotty [scant altern-ative]'. No point arguing: he has struck a rich vein. Most people live in towns, so that '… Nature / itself' is as 'anachronistic today / as a poem about it'. So, 'Phoney-rustic bards, / spare us your thoughts about birds …'. Well, out in the field this morning there was a single thrush, the first round here for years. I had no 'thoughts' about it, but some feelings: pleasure, disappointment there was no mate, and it was oddly small. As for the last one seen round here, who can compute? No one is going to say, 'That's my last thrush' and note the date. It was a long time before I noticed that Lyons Corner Houses in London had melted away like snow. 'Bumpkins, from whose bums / you consider the sun shines, / think you're townee twits.' Probably, but there are bumpkins here who would have remarked on that thrush. Thrushes have been missed.

Nevertheless, it does make the heart sink to have to mention celandines. They have been done to death. Wordsworth has no less than three poems about them; gnarled and sinewy campaigner that he was, he is defiant: 'I will sing, as doth behove, / Hymns in praise of what I love!' They are a small ground-hugging flower that could be mistaken for a buttercup, and were yesterday so mistaken by a visiting townee. Buttercups flower later, celandines are not so tall, are almost hidden in the grass, and are not cup-like. This year they are everywhere, in such abundance that when the sun shines and their flowers open the field outside my window looks as though covered with Advocaat-coloured confetti. Wordsworth (in 'To The Small Celandine') warns, almost Reading-like, against poets, who follow fashion, who don't notice anything so humble, and are therefore ... 'Wanton Wooers / But the thrifty cottager, / Who stirs little out of doors, / Joys to spy thee near her home, / Spring is coming, Thou art come!'

Celandines do raise the spirits, opening in the light, and that sunlight is also the point, because for the last week the sun has shone. Spring, even without the distraction of Foot and Mouth, can take place under wraps, dark, cold and you've missed it. This year it has happened in broad sunlight, under cloudless skies – though latterly with an East wind that makes your eyes water. You can watch it uncoil.

Lambs too are a tricky subject, on every calendar, difficult to make fresh, but fresh they are, and so white they make their mothers, hitherto white enough, look grey. For the first week they lie by their mothers, emphasising this contrast, or they totter a bit. After a few days they begin to play – impossible not to anthropomorphise – they play like children, play tag, chasing each other, or the daring ones do, others stay by their mothers, don't join the gang. They run, stop, then run again, doing vertical takeoffs, twisting their bodies in mid-air, for the sheer joy of it. Why else? They're not catching flies. When Henry Moore built a glass extension to his studio, sheep came right up to it and he became fascinated by the slight difference in their characters, began to draw them.

Talking of character (and genetics), about a dozen years ago one of them took to jumping our wall, built long before by a shepherd wise in the ways of sheep, but not of this one. Its fleece was so long you could not tell its sex, but because of its unblinking gunman's gaze we called it Clint. Now, another has taken to jumping in, and remaining, with a dowager-like imperiousness, so we call her Madam. Her owner, nervous for our garden, confessed that Clint was her grandmother. (If that strain ever triumphed, sheep walls all over the world would have to be raised two feet.) She once trained a ram to jump with her. He went on jumping further walls and ended up fields away, bewildered, whereas she was called back to her own field by her lamb, by reality.

The major glory of this spring has been the sloe, the blackthorn. So called, for those who cannot tell their celandines from their butter-cups – and why should they? Wordsworth says it took him thirty years to recognise and name that little flower – 'blackthorn' because the flowers appear before the leaves, are on the black thorny twigs. This year these flowers are unusually luxurious, flames of white among the bare, still-leafless hawthorns. In the hedge three have been allowed to grow unchecked, maybe twenty-five feet of snowy drifts. On the other side of the lane they have been cut waist-high, so as not to shadow the wheat. Even there, they have put out a white, flat cushion of flowers. 'Hymns in praise of what I love' seems only meet and just, even if others have sung them before. Besides, the blackthorn flowers only last a few days, turn brown. You have to keep on your toes round here.

*April 2002*

# Czeslaw Miłosz

Keep us ignorant for centuries,
generations, decades, we'll start getting born
stupid, the murder-machine
works: young rebels
don't even know how to rebel …

These lines, from 'Spain '67' by Pearse Hutchinson, were written in Barcelona, under Franco, and it was in Barcelona in the early 1960s that Hutchinson put into my hands Czeslaw Miłosz's *The Captive Mind*: a book which concerns itself, precisely, with such an attempt. Yet Miłosz has been partly misunderstood. As a survivor of the Nazi invasion of Lithuania, of the Stalinisation of Poland, he is not merely an 'anti-Communist' writer. Some writers suffer this journalistic reduction.

For example, in the interviews that filled the Irish airwaves in celebration of the recent publication of Hutchinson's *Collected Poems*, the
questions were almost wholly directed at the political, historical
content of his work; this is the despair of poets. Hutchinson could be
as well described, or better, as a love poet, or as one who celebrates
sudden enlightening glimpses, afforded by a face, a tune, or the reflection of light on water. Miłosz is misused in the same way. Born in
Lithuania in 1911, as late as 1988 he is forced again to protest: he has
been congratulated by a critic for his 'witness' to the post-war barbar-
ities inflicted on the Baltic countries. He will have none of it.

> We, natives of hazy Eastern regions, perceive History as a curse
> and prefer to restore to literature its autonomy, dignity and inde-
> pendence from social pressures ... The voice of a poet should be
> purer and more distinct than the noise (or confused music) of
> History.

'Confused music' is interesting. Caught as a young man in Poland,
in the claws of 'dialectical materialism', 'historical necessity' and 'the
class struggle', aware there is some sense in the last, but not enough,
Miłosz nevertheless struggles against the near-impossibility 'of
communicating to people who have no experience of it the indefin-
able menace of total rationalism'. Art is not rational in that sense,
which is the point.

For Westerners to try to imagine what it is like to be Miłosz (and
millions of others) becomes more clearly an impertinence when they
read his description of the various fates that befell the town where he
went to school and university. Vilna, Wilno, Vilinus – even the name
fluctuates with its 'history' –

> has, in the last half-century belonged to various countries and seen
> various armies in its streets. With each change painters were put to
> work repainting street and office signs into the new official
> language ... The city was ruled in turn by the Russians, the
> Germans, Lithuanians, Poles, again the Lithuanians, again the
> Germans, again the Russians.

How does one accommodate to these different ideologies, at least
two of them 'murder-machines'? (In Stalinist Poland, Miłosz partly
owed his survival to what was called his 'feudal' background; fairly
distant forebears had been small landowners which saved him from
the fatal category 'bourgeois'. This would be comic if the stakes were
not so high.)

In his analysis of the various types of dissimulation necessary under an intelligently heartless régime in pursuit of a Greater Good, the end of the exploitation of man – 'it is better to chop human trees down blindly than to wonder which among them is really rotten' – Miłosz is exhaustive and brilliant. For some, deceit (and self-deception) becomes almost a delight: 'For most people the necessity of living in constant tension and watchfulness is a torture, but many intellectuals accept this necessity with masochistic pleasure.'

It is here, in 1953, that Miłosz touches one of our most pressing concerns in 2002. How do you gain information from one whose faith not only permits but commands him to lie? It is the problem that agitated the Elizabethan Reformers – and the word 'Jesuitical' entered the language. It exercised Charles Kingsley, who accused John Henry Newman along the same lines. Miłosz finds a parallel in Gobineau's *Religions and Philosophies of Central Asia*, though he finds Gobineau 'rather a dangerous writer'. Gobineau calls the practice of the devout lie 'Ketman'. 'The people of the Mussulman East believe that he who is in possession of truth' must not expose himself to the perversity of those in error. However, if his silence can be interpreted as avowal, 'he must not hesitate. Not only must he deny his true opinion but he is commanded to use all ruses ... it is a dangerous beast you disarm. What a wealth of pleasures!' Miłosz, via Gobineau, is, of course, not attacking Islam – indeed, such devotion to the Divine is attractive. He is talking about an equivalent but secular devotion to the Politburo, to Stalin. Nevertheless, it does suggest the difficulty of gaining information from fundamentalist believers whom we do not understand, ones the West is at present clumsily interrogating.

In the 1950s, Miłosz nearly despaired of himself and his like being understood by the materialist West. Now he lives and teaches in America. His refuge, or rather his solution, was in art, 'its autonomy, dignity and independence'. Even as a youthful Marxist, hating the Nationalist Right, he felt ill at ease with his friends and fellow revolutionaries: 'What was I, with my liking for St Augustine, doing here?' To this day, he is chided for traces of Christianity in his writing, which are called, by one admirer, 'errors in logic'. However, a doubting poem is quoted in mitigation:

> With almost goodwill but not quite
> We plod on with hope. And now let everyone
> Confess to himself. 'Has he risen?' 'I don't know'.

But, as Miłosz knows, no one can know; and as Hutchinson says, 'If granted another hundred years, / I might learn / how to say prayers.'

Caution is desirable. It could be called humility.

The epigraph to *The Captive Mind* claims to be a saying 'Of an old Jew of Galicia':

> When someone is 55 per cent right, that's very good and there's no use wrangling. And if someone is 60 per cent right, it's wonderful, it's great luck, and let him thank God. But what's to be said about 75 per cent right? Wise people say this is suspicious. Well, and what about 100 per cent right? Whoever says he's a 100 per cent right is a fanatic, a thug, and the worst kind of rascal.

*March 2002*

# Index

*A Glastonbury Romance*, 8–9

Abercrombie, Lascelles, in *Georgian Poets 1920–22*, 27

Aberystwyth, seaside fashion; National Library; starlings, 189–91

Ackerley, J.R., quoted by E.M. Forster, 51

'Æ', *see* Russell

Air-conditioning, effects of, 83

Akhmatova, Anna, 4

Alexander, Cecil Frances, hymn-writer; 'Burial of Moses', 182

Alexander, William, Church of Ireland Primate; brief meeting with Mark Twain, 181–2

Allingham, William, Turgenev on *Laurence Bloomfield*; *Letters*; *Diary* (ed. Grigson), conversations with Tennyson, 82, 160–1; Darwin, Carlyle, Emerson, 160–1

America, CNN war news (1990), 60–2; upstate New York 61–2; sport in, 97–8

Alvarez, A., 167

Amichai, Yehuda, 156

Andrewes, Lancelot, 'A cold coming…' and Eliot; on public worship, 159–61

Angels, guardian; in paintings; Montaigne's view of; in Angers tapestry, 127–9

Angers, tapestry of Apocalypse, 128–9

Anti-Papist prejudice, Oxford conversation, 16; O'Faoláin on, 65; Charles Kingsley's, 112; at Godstow, 135; in C19 Ireland, 182; in Northern Ireland, 65, 185

Aphorisms, bullying nature of, 37

Argentina, Buenos Aires; W.H.Hudson's youth in; birds on the pampa, 138–40, 142–3

Armstrong, Karen, *History of Jerusalem*, 219

Arnold, Matthew, 86

Arts Centres, perils of, 6

Ashbery, John, sleep-inducing difficulty of; James Fenton on; Marjorie Perloff on, 39–40

Auden, W.H., on language, 51; on starlings, Hopkins-style, 151

Augustine, St, Peter Brown biography, 220; *Confessions*; on distractions, 120–1, 162; on martyrs, 121; Belloc quoting, 144; on time, T.S.Eliot possibly borrowing from, 159; on memory; on desire for happiness; on truth, 162–4; and Neoplatonists, 164, 225; preoccupation with demons, 220, 224–5; on goodness of creation; on creation of angels; Marcus Dods, translator and editor of, 221–2, 224; writing *City of God*; admired by Erasmus; Christianity and the fall of Rome, 224–5; Miłosz and, 230

Australia, Anzac day in Melbourne; Tasmania greeted, 21; genealogy frenzy; 'New Australians'; Australian beer, 22; the 'Australian pause', 25; Irish in, 35; literature, 88; *see also* Tasmania.

Awdry, Rev.W., 126

Bacon, Francis, 87

Bali, religiousness in, 63

Ballyjamesduff (Cavan), and Percy

French, 184

Barker, George, contrasted Roy Fuller, 71–4; quoting Loyola, 73

Bate, Walter Jackson, *Samuel Johnson*, 176–7

BBC, golf commentary, 31; MacNeice in; Radio Features Dept., 100

Beaconsfield, G.K. Chesterton's church; G.K.C.'s grave, 136–7

Beardsley, Aubrey, Yeats on, 41

Belloc, Hilaire, *The Path to Rome*, 144–5

Bellow, Saul, *Herzog*, 86; *Ravelstein*; quoting Schiller; on the soul; on the dead, 170–2

Benedictines, on pilgrimage, 154–6

Bennett, Alan, on writing about himself, 170

Bergonzi, Bernard, *War Poets and Other Subjects*, 173, 175

Berryman, John, at Spoleto (1967), 44

Birds, greenfinches, 3, 28; racing pigeons, 3; goldfinches; bird variations, 28; Melodious Warbler; *Hamlyn Guide*; in August, 34; fieldfares, starlings, pigeons, 78; death of sparrowhawk, 79; linnets, 92; blackbirds, finches, 96; odd behaviour of blackbird,108–9; dead gull, 120; in Argentina; kiskadee (*bienteveo*); W.H.Hudson and, 139–40, 142–3; modest English birds, 143; starlings and rooks in January, 149; in Uruguay; parakeets nesting; 164–5; in Chile; brown pelicans, 166; ill-fated blackbird and hawk, 179–80; Brent geese at Strangford Lough, 185–6; starlings at Aberystwyth, 190; arrival of fieldfares and redwings, 220; a single thrush, 226

Bishop, Eric F.F., *Prophets of*

*Palestine: the local background...*; Isaiah's 'familiar walk', 217–19

Bizet, *The Pearl Fishers*, 115

Blackthorn, 228

Blake, William, visions and imagination, 86; 129

Böll, Heinrich, on folklore, 126

Bonhoeffer, Dietrich, biography by Eberhard Bethge; letters from prison, 186–8

Botticelli, illustrating Dante, 201

Boucher, paintings in Wallace collection, influence of 181, 183

Brown, Peter, biographer of Augustine, 120, 220

Browning, Robert, Tennyson on, 72

Bryony, 76–7, 151

Buddhism, in Dublin, and Catholicism, 151–4

Buenos Aires (1998–2000), trees, birds in; Hudson's birthplace; artists in, 138–40; beggars in; Recoleta church, 166–7

Bunbeg (Donegal), new church in, 131

Bus, pleasures of, 95

Butler, Samuel (author of *Erewhon*), notebook, 18

Butor, Michel, editor of Montaigne, 128

Butterflies, 108, 110; in Italy, 146

Carlyle, Thomas, and Allingham 134, 160

Carroll, Lewis, on believing impossible things, 21

Celandines, 226–7

Chaucer, Geoffrey, a 'consolation', 87

Cheltenham, literature festival, 157

Chesterfield, Lord, quoted by Sisson, 15

Chesterton, G.K., on Holbrook Jackson, 38; suggesting place-bylines, 58; in Beaconsfield, his church, his grave; Frances (his wife); Dorothy Collins (his secretary); *A Short History of England*; on choosing statue of Virgin, 136–7; on Belloc, 144; on Wilde; on Dickens; on Little Nell, 215–16

Chile, Neruda's houses, Santiago, Valparaiso, Isla Negra, 165; Neruda on; Ortega y Gasset on; ghetto estates 165–6

Christian, R.F., translator of Tolstoy, 194–5

Christianity, danger of words, 47; and 'disturbing', 87; and confrontation, 102; guardian angels, 127; post-reformation antagonism; portrayal in media; Chesterton and, 136–7; Belloc and, 144–5; Thomas Merton and, 149–51; President McAleese to Dublin Buddhists, 151–4; Gandhi on Beatitudes, 157; T.S.Eliot and Augustine; Jonathan Miller on metaphor of, 161; the Reformation in Ireland, 181–2; a pilgrimage, 154–7; Dietrich Bonhoeffer, 187–8; Philip Toynbee; von Hügel, 200–2; and the fall of Rome, Augustine on, 223–5; the 'Jesuitical' problem, 230; *see also* Religion, Augustine

Churchill, Winston, and de Valera, 102; and anti-Hitler Germans, 187

Clare, John, 'nature' and sanity, 121–2

Clarke, Austin, and nature of Irish language, 94

Clonfert (Galway), C. of I. cathedral, 146

Coburn, Kathleen, *In Pursuit of Coleridge*, 12–13

Coleridge, Samuel Taylor, *Notebooks*; on authors avoiding 'I'; on not judging by defects, 12–13; 19; on nature as language of God, 96; 101; Hopkins and, 174

Colgan, John, Franciscan historian; on despoliation of Abbey of St Mura (Fahan), 181–2

Coliseum, English National Opera, Bernhardt and W.C. Fields sharing poster, 115

Collins, Billy, Library of Congress Poet Laureate; poem quoted, 225

Collins, Michael, and 'Æ', 90

Conrad, Joseph, on Hudson, 138

*Consolations, A Book of* (P.J.K.), 'console' vs 'disturb', 85–6

Cope, Wendy, quoting Doris Lessing, 20

Corcomroe (Galway), abbey ruins; Yeats's *The Dreaming of the Bones*, 147–8

Corkery, Daniel, *The Hidden Ireland*, 35

Cotán, Spanish still life, 104–5

Country life, attempts to write about, 27; Brussels colours, 92; threatening helicopters, 93, 186; quick changes, 96; ploughing, 119–20; scything, 141–2; hunting scene, 197; Foot and Mouth anxiety, 197, 226; Minister's idea of; non-tranquillity of, 178; blackthorn, 228; *see also* Birds, Grass, Farming, Seasons.

Cow parsley, 91, 141

Cows, dignity of, 4; in snow, 77–8; peace-inducing, 92; at Fore abbey, Co. Westmeath, 183

Cricket, Richie Benaud, 26; radio commentaries; Brian Johnson; Test Match vs West Indies (1988), 33–4; Trevor Bailey, David Lloyd; Botham vs Boycott, 50; Test 1992, 80; Test vs Australia 1997; Lord's in rain; John Jameson, 124–6; Test Match vs Pakistan 2001; Bill Frindall, 'Mr Stats'; discussion on nature of bails; 210–11; and scything, 211

attacking Newman, 112, 230
Korean War (1951), 203–4

Latin, 5
Lawrence, D.H., and Frieda, and
foxgloves, 93
Lee, Laurie, 149
Lehmann, Rosamond, her
obituary, 48–9
Leitrim, pleasures of, 48
Leopardi, 86
Lessing, Doris, mental argument
with, 20–1
Little Nell, 215–17
Levi, Peter, in Toronto 85;
memorial service; attitude to
'mistakes' in books; *Pausanias*;
footnotes on; *A Bottle in the
Shade*; *The Frontiers of Paradise*,
167–70
Lewis, C.S., *The Allegory of Love*, 35
*Lignum vitae*, cricketing discussion
of; cure-all, 210–11
London, observing from bus,
95–6; Stamford Bridge football,
114–15; farcical day in; changes
in, 132–4; unhappy faces in,
163; Wallace Collection, 180–3
Lord's, cricket ground, tannoyance,
50; in rain, 124–6
Lubianka prison, Moscow,
deposition of statue; Czapski's
account of, 65–6

MacCaig, Norman, Edinburgh
chilliness of, 6; *Collected Poems*
(1991); abandoning 'form';
'Cock before Dawn', 59
MacCarthy, Desmond, staying with
Tolstoys, 192
MacNeice, Louis, superb rhymer,
58; claimed as Ulster poet; grave
in Co. Down, 75; Stallworthy
biography, 99; at BBC, 100–1;
'The Gone-tomorrow', 101;
epitaph, 102; on India;
'Didymus', 114, 116; on poets,
170; 'Forty-two years ago…';

'Elegy for minor poets', 203
Mann, Thomas, 45
Mansfield, Katherine, on the
Lawrences, 93
Martyn, Edward, and Dunguaire
castle; starting Abbey theatre,
147–8
Matisse, 60
Matthews, James, biographer of
Frank O'Connor, 129, 131–2
McAleese, Mary, Irish President,
speech at Buddhist Centre,
Kilmainham (Dublin), 151–4
McEnroe, inspired tennis, 31–2
Melverley, on Severn walk, fabulist
in, 29–30
Memory, Vittorio Sereni on, 3;
Edward Thomas on, 122–3;
Augustine on, 162–4
Merton College, Oxford, status
conversation at Gaudy; garden,
16–17; dining at; chaplain on
saints' days, 137
Merton, Thomas, and Hindu life-
divisions; as Trappist in
Kentucky; bizarre death; *The
Sign of Jonas* (his journal); on
rain, 149–50; PhilipToynbee on,
201
Michie, James, *Possible Laughter*, 18
Middleton Murry, on George
Moore, 112
Milford, Wogan (Philipps), farmer,
painter, communist, 198–9
Miller, Jonathan, 'Christianity as
metaphor', 161
Miłosz, Czeslaw, on Aleksander
Wat, 68; *The Captive Mind*,
228–31; on Gobineau and the
'devout lie', 230
Milton, on angels, 128
Mitchell, Adrian, on Arts Centres,
7
Montaigne, on Socrates; on
Archangel Michael, 128
Moore, George, Yeats on, 42; *Ave,
Salve, Vale* (*Hail and Farewell*);
betraying class-consciousness,

Powys, Littleton, in MacNeice's
'Autumn Sequel', 100
Powys, Llewelyn, 9
Powys, T.F. 'moods of God', 186
Pritchett, V.S., on Dublin; English
view of Irish religiousness, 63
Pryce-Jones, David, on Peter Levi,
167
Puns, in poems, 19; and Irish
language; irresistability of, 94–6

QE2, tale of the gaunt dancer,
10–11
Quilp, in *The Old Curiosity Shop*,
embodiment of evil, 216–17

Raftery (Irish poet), naming places,
54
Ram, cautionary tale of, 4
Reading, Peter, anti-Nature Poem,
226
Rehearsing, meticulous nature of;
bonding, 133–4
Religion, Doris Lessing's dismissal
of, 20; value of ritual, 35, 202;
V.S. Pritchett's view of in Irish
life; in Bali; English attitude to,
63; Newman and Kingsley, 112;
in media, in detective stories,
136; Catholic literal-
mindedness, 180; illogical belief
in afterlife, 122–3, 202; Holy
Land, 154–7; Tolstoy, 196;
Fénelon and Jansenism, 208; *see
also* Anti-Papism, Buddhism,
Christianity, etc.
Ridler, Anne, 'A Phoenix
Answers', 180
Rumens, Carol, against 'console',
for 'disturb', 86
Russell, George ('Æ'), and Yeats,
55, 90; and Michael Collins, 90;
consulted by statesmen; shaping
Catholic Ireland; against
Kipling; on national differences,
90–1

Santiago, Chile, 165–6

Saints: St Jerome, hearing of sack
of Rome, 223–4; St John, in
Apocalypse tapestry, 129; St
John of Damascus, 223; St
Maignenn (Kilmainham),
153–4; St Molaise, President
McAleese introducing Colum
Kelly biography, 154; St Mura,
abbey ruins at Fahan,
Inishowen; bell in Wallace
Collection, 181–3; St Patrick,
apologising for clumsy Latin,
75–6
Sassoon, Siegfried, 'The General';
wrong sort of indignation, 213
Scything, and Ivor Gurney;
availability of scythes (c.1985),
141–2; helpful instruction from
radio Test commentary, 211
Seaside towns, 188–9; Whitley Bay,
Deal, 189; Aberystwyth, 189–91
Seasons, bryony in January, 76–7,
151; January dawn, 149;
February snow, 77; February
wind, 111; February
muckspreaders, 135; Spring
equinox, 119; April; celandines;
blackthorn, 228; hawthorns in
June, 209–10; midsummer
hogweed, 91; cold midsummer;
cold midsummers past (Gilbert
White, James Woodforde), 212;
August untidiness, 50; hot
August, 108; November floods,
186; Christmas afternoon, 3–4
Sereni, Vittorio (Italian poet), 3
Severn, River, walking along,
29–30
Shakespeare, Tolstoy like, 193;
Tolstoy dismissing, 196
Shanks, Alastair, English teacher of
Islay, 6
Sheep, in February, 112; ill-fed,
121; spring lambs; Henry Moore
and; wall-jumping, 227–8
Sisson, C.H, *English Poetry
1900–1950*, 15; translation of
Vauvenargues, 37

Smart, Elizabeth, on George Barker, 72

Smith, Sydney, on Irish Penal Laws, 102

Socrates, Montaigne on, 128

Spoleto festival (1967), 44–6

Sportsmen, inspired (Ballesteros, McEnroe), 31–2

St Margaret's Bay (Kent), chalk cliffs of, and 'possible laughter', 18; 189

St Michael's Mount, 51

Stallworthy, Jon (poet), biography of Owen; Arts Centre experience with, 7; biography of MacNeice, 99

Stamford Bridge (football ground), 114

Stephens, James, *Irish Fairy Stories* (on Finn McCool), 81; *The Crock of Gold*, 109; describing himself; *The Demi-Gods*; retelling Irish sagas, 110

Stevenson, Anne, 7

Strangford Lough (Down), 185

Strand, Mark, 85

Straw, 50

Sutherland, Kathryn, academic on language, 5

Tadpoles, and J.C. Powys, 103; pond life scenario, 104; decline of, 119

Taj Mahal, 115

Tasmania, greeted affectionately; like Ireland; Queen in Launceston, 21; New Norfolk; Port Arthur, 22; modern myths, 23; animal road casualties, 24; Uruguay like, 165

Tasso, Fenton on; compulsive reviser, 55, 57

Taylor, John, unhelpful Northern Irish language, 185

Tennyson, on Browning, 72; and Allingham; on immortality, 82, 160–1

Thistles, 209–11

Thomas, Edward, 'nature' and the self; defining memory; compared with Unamuno; 'The sorrow of great love…', 122–4

Tolstoy, diaries; on critics; different views of *Anna Karenina*, 191–2; A.N. Wilson biography; Desmond MacCarthy visiting; on gentlemen; 192; novels as 'surrogate diaries'; Vronsky; Levin; devoted daughter, 193–4; R.F. Christian, translator and editor; struggles to eliminate 'I', 194; *Resurrection*; against Tolstoyanism; 'secularised Christianity', hared of blur, 195–6

Toronto, poets in; hotel life in, towers of, 83–5

Toynbee, Philip, journals: *Part of a Journey*; on Thomas Mann; on depression; on difficulties of a commune; on God and beer; *End of a Journey*, 45–6; on religion after 50; 'the banana skin!'; and von Hügel; on the importance of literal truth, 200–2

Trout Inn, Godstow, 135

Tsvetayeva, Marina, 4

Tuscany, the *Crete*; Chianti; hill-towns; Chiusure; Belloc in, 143–6

Unamuno, Miguel, *Tragic Sense of Life*; compared with Edward Thomas, 122–4

Untermeyer, Louis, *Modern American/ Modern British Poetry* (1942); forgotten names in, 204–5

Uruguay, birds in, 164–5

Van Gogh, 86

Vauvenargues (C18 aphorist), *Maximes et Reflexions* translated by C.H. Sisson; on Enlightenment believers;